THE SCRIPTURE PRINCIPLE

BY THE AUTHOR

A Defense of Biblical Infallibility

Set Forth Your Case

Biblical Revelation

Truth on Fire

Reason Enough

Toward a Theology for the Future (editor, with David F. Wells)

Grace Unlimited (editor)

The Scripture Principle

CLARK H. PINNOCK

1817

Harper & Row, Publishers, San Francisco

Cambridge, Hagerstown, New York, Philadelphia
London, Mexico City, São Paulo, Singapore, Sydney

To Donald Bloesch, Gabriel Fackre, and Millard Erickson,
who are friends and colleagues,
and who represent the growing company of good evangelical scholars,
valiant for truth and creative in expression,
currently at work in the service of Christ and his church

FIRST EDITION

Library of Congress Cataloging in Publication Data

Pinnock, Clark H., 1937–
   THE SCRIPTURE PRINCIPLE.

   Bibliography: p.
   1. Bible—Evidences, authority, etc.—Addresses, essays, lectures.   I. Title.
BS480.P63   1984   220.6'01   84-47732
ISBN 0-06-066620-X

84   85   86   87   88   10   9   8   7   6   5   4   3   2   1

Contents

Preface

I have three aims in mind in writing this book. The primary aim is to present an understanding of the Scripture principle and the authority of the Bible in a positive, systematic, and relevant way. My purpose is not negative, as if to answer errors on the left or on the right; nor is it parochial, as if to speak only to the Protestant conservative community, of which I am a member. I write first of all for the person who asks, "How should I regard the Bible and respond to it?" My emphasis is upon that vital, practical certainty one can have in the Bible we now possess as the transforming medium of the saving message of God. Such a reader may well have an advantage over me, his or her teacher, in that the over academic study of theology has distorted some of the most basic issues in connection with the Bible. It has given people the impression that what is crucially important is the ability to rationally comprehend these matters rather than to come to know, love, and obey the God who speaks in the Scriptures. There is a spiritual dimension in the recognition, interpretation, and application of the biblical text as the Word of God that does not easily fit into scholarly technique and comes more naturally to those "uncorrupted" by it. For this reason, in my own approach I consider it essential to listen to the Spirit, not only in scholarly circles, but in the community of faith, which tends to keep a healthier balance in the dialectic of mind and spirit. Writing for the general, unspecialized reader I also bear in mind the vulnerable inquirer who may be disturbed by the quantity and depth of the problems that must perforce be discussed in a book that strives to be responsible to the state of the discussion as it exists today. Some of us must face up to them, for the good of the church and the defense of the gospel, but the reader may well ask at this point if he or she is one who ought to do so. For there is a spiritual danger involved in exposing ourselves, as I intend to do, to the starkest and most vehement objections to faith in the God of the Bible. In doing so we, in effect, pit ourselves against the most seasoned critics of the gospel and expose ourselves to some of the most penetrating of the "fiery darts of the evil One." We ought then to be clad in God's armor and in prayer, for in seeking to guard the gospel, one becomes exposed to increased assaults. Let the reader take care, then, in approaching this subject and this book, and be looking to God and his strength for sustenance in the exercise of testing basic truths of faith. God's promises are, of course, sufficient also for this.

My second aim in the book is to speak out, in the context of the crisis of the Scripture principle, in defense of the full authority and trustworthiness of the Bible. Unfortunately, this is necessary because of a major and widespread shift in contemporary theology toward seeing the Bible as a fallible testament of human opinion and religious experience, not the reliable deposit and canon of normative instruction. Although the number of those involved in such a depreciation of the normative authority of the Bible is few in relation to the faithful church as a whole, they are often influential scholars and teachers whose opinions sway the unwary and subvert the faith of those who are weak. The seriousness of the crisis is plain once we consider that a decline in respect for the Bible results in the church not hearing the saving message of the Scriptures and in her becoming liable to being overtaken by the religious philosophy of the moment. Thus, a crisis of the Scripture principle is one of the greatest crises of all. Polemical theology, following the didactic, is sadly unavoidable in the age of theological decline in which we live. I can only promise that I will not permit unavoidable controversy to steal the limelight from my basically positive and joyful presentation. Unsound theology ought not to succeed even in making orthodoxy feisty and ill-tempered.

My third aim is to assist classical Christians who hold to the full authority of the Bible to move ahead in the understanding of their conviction. It is sad when our critics are able to "nail" us on one point or another simply because we have not done our work very well. Too often we have been smug in our belief and not faced important issues squarely and honestly. We have made "cheap shots" and taken shortcuts, deserving some of the ridicule we have received. Low intellectual visibility also accounts for internecine skirmishes in the evangelical camp, which could be avoided with a little clarity of thought. I hope to provide the reader with a systematic proposal about biblical authority that will cover all the bases tolerably well and reach home plate standing. My sense is that large numbers of Christians are yearning to move ahead in their understanding and get beyond futile arguments about imponderables. They do not like to be running scared before the religious liberals and having their beliefs defended in neurotic and unconvincing ways that glorify neither God nor his cause. I think we can move ahead, and this is the time to do it. On so many points of the theological spectrum today believers are longing for an evangelical confidence in the Bible, and many minds are open as never before to a serious consideration of the classic Scripture principle presented in a viable and convincing way. I only hope that this book offers the kind of presentation that is needed.

I will admit that I have not found this an easy book to write. Indeed I have written and rewritten it several times. I agree with James Orr, who said: "There is perhaps no subject at the present moment more difficult to write upon, and above all to write upon wisely, than this of revelation and inspiration."[1] As in trying to smooth down a large rug, one gets rid of a wrinkle here only to find it reappear somewhere else. It is a task that brings out the finite nature of the writer's own resources. My aim has been not so much to uncover new data as to produce a better understanding of what we know already. I offer wisdom rather than expertise, and the measure of my success will be the fruitfulness people find in looking at the subject in this way.

I take this opportunity to thank Fuller Theological Seminary for the invitation to deliver some of this material in the Payton Lectures for 1982. I am grateful, too, to the students at Regent College and McMaster Divinity College, who helped me work out some of the ideas in the book. I thank the board and faculty of the Divinity College for permitting me to teach in such a stimulating context, and I thank my wife, Dorothy, and daughter, Sarah, for the loving support they never fail to provide me.

Introduction: Maintaining the Scripture Principle Today

The adoption of the bipartite Christian Bible as the authoritative Scripture of the church was probably the most momentous choice ever made in the history of doctrine. By doing so, the church provided herself with a standard of identity by which to evaluate and shape her theology, life, and mission. Therefore, the place to begin a discussion of biblical authority is with the simple fact, not really disputed, that entrenched in Christian thinking of every kind is a belief in the Bible as the written Word of God. Even if we are not impressed with this belief or persuaded by it, we have to acknowledge it and appreciate why it is held to so stoutly. For better or for worse, belief in the Scriptures as the canon and yardstick of Christian truth, the unique locus of the Word of God, is part of an almost universal Christian consensus going back to at least the second century. Until the recent rise of revisionist theology, Christian thinking was done in the house of authority, a fact that is not doubted even by the writer most eager to overturn such belief, Edward Farley.[1] Theology in the premodern period was always done on the assumption that the Bible was the written Word of God.

As a Baptist evangelical Christian, I will quote an eloquent paragraph from the New Hampshire Baptist Confession of 1833 to represent this belief, but it can be documented from a hundred other authors and documents:

We believe that the Bible was written by men divinely inspired, and is a perfect treasure of heavenly instruction; that it has God for its author, salvation for its end, and truth without any mixture of error for its matter; that it reveals the principles by which God will judge us; and therefore is, and shall remain to the end of the world, the true center of Christian union, and the supreme standard by which all human conduct, creeds, and opinions shall be tried.[2]

The Roman Catholic scholar Bruce Vawter and the Anglican evangelical Geoffrey Bromiley have both observed that the early fathers of the church everywhere and always presuppose the divine authorship of the Bible and never betray any other view of it.[3] This is true even more obviously of the people of the Reformation and their successors to this day, since their entire ecclesial project was founded upon the infallible teaching of the Scriptures as opposed to supposed errors that had crept into the church's traditions. Hence, it is from this period that we receive the most explicit and tightly drawn statements about the authority of the Bible. Luther and Calvin expressed themselves in the strongest terms on this matter. They regarded Scripture as the divine teacher that reliably delivers to us the doctrines of God. If there is a "Protestant principle," then this is it.[4]

More than an isolated belief, this conviction about the Bible was an integral part of a larger package of classical convictions and cannot be discarded without tearing the fabric of the whole garment of traditional Christian beliefs. Without much exaggeration one could say that the history of theology is a history of the interpretation of the Bible, so basic to this message was this medium. The way Christians have thought about God, Christ, humanity, salvation, and church is indebted to the teachings of the Bible. This is not to deny that cultural factors have entered into the various formulations at different periods, but simply to point out that the creed as we all know and accept it is utterly tied up with its scriptural foundations, making the authority of the Bible, if not a soteriologically indispensable belief (one can be saved by believing in Christ whatever one thinks of the Bible), then certainly an epistemologically crucial belief. Without belief in the authority of the Bible, there would not have been any creedal backbone to the Christian movement, and certainly not the bony structures of Nicaea and Chalcedon. Beliefs like the atonement and the resurrection unquestionably stand or fall with belief in biblical authority, and that is the measure of the seriousness of the modern debate about it. We are not arguing over some minor detail in Christian belief, like the rapture or the classes of angels, but over the basis of religious knowledge as such and how we know what God has promised and commanded. How can we worship God if we do not know who God is? How can we trust his promises if we do not know what they are? How can we obey God if we have no sure knowledge of his will? The reason Christians have felt historically that the authority of the Bible is a crucial conviction is that they have realized the Bible is needed to give us a reliable knowledge of the truth, without which we cannot exist long as Christians. Calvin spoke of this so practically when he referred to the Bible as the spectacles our dim eyes require to make out what the will of our creator is (*Institutes* I, chap. 6).

Now, the fact that belief in biblical authority has been the majority opinion traditionally and that the orthodox creed depends upon it does not prove it is right or make it viable for us if it is not. But it does prevent us from saying a really foolish thing: that the Scripture principle can just be jettisoned without having much effect upon anything else. And it also helps people realize why conservative-minded Christians get so upset when their belief in biblical authority comes under attack, or even seems to. This belief is a very fundamental one epistemologically, with far-reaching consequences in every area of doctrine and practice, and thus one that will not be overturned without a momentous struggle in the churches. The objections to it are going to have to be very impressive to get more than a handful of turncoats to be convinced. Thus far, only a few critics of orthodoxy seem at this point to be aware of what they are up against. Even James Barr, who has given it a lot of thought and hopes to lure Christians away from what he calls fundamentalism, does not seem to have taken proper measure in his mind and in his emotions of the conviction he dislikes so much. Notice may as well be served right here that large numbers of us are not going to abandon our belief in the Bible as the written Word of God in favor of some view of it as mere human tradition without a very severe struggle—simply because we know, as our opponents ought to know, that Christianity in any sense deserving of the name stands or falls on that belief.[5]

I will be using the term *evangelical* to refer to those believers who, like myself, are committed to the gospel as it is biblically defined. Our basic concern is with the gospel, not with the Bible per se, but we are convinced that the one will not remain pure very long without the other. When I was a student three decades ago, the fortunes of evangelical theology were not very good, but nowadays, I am glad to note, a strong recovery is under way and a renaissance likely in such convictions.[6]

To be candid, however, the classical conviction about Holy Scripture was not always developed in sound and healthy ways, and some of our difficulties today are due in part to inadequacies in it. Given the polemical atmosphere between evangelicals and more liberal Christians, it is uncommon for conservatives to admit any un-ideal elements in the orthodox view of the Bible, but admit them we must if we hope to gain a fair hearing and to advance in our own undertanding. There has been, for example, a tendency to exaggerate the absolute perfection of the text and minimize the true humanity of it. One of the weaknesses of the fathers, as Bromiley notes, was their failure to give full weight to the human and historical aspects of the text. "The truth is that the fathers seem not to have appreciated the real significance of the human dimension nor to have grasped the possibilities of a better exegesis that lexical, literary, and historical inquiry would present."[7] This docetic tendency, as Berkouwer would call it, has meant that many features of the text were left unobserved and we were badly prepared for advances in literary criticism that the modern age would produce.[8] Barth has taken note also of the mechanical view of the Bible that many of the fathers held.[9] In addition, there was a strong, "catholic" tendency to link the authoritative Scriptures to an infallible ecclesiastical institution, thus providing even more security for the believer—more, in fact, than the Lord had planned for us. It must be obvious to any reader of classical theology that the people who spoke so highly of the infallibility of the Bible very often spoke just as highly of the church's creeds and hierarchy, and that they do not witness to what we today would regard as an evangelical position, though they are repeatedly cited by evangelicals today for that purpose.[10] Evangelicals who hold to the sole authority of the Bible do not do justice to themselves when they appear to be uncritical of tradition, even when it happens to be tradition about the Bible. Rather than trying to argue unconvincingly, as Rogers and McKim did, that the traditional view of authority was less rigorous than we have thought (Woodbridge has shown it was very rigorous indeed), what we have to do is admit honestly that the old view of the Bible that we treasure is not biblical and serviceable in every detail today and, like every other theological topic, can use some improvement and development by the thinkers and scholars of our generation.[11] We simply must transcend the neglect of the humanity of the Bible, so familiar in orthodoxy, and liberate the Bible from too close an association with mother church, an association that can easily smother its independent voice. The legacy we honor is noble and true, but it is not infallible or perfect, and we must be free to improve it if we can.

The Crisis of the Scripture Principle

Despite the ecumenical range and great antiquity of the classical conviction about the Bible as the written Word of God, we face a "crisis of the

Scripture principle" today and with it the unmaking and unraveling of traditional Christian doctrine.[12] Farley and Hodgson put it succinctly and accurately when they write:

Until recently, almost the entire spectrum of theological opinion would have agreed that the scriptures of the Old and New Testaments, together with their doctrinal interpretations, occupy a unique and indispensable place of authority for Christian faith, practice, and reflection. But this consensus now seems to be falling apart.[13]

Out of the liberal theological revision has come a flat denial of the Scripture principle in the classical sense, the collapse of the house of authority based upon it, and the subsequent disintegration of the orthodox creed. Whether the denial comes in a direct[14] or in an indirect form[15] does not matter much: the point is that the normative authority of the Bible has been called into question deliberately and repeatedly since Schleiermacher by adherents of the new theology.

But what can possibly explain such behavior? Why would obtensibly Christian theologians deny the Scripture principle, when the Christian message has historically always depended on it? It seems on the surface to be a suicidal act. How could it do anything but harm to Christianity, and who could it possibly please except the enemies of Jesus Christ? There are three basic reasons for this far-reaching change of theological opinion. The first and most important is the cultural shift to secular modernity beginning in the Renaissance, and to rationalist modernity, brought on by the Enlightenment, and the liberal response to it. The modern mind dislikes traditional authorities such as the Bible and insists on subjecting them to rational scrutiny. Alongside this fiercely independent spirit of inquiry, in itself not such a bad thing, goes a deeper antipathy to a book that speaks about God and humanity in premodern categories. Speaking as it does of a sovereign God and subject humanity, of resurrection and atonement, of grace and wrath, of incarnation and cognitive revelation, the Bible lacks credibility in the eyes of those taught to prize human autonomy and self-sufficiency. Lack of belief in the message of Scripture lies behind denial of the Scripture principle. The final authority of the Bible can hardly stand if the message it conveys provokes, not belief, but unbelief. Ed Farley makes it plain that this is a fundamental reason for his own rejection of biblical authority.[16] We face a rebelliousness in the modern period that seeks to edge God out of the world and leave humanity autonomous in it. To achieve this, the Bible that challenges this insurrection must be silenced as divinely authoritative.

The second reason, second also in importance, is the rise of biblical criticism of the kind that treats Scripture as a merely human document and frequently debunks its claims on various levels. At first this criticism consisted in a discrediting of traditional views as to the literary nature of the books of the Bible; then it questioned the historical details of the biblical narrative; and then it exposed difficulties in the truth claims themselves. Pretending to be a key to the elucidation of the text, criticism had the effect of situating the Bible so thoroughly in the human context as to make it well nigh impossible to consider its authority as anything more than human. It became less and less natural to regard the text as divine communication and more and more plausible to regard it as fallible human utterance.[17] What made it even more difficult for the conservative believers who wanted to be honest in their study of the Bible was the burden of their own heritage, which had erred in both exaggerating the absolute perfection of the text and obscuring its genuine, humble humanity. They were thus not in a strong position to distinguish between the positive and the negative proposals that the new criticism advanced. To this day, this is the conservative burden. It makes it difficult for those who keenly desire to respect the Bible highly but are put off by the form the conservative tradition often still takes.

The third reason, though it is more in the nature of an afterthought, I suspect, is theological in character. Orthodoxy, it is felt, silences God from speaking today—locking him up in a book—and creates a petrified and rigid style of faith that is false to the dynamic transcendence of the Bible. It closes us off from appropriating fresh truth and creates a whole set of oppressive attitudes and dogmas. Surely, as Auguste Sabatier argued, religious experience is the heart of Christianity, and though this gives rise to dogmas in time, such are the work of human beings, not the declarations of God.[18] Why should a religion that celebrates an inner spiritual guide be so concerned with written rules and doctrines? Christianity is a religion of the Spirit, not of a book.[19] A rigid Scripture principle would tend both to inhibit each new generation from seeking the will of God afresh and to lose touch with the glorious fact that God is at work in us, too. Of course we will need the New Testament, but we will not need an infallible testament incapable of error, only a kerygma collection to bear witness to the originating experiences of revelation through Christ.[20]

Leaving aside for the time being how the conservative theologian might counter these three contentions, it is obvious that we have here a confrontation between classical Christianity based upon the Scripture principle and a neo-Christianity without a Scripture principle, a collision that, in the realm of theological ideas, makes the differences between Roman Catholic and Protestant seem trivial by comparison. Theology without the controlling influence of the Scripture principle could only degenerate into open-ended pluralism of belief that none could adjudicate, and its classical concepts could only suffer unlimited revision. The crisis of the Scriptures is in fact the crisis of Christian theology itself and the cause of the deepest polarization of all in the churches. The gap is unbridgeable between those who stand by the historic confidence in the infallible truth of the Bible and those who adopt the pancritical view, which relativizes the entire theological enterprise. Seeking reconciliation is always a good thing, as it is between theological liberals and conservatives, but when the full measure of the difference here is taken, I doubt that reconciliation is possible.[21]

At stake here is the well-being of the church and the effective proclamation of its message to the world. The church depends upon a sure word of instruction in regard to her gospel foundations. We need to possess a true knowledge of God and his salvation, and this is what the inspired Scriptures provide for us. Should they be discredited, we would lack the requisite knowledge of God's Word and the necessary foundations for the life of faith. It is as if a person were to place a great charge of dynamite at the base of orthodox Christianity that caused the structure to crumble to the ground, collapsing of its own weight. Now, given that confidence in the Bible is so basic to the memory, theology, and liturgy of the church universal, it is most unlikely that the crisis of the Scripture principle will last or have the effect of carrying more than a small percentage of Christian people with it. Like the false teachers Paul faced, these unreliable guides are not likely to get very far (2 Tim. 3:9). Nevertheless, a definite threat is posed to the solidity and soundness of the teaching office in the church today, a threat that can harm believers who come under its influence.

James Barr rightly protests when conservatives link salvation and belief in the Scriptures so closely as to suggest that those who hold a nonconservative view of the Bible have no right to even the hope of salvation. He correctly points out that the judgment of God turns upon a person's response to Jesus Christ, not to the Bible, and that this decision and no other matters ultimately.[22] Warfield granted Barr's point when he said that Christianity does not depend upon the Scriptures for its truth or saving power.[23] Yet there is something very important at stake here nevertheless. It is the well-being of the church, which draws its sustenance and instruction from the Bible. The necessity of the Scripture principle is, I admit, practical rather than absolute, but a practical necessity of the greatest importance.[24]

Of scarcely less importance is the necessity of presenting to a lost

world the sure Word of salvation. Now that the entire world is being
sucked into the vortex of atheism and self-destruction, as Solzhenitsyn
puts it, it is more important than ever to be able to declare God's Word
of good news, which comes to us from outside the human situation
with clarity and forthrightness. How will people of the modern world
recognize truth of eternal validity and saving power unless it originates
outside the flux of the human situation? How else will they come into
contact with the basis of meaning and hope that they need? And how
will the church be able to communicate effectively her confidence in
such a gospel if confidence in the sources of the knowledge of God fails
her? Not only does the church herself need the Bible for her own
renewal and health, the fortunes of the nations as well depend upon
the validity of the good news and its scriptural vehicle.[25]

The Struggle to Maintain the Scripture Principle

Seeing a real threat to the authority of the Bible and to the *bene esse*
of the churches, classical Christians today respond by wanting to defend and explicate the Scripture principle in this newly critical context.
In one sense, they are in a strong position to do so. The conservative
position is deeply rooted not only in the most ancient traditions but
also in the Bible itself, as we shall see, and the task is made easier by
the fact that the liberals are scrambling to find a viable alternative to
it—not an easy thing to do. The church as a whole is not likely to
respond well to a denial of the real basis of her apostolicity when nothing solid is proposed to be put in its place. In another sense, however,
it is not so easy, because in the course of the criticism of the Scripture
principle some very tough questions have been raised and placed on
the agendas of all serious students of the matter. How shall we use as
authority a text that was written when people thought in very different
ways than we do? How shall we respond to critical "discoveries" on a
host of issues pertaining to biblical literature and history? What about
the diversity of biblical teaching? How should we think about the
present defective copies and translations? What books properly belong
to the canon? How is the Old Testament authoritative when the New
Testament appears to correct it? What is the nature of the claim the
Bible makes for itself? Those who are honest in pursuing these issues
(not all Christians are) know there are some hard questions for the
conservative scholar to answer and know also that there is little agreement among such scholars how to answer some of them. Even though
there is agreement on the basic approach to the Bible as God's written

Word, and a widely felt desire to preserve unity among Bible-believing Christians in face of the present crisis, there is lack of consensus on some rather important questions and on what to do about it. From a distance it seems that everyone dwells in the same house of biblical authority, but closer in, it becomes quite apparent that the house contains various rooms and closets in which one or another of this mixed multitude resides. Thus there are debates among conservatives, despite the need for a united front.[26]

Some would take their stand with the inerrancy of the King James Version, seeing the need to locate the truth in an accessible text, not in lost autographs. Some posit the perfect errorlessness of the original Hebrew, Aramaic, and Greek texts and try to make that meaningful. Some work with terms like *infallible* and *inerrant* and find a good deal of room to move there, since these terms are a great deal more flexible than they seem at first sight. Some suggest a lesser claim of inerrancy, one that would apply to the purpose of a biblical writer rather than to everything he may have written. Some speak of a set radius of biblical authority that encompasses a plurality of theological styles not to be forced into systematic unity. Some refer to the time-conditioned and culture-bound character of the Bible at certain key points that obviates the need to bring those elements forward into the twentieth-century church. And there are still others who fancy themselves "catholic" evangelicals, who appeal to ecclesiastical authority in order to buttress biblical authority. Although *evangelical* may be a good umbrella term to describe this company of conservative believers, there is an obvious lack of theological unity in how we ought to maintain the Scripture principle today, differences that are not trivial but well worth debate and resolution. It is easy to become impatient with those who attack other evangelicals for holding what they consider unsound positions, but one must recognize that the differences can be quite important, and positions can be taken for well-considered though differing reasons. There is often a logic at work that it is easier to deplore than to answer, and rhetorical shortcuts will not get us anywhere. The problem is aggravated by the success of the evangelicals. In the past few decades, they have moved out of a subculture where their disagreements went unnoticed to a position in the public limelight where their differences are given attention and subjected to some analysis. The opportunity is now given to them to set forth the evangelical understanding of the Bible before a listening world, and they are caught without having a united opinion on a host of detailed questions.[27]

What obviously is needed is a systematic treatment of the Scripture principle that faces all the questions squarely and supplies a model for understanding that will help us transcend the current impasse. Though one has the impression that evangelicals are always writing such tomes, there are in reality almost no full-scale expositions that cover the ground adequately and set forth the evangelical conviction in a balanced and sensible way. Much of our work operates within a circle of limited visibility, presupposing evangelical readers, and never raises its eyes to the larger perimeter of the theological mainstream where such issues are discussed professionally and in depth.[28]

In broad outline, as a glance at the table of contents will reveal, I suggest a paradigm utilizing three dimensions: first, the divine inspiration of Holy Scripture that arises organically out of the Christian pattern of revelation; second, the human character of the biblical text as the form in which the Word of God was communicated to us; and third, the ministry of the Spirit in relation to the Bible and the dynamic interaction between the two. Such a paradigm is sufficiently broad to capture the major themes and specific enough, when opened up, to introduce the reader to a large number of issues without losing his or her attention.

More specifically, my treatment of the Scripture principle will focus on and orient itself to the kind of practical, evangelical emphasis found in 2 Timothy 3:15–17:

From childhood you have been acquainted with the sacred writings which are able to instruct you for salvation through faith in Christ Jesus. All scripture is inspired by God and profitable for teaching, for reproof, for correction, and for training in righteousness, that the man of God may be complete, equipped for every good work.

In this wonderful text Paul places his emphasis on the plenary profitability of the Scriptures in the matter of conveying a saving and an equipping knowledge of God. He does not present a theory about a perfect Bible given long ago but now lost, but declares the Bible in Timothy's possession to be alive with the breath of God and full of the transforming information the young disciple would need in the life of faith and obedience. I think we can all learn from this kind of concentration and orientation.[29] It is important for us to stress the practical effectiveness of the accessible Bible in facilitating a saving and transforming knowledge of God in Jesus Christ. We must not shift the emphasis to the unavailable Bible of the past, about which one can speculate, or to the inaccessible Bible of the future, after the experts will (supposedly) have cleared away every perplexing feature of the text, removing all possibility of doubt. It is this present Bible we need to be able to trust, this New International Version or King James Version, and this practical purpose of communicating the saving knowledge of God we need to be focusing on. Furthermore, it is this Bible that all Christians have come to trust through the grace of God, and this purpose that has proven valid in their experience. Given by God's breath, the Bible proves to be quick and powerful and sharper than any two-edged sword and gives life and truth to the one who trusts in Jesus. This is the doctrine of Scripture I am concerned to discuss and defend: Not the Bible of academic debate, but the Bible given and handed down to be the medium of the gospel message and the primary sacrament of the knowledge of God, his own communication, which is able to reconcile us to God so that we might come to love and obey him. Not a book wholly free of perplexing features, but one that bears effective witness to the Savior of all.

Why, in the last analysis, do Christian people believe the Bible is God's Word? Not because they have all studied up on Christian evidences and apologetics, however useful these may prove to some. Christians believe the Bible because it has been able to do for them exactly what Paul promised it would: introduce them to a saving and transforming knowledge of Christ. Reasons for faith and answers to perplexing difficulties in the text, therefore, are supportive but not constitutive of faith in God and his Word. Faith rests ultimately, not in human wisdom, but in a demonstration of the Spirit and power. Therefore, let us not quench the Spirit in our theology of inspiration, whether by rationalist liberal doubts or by rationalist conservative proofs, because both shift the focus away from the power of God in the Scriptures and onto our ability to rationally comprehend these matters. There is, of course, a place for ordinary understanding with the mind and a place for scholarly discussion and vindication. But it is greatly overdone if we leave the slightest impression that we are able to ground faith in Gods' Word by rational arguments alone and that God's working in the human heart in response to faith is not the main cause of faith. The Bible is not so interested in our academically proving, as in our holistically seeing, the truth, in our believing the gospel and obeying God. This is something I have had to learn myself, and it is a liberating truth.[30]

We conservatives should ask ourselves why it is that ordinary believers can go on trusting the Bible, even though it appears to have defects due to transmission and discrepancies due to unknown causes. How do they go on believing the Bible when so many technical details remain unresolved? The answer is obvious and important. Believers do not depend for their certainty at this crucial point upon the experts in some seminary but upon God, who speaks to them in the Scriptures. They can tolerate some uncertainties and perplexities because their confidence does not rest on human expertise, liberal or conservative, but on God himself. They are not tied to human authorities but free in the liberty of the children of God. They know that what is primary is the saving and transforming truth of the Bible and what is secondary are those curious numbers, those details that will not line up, those obscure allusions that do not begin to upset the truly fundamental point. It has always been a marvel to me how ordinary believers show themselves so much wiser in these matters than those who would be their teachers, who often introduce them to arcane discussions that never end and never deliver the kind of certainty these ordinary believers already possess.

As we proceed it will become obvious that I am not proposing that we restrict the degree of trust we accord the Bible in our understanding of it. I am not saying that we need to believe it only when it seems to be speaking about saving matters as opposed to other things. This would be to introduce a distinction of true and false into our attitude to the text that would be unfruitful and even, quite possibly, dangerous. On the contrary, our experience of the truth and power of God's Word predisposes us to be open in an unlimited way to all of its assertions, even when they are perplexing. Even a small detail can prove to be important and not incidental at all. An emphasis on an evangelical certainty implies that we will be open to the sort of text God actually gave us and not tend to predetermine according to rationalistic criteria the form it ought to take and then twist it into that form by scholarly devices.

Concentration on the saving truth of the Bible does not mean that we ought to make a distinction between value judgments and speculative judgments, as Ritschl and (following him) Bultmann did. It does not mean we ought to depreciate in the slightest the cognitive substance of what the Bible teaches. But some who stress it do not always guard themselves against such implications—which would be truly dangerous. Rather, it means that we should focus our attention on the transforming message of the Bible, which comes across with tremendous power from the texts we now possess, and place the great bulk of our concern upon heeding and digesting that glorious and liberating Word.

Part I

THE WORD OF GOD

Pattern of Revelation

The goal of this first major section of the book is to determine the pattern of revelation as it is laid down in the biblical witness and to locate the place of the Bible itself in it. I will argue that the provision of inspired Scriptures was integral to the divine self-disclosure and cannot be put aside. In the first chapter I will present the general picture, painting with a broad brush. We will look in greater detail at the crucial biblical testimony to inspiration in Chapter 2 and go on in Chapter 3 to a consideration of the Bible's normative authority as the school of the Holy Spirit.

In the context of religion, revelation refers to the vision people have of what is ultimate and sacred to them; it gives them an orientation for life and a criterion of what is true and valuable. In theistic religions, like Judaism and Christianity, revelation refers to the self-disclosure of God, there being no other way for us to know him unless he has made himself known to us. How could we know the One whose ways and thoughts are higher than our ways and thoughts unless he had given us his Word? (Isa. 55:6–11). Without revelation we would be left groping in darkness. A term such as *salvation* might be a more central category in the biblical proclamation than revelation is, but revelation nevertheless enjoys a certain logical priority, since God's way of salvation still has to be disclosed. Thus we cannot take too seriously those who suggest that Christianity has no revelation when it is so apparent that it rests on a definite vision of what is ultimate and true based in the revelation of God.[1] "For he has made known to us in all wisdom and insight the mystery of his will" (Eph. 1:9).

What sort of revelation, then, does Christianity claim to possess, and what is its pattern? A great deal hangs upon getting the answer to this question right, because the essence of Christianity is bound up in it. What one decides revelation to be will be reflected in what one defines Christianity to be. If revelation is taken to be primarily a matter of personal encounter, as it is in Bultmann then the historicity of salvation history and the infallibility of apostolic teachings will not seem important. If revelation is a universal intuition that takes form in all world religions, then the Christian revelation will be handled as a human construct and assimilated with insights from other quarters. If revelation consists primarily of historical acts of God, not verbal communication, Christianity must be divined from the meanings inherent in those events in the context of universal history. Or if revelation comes with cognitive substance intrinsic to it, the shape of Christianity will be determined by the information revelation delivers. There are few questions more important to theology and the essence of Christian faith than the nature of revelation, and no better way to answer it than to interrogate the revelation itself. As Dulles says, "To construct a sound and credible notion of revelation is an urgent task in our day, both for the church's dialogue with the surrounding world, and for her own internal development."[2]

Revelation According to the Bible

The first point to make about revelation, as the Bible presents it, is its complexity. It is not a single activity or a simple entity but a complex web and set of actions designed to disclose the divine message of salvation. As it is put in Hebrews, "In many and various ways God spoke of old to our fathers by the prophets, but in these last days he has spoken to us by a Son, whom he appointed the heir of all things" (1:1–2). Revelation appears to be multifaceted, and we need to try to avoid losing any of the richness of it. Its unity consists in its overall function of communicating the gracious truth and action of God, and its diversity, in the various forms and features of this communication. God's Word has a rainbowlike effect when it breaks into the world, and we have to speak of a *pattern* of revelation to do any justice to it.[3] We will find as we look into it that God acts in human history, gives some understanding of his will to prophets and apostles, becomes flesh in the person of Jesus, moves in power in the Spirit of Pentecost, and provides written Scriptures for the church. Each facet contributes something vital to the disclosure, and we ought to view each in complementary relationship with the others. The temptation to select one aspect, such as experience or event or oracle, and make it the whole—with revelation being nothing but that—is a bad mistake. It can only distort the total picture. The only valid model of revelation will be one that welcomes into it each of the original elements in the ancient pattern and does not pick and choose arbitrarily among them. Among modern theologians, some see revelation chiefly in terms of content, some in terms of historical events; others see it as inner experience or transforming encounter. Much of the disagreement could be removed if arbitrary selectivity were avoided.[4]

A second point to notice from the outset, because of its contemporary relevance, is the bipolar structure of revelation, objective and subjective. We always ought to be concerned about both the content of what has been revealed and the way it is being received and appropriated, and we ought to be careful not to suppress either aspect. Orthodoxy often tends to highlight the propositional nature of revelation at the expense of the existential, whereas contemporary liberal thought certainly stresses the inner, subjective dimension. One jeopardizes the vitality, the other, the noetic content, of revelation. I am concerned to correct both errors and, in this chapter, particularly the precarious shift to the subjective in the contemporary theologies of revelation.

As we now begin to distinguish the various facets of God's multifaceted revelation, the first thing we notice is a distinction between what has been called "general" and "special" revelation. On the one hand, the whole of nature declares the glory of God and is revelational of God, and on the other hand, a more focused and specific revelation of the will of God to Israel is the main emphasis in the Bible. There is a cosmic revelation accessible to all peoples as well as a special initiative in history to reveal the heart of God and make his saving plan effective. "For ask now of the days that are past, which were before you, since the day that God created man upon the earth, and ask from one end of heaven to the other, whether such a great thing as this [Sinai] has ever happened or was ever heard of. Did any people ever hear the voice of a God speaking out of the midst of the fire, as you have heard and still live? Or has any God ever attempted to go and take a nation for hmself from the midst of another nation, by trials, by signs, by wonders, and by war, by a mighty hand and an outstretched arm, and by great terrors, according to all that the lord your God did for you in Egypt before your eyes? To you it was shown, that you might know that the Lord is God; there is no other besides him" (Deut. 4:32–35).[5]

Although the Bible does not dwell upon it, it does present a form of revelation that is universal in scope and accessible to all peoples. God is, after all, the creator of the world and is revealed as its Maker in all things. His power and divinity are plainly evident before our very eyes

(Rom. 1:19). Human beings exist necessarily and inescapably in the presence of God, being created for God and by God. Though we can certainly rebel and even curse God, we cannot escape him altogether, at least in this life, but must encounter him everywhere and always. For those who come to know God, God is the meaning and truth of their being.[6] Just as individuals reveal themselves in their general conduct and also, more self-consciously, by means of specific acts, so God reveals himself in both these ways and never leaves himself without a witness (Acts 14:17). General revelation in the creation provides valuable common ground between the Christian and all others and can prepare the way for and open the door to an encounter with special revelation through Christ.[7]

Among the theologians, Karl Barth, was most reluctant to speak positively about general revelation, because of the danger of it eclipsing and even distorting the revelation of the Bible. Just because it is so minimal and inarticulate, general revelation lends itself to human rebelliousness and to being twisted in support of some favorite project. Barth saw this happening in the Nazi ideology as the propoganda machine appealed to general revelation in support of its twisted notions of race and calling. Furthermore, an overemphasis upon it can easily lead to the conceit that human beings can apprehend truth about God by their own powers of reason and experience and not rely upon the saving revelation of the gospel. Liberal theology is largely a theology built upon supposed general revelation coming through human consciousness, and it distorts the biblical revelation by means of the insights drawn independently of it. In it, the knowledge of God is sought by delving down into the depths of experience and finding revelation there. When God has been found in the depth of everyday experience, there is no great need to seek him elsewhere, either in heaven or in the pages of the Bible.[8] Thus, the danger Barth feels is not an imaginary one.

Nevertheless, the Bible itself speaks of such a revelation. The creation bears the mark of the handiwork of its maker and proclaims the glory of God (Ps. 19:1). No one is far from God's presence, because we all live, move, and have our being in him (Acts 17:28). The light of creation falls upon the heart of everyone coming into the world (John 1:9). Far from negating special revelation, it holds out the promise of it. It opens the door through which God can then approach his creatures, not as an alien and a stranger, but as the one who has a proper claim upon them, a claim of which they are already aware. Just as salvation is the restoration of creation, so Christian revelation is the representation and amplification of the offer of salvation already present in general revelation. It is true that many evangelical theologians are nervous about recognizing any saving significance in cosmic revelation. Like Barth, they too are jealous for the utter uniqueness of Christian salvation. They allow themselves to see it only in terms of a restraining influence upon sinners that keeps them from degenerating into utter bestiality. In general revelation God presents himself only as a power to be encountered, whereas in the gospel he comes as a person to be known in faith and trust. For my part, I cannot see how any revelation from the God of the gospel can be other than saving in its basic significance if it is truly a revelation of him. If we grant such a revelation to all peoples, such as Scripture describes, then it must be the disclosure of the gracious God from whom our creaturely existence flows. God is the mystery of created life and offers himself for trust to everyone. We meet him in a thousand ways: when we ask if there is anything to trust in, or any justice to be had, or any basis of final meaning. God is present even when he is not named. Now, this is not to say that people always respond favorably to this fact—they do not. God is near and they ought to seek after him, but often they do not (Acts 17:27). But if they do respond, God proves to be "the rewarder of them that diligently seek him" (Heb. 11:6).

In relating general revelation to special revelation, we ought to see the first as leading into the second. In general revelation, God offers himself to everyone in the secret of each person's heart. I believe, in contrast to the usual Protestant position, that God by his grace makes an offer of salvation to them all, in keeping with his stated desire (1 Tim. 2:4). This offer can be accepted or refused and is a genuine subjective possibility. But the revelation remains rather hidden and unclear and calls for further revelation that is definitive and out in the open. This is exactly what we have in special revelation. In the biblical history of salvation, we have a segment of world history in which God has made good on his offer of salvation. Indeed, I would affirm that the whole world was created for the salvation brought by the Word made flesh. What all humanity has hoped and longed for, the dwelling of the gracious God with them, has come to pass. The God who "never left himself without witness" has surpassed the mute witness of general revelation by granting the supreme miracle of reconciliation by the divine Son of God. The world and its history was made by him and for him, and fitted to become the stage of his incarnation. He who loves the world and presents himself to every soul has communicated himself without reservation for the salvation of all believers.

The Pattern of Special Revelation

But the glory of revelation in the Bible is that it presents an infinite, personal God making himself known as the saving Lord who desires a covenant relationship with his human creatures, (unlike the god of the Greeks, who never spoke to humankind and never revealed himself in historical deeds). We have no interest in revelation as an abstraction or as the linchpin in a philosophical theology but in revelation as the unveiling of the grace and mercy of God, which calls for trust and commitment from us. This, in the last analysis, is what makes the Christian revelation so convincing: not the objective proofs extrinsic to its substance (though proofs there are), but the intrinsic appeal of the pearl of great price that is made available in it. Revelation by itself might have no appeal—if, for example, it portrayed a remote and austere deity. However convincing its external credentials might be, we would turn away from it in disgust, and go to any hell defiantly. The Koran, for instance, makes the highest claims for itself (higher indeed than the Bible does) and, in a tight apologetic case for Islam as God's truth, offers to supply the revelational axiom. Yet it has no good news to offer, only law and submission. What makes Christian revelation, and the Bible as its medium, different is simply the message of grace and forgiveness it enshrines, which draws sinners almost irresistibly to the mercy seat of God. It drew them before there even was a Bible, and it draws them still.[9]

Revelation in the Old Testament occurs in the context of establishing a covenant with Israel and calling forth trust in the divine promise.[10] In a variety of ways God made himself known to the people as the true and living God. He gave his word of promise to their forefather Abraham that he would bless the whole world through his descendants and, in his dealing with the other patriarchs, continues to show his fidelity to that pledge. Later on, God makes himself known to Moses and calls him to be the leader of the people and to liberate them from bondage in Egypt. At Sinai God gives his ten words of holy law and opens up deeper dimensions of his contract with Israel. History became the theater in which God showed himself to be the redeemer and savior of humankind. He wants to be known, not so much from nature, but from the acts he performs before human eyes, as Pannenberg emphasizes. If sin has twisted and corrupted history, grace will come in and begin to put it right.[11] But the events are not left uninterpreted, according to the biblical record. The Old Testament does not downplay the importance of the Word of God that comes in to bring out the redemptive significance of

God's acts of salvation. Just as the words of a person have as much importance as his or her deeds in determining character and intention, so God acts in order to achieve redemption and speaks in order to communicate his plan in detail. It is fruitless to ask which is more important for revelation, history or language; the Scriptures give them equal emphasis and refuse to choose between them. Facts without words are blind, and words without facts are empty. The old Testament presents revelation as the story of what God has done and the witness to what God has spoken—content and confirmation.[12] The pattern is abundantly plain in the case of Moses himself, who was both the agent of a great deliverance and the prophet par excellence, who spoke to God "mouth to mouth" (Num. 12:8). Deuteronomy makes it clear, too, that the Word of God thus communicated embraces the whole corpus of legislation and not simply the original ten words of Sinai. There is revelation also in the messianic and eschatological prophecy scattered throughout the Old Testament in which the coming king is described and the kingdom that shall not be overthrown is promised. A blessed era is foretold in which there will be a new David, a new Moses, a new covenant, and a new exodus. And there is revelation in the books of wisdom that, although it sounds like ordinary human insight, is understood to be the product of divine illumination. As the First Book of Kings says, "God gave Solomon wisdom and understanding beyond measure, and largeness of mind like the sand on the seashore" (4:29). Wisdom comes from God, and we are given to understand that the Old Testament wisdom literature reveals a divine pattern of behavior disclosing the will of the Lord. Even the psalms are more than merely human response to God, because they are linked to inspiration and prophecy, as when, for example, Miriam the prophet of God sang her canticle. Even the narratives in the historical books are not just interesting tales but a form of instruction for our sakes to spell out the shape and directions of the life of faith. In many and various ways, indeed, did Yahweh God of Israel reveal his name as the holy, loving, and saving God that he is.[13] He manifests himself as the Lord of history, performing acts of deliverance and giving messages for the people, and although the focus is upon a single nation, the horizon of his salvation reaches out to include all peoples.[14]

Revelation in the New Testament builds upon the modalities of the Old and focuses upon a new covenant, made effective in Jesus Christ and open to all who believe from every tribe and nation. In him the promises formerly directed toward Israel are made universally available, extended, and transformed. The witness is now borne to a new set of realities brought about by the coming of Jesus in the fullness of time, the Word made flesh, and in the sending of the Spirit to empower the church to proclaim the gospel to the whole world. Not simply the fulfillment of discrete prophecies concerning the coming of a great king, his advent is the fulfillment of the great promise to save the world through Abraham's seed. Yahweh is once again actively bringing salvation to earth.

Jesus Christ is and must be the centerpiece of the Christian revelation, because in him God entered our world within the parameters of a human life. Quite properly, Luther pointed to him as the material center of the Christian message and inquired of every book of the Bible how it preached Christ, the Word of God, supremely. The Scriptures exist to bear witness to him (John 5:39), and he is the sum and substance of their message. No mere emissary of the prophetic sort, the very Son of God is incarnate, dwelling among us, the revelation of God without peer. Of all the forms of revelation, this is the best. We are not able to come to God on the basis of our own wisdom or righteousness, but a way has been opened for us to come, and the life has been made manifest—visibly, audibly, and tangibly. Small wonder that orthodoxy has made response to him the touchstone of a sound confession. In him, the divine nature is mirrored and a fulfillment of the divine plan to restore fallen humanity to a true and saving knowledge of God.

But the moral miracle of the incarnation is as great as the metaphysical. For God came into the world, not as might be expected, in the form of a king, but in the form of a servant. Shattering the almost universal stereotype of God as one who is too high a being to be much concerned with lowly human affairs, one who keeps his distance and protects his honor, God does the utterly unexpected thing and humbles himself in the service of humanity, even unto death upon a cross. The pagan philosopher Celsus was right to feel that this claim is something incredible, judged by the standards of religious opinion he was familiar with. But nothing could have more effectively revealed the heart of God as the loving shepherd of humankind than this. In the incarnation, God makes full use of the human receptor culture and interacts with people in it in dynamic human terms. Though by no means devoid of content, revelation in this mode is much more than a set of lifeless propositions, and the information conveyed through it is personal and inexhaustible. For this reason, perhaps, John said that he did not think all the books in the world could tell the story exhaustively (John 21:25). God does not keep his distance, as in Islam, but crosses the great divide between heaven and earth and communicates with us in human terms.[15]

But is it true? From the standpoint of ordinary people in history, it certainly rings true. It has to be the greatest story ever told, the fulfillment of the bravest human dreams. No other symbol can give such a basis to the dignity and worth of human life and at the same time promise us healing and deliverance from the forces that enslave us. It tells us what we most need to hear, and if it be false, then there is something amiss in those needs themselves. The incarnation is not so much the projection of a mere wish as the promised fulfillment of the deepest needs of the human heart. What kind of world would it be in which what we most desperately need is impossible of fulfillment? From the point of view of Judaism and Islam, the incarnation is certainly possible. The God of Abraham, Isaac, and Jacob came near to redeem his people and cares passionately for them. He is the kind of God who could (because of his power) and would (because of his love) be able to make such a gesture of his concern as the incarnation is. The claim goes beyond, but not against, anything in those religions. God is free and merciful, and therefore these believers must be open to the unexpected and not shut themselves against it. One can only respect Rabbi Pinchas Lapide for admitting that if it turns out that Jesus is the messiah of Jewish hope he would have no objection to that. "Who am I as a devout Jew to define a priori God's saving activity?"[16]

The question of truth, so deceptively simple, can be asked on so many levels at once that the answers must tumble over one another. Did Jesus himself claim any such thing? It would seem that he did when he set himself apart from all others in the authority of his word and the uniqueness of his relation of sonship with God his Father.[17] Was the claim in any way justified? It seems that it was when the mighty power of God raised him up and left the tomb empty to testify of that wondrous vindication.[18] Did the apostles claim incarnation or only something less? Saint John affirms the incarnation in those very words, but other writers say as much in other terms.[19] Does incarnation make theological sense—Godhead united to manhood? A mystery, without doubt, but one in keeping with human beings being made in the image of God and God limiting himself to the lowly conditions of that earthly life.[20] But how reasonable is it? As reasonable as need be, if we grant the reality of a living Lord and Creator, within whose possibilities even incarnation must surely lie.[21] But these issues, important as they are, cannot be explored in this chapter, whose more modest purpose is to call attention to Jesus Christ as the center of the claim to revelation in the New Testament.

The coming of the Spirit on the day of Pentecost is the second crucial feature of the New Testament revelation claim, after the incarnation. It fills in the subjective side of revelation in the Christian understanding and balances the objective pole. It answers the human need for subjective immediacy in religion and forces us to the dynamic and contemporary dimensions of revelation. The Spirit makes it impossible to construe revelation in a static way and removes the need to defend the authority of revelation in ways wholly objective. If it requires the Spirit to make revelation real in our lives, then the Spirit cannot be so easily squeezed out of the picture when it comes to questions like the ones we are facing in this book. The neglect of this factor may be what has led to some of the difficulties that will not seem to go away.

Jewish belief in the first century had it that the Spirit had been withdrawn because of human disobedience, but the Christian claim is that the Spirit was restored in connection with the messianic work of Jesus.[22] Each of the main New Testament writers is very conscious that the Spirit was poured out afresh and in power and was rendering the lordship of Christ effective in the world.[23] Luke and Acts are full of the conviction that the Spirit has come to empower believers to proclaim the gospel effectively to the whole world. John's Gospel presents the Paraclete Spirit, who bears witness to the truth in Jesus, and his First Epistle refers to the anointing of the believer for the knowledge of God. Paul gives us an extensive doctrine of the Spirit. Preaching, in order to be effective, has to be done in the power of the Spirit. The experience of salvation and the assurance of adoption is made possible by the Spirit's witness in us. Believers can expect the Spirit to lead and guide them and give them gifts to equip them in the work of building up the community and ministering love. The Spirit searches the deep things of God and reveals them to the apostles, inspiring their teaching and, in turn, enlightening their hearers (1 Cor. 2:10–16). Paul speaks of the Spirit "interpreting spiritual truths to those who possess the Spirit" (v. 13). The spirit gives an ability to receive and understand spiritual things that the unbeliever lacks; things will remain enigmatic until the Spirit opens the believer's eyes to them. Of course the words can be comprehended and the sentences understood before the Spirit does his work, but they do not register in their full significance and do not carry conviction until that time. The overall picture the New Testament gives us of the coming of the Spirit is that he desires to make the Word of the gospel in all its forms existentially real to people, so that they awaken to the reality of God's grace and love and receive what Christ has done for themselves personally. Mere information about these topics will not be effective until the Spirit renders it dynamically effective in a human heart.

The coming of the Spirit does not mean that the norms of the gospel established by Jesus and the apostles have lost their authority and can be transcended at any time by persons claiming the Spirit. There are some today who would want to construe their spiritual "liberty" in this way and launch out in altogether new directions of belief and praxis for which there is no scriptural support—and even opposition. What Christianity is or will be would, then, be an open question, not to be decided on the basis of past norms but open to creative change as the "Spirit" leads.[24] Thus, the Spirit could be appealed to in order to break out of the restrictions of orthodoxy, leaving us free to shape religion for ourselves. Tempting though this perspective is, it is not true to the New Testament witness about the Spirit. In John's Gospel, for example, there is no idea of the Spirit canceling the truth given through Jesus but, rather, the Spirit freshly focusing that truth for the current situation. The Spirit works to bring each generation of believers as close to the Lord as the first apostles were and enables them to penetrate the same truth in relation to their different context. It is not that a new message will be given, but that the old message will continue to be made effective by the Spirit, as he helps us to reinterpret and apply the truth once delivered to meet new challenges. Even these fresh interpretations depend for their validity upon the original truth and are limited in their authority to the special circumstances they address.[25]

What the coming of the Spirit does mean for our doctrine of revelation is that the norms given in the classical disclosure are dynamic in the sense that they can be dynamically interpreted and freshly applied in ever-changing situations. It means that revelation is not locked in the past as a collection of inflexible rules but is a disclosure that comes alive today, opening up a relationship with God and transforming human life. It means that the Bible, for example, cannot be seen as simply a set of ancient propositions, but as a means of grace by which God is able to speak to us in new ways. For this reason, Paul prays that believers will be given "a spirit of wisdom and revelation" so that the truth of what he is teaching them will come alive in their experience and they will begin to understand its significance for their own circumstances. Obviously, the issues surrounding revelation and inspiration cannot be handled simply from the outside in an academic way but will have to be considered from the inside in relation to commitment.

A further dimension of revelation in the New Testament is brought out by the phrase so often used in it: "the word of God." In our day it is common to hear it used to refer to the Christian Bible, which is quite an extension of its original meaning. In the New Testament, apart from the special instance where it refers to the incarnate Word (John 1:14), it refers to the message about Jesus that the apostles proclaimed. "They spoke the word of God with boldness" (Acts 4:31). It is sometimes called "the word of the Lord" or the "word of Christ" or "the word of the cross" or "the word of truth" or "the word of reconciliation." Hebrews calls it a living and powerful sword, whereas Peter credits it with the ability to create life in us. The word of God in the New Testament refers primarily to the proclamation of the gospel at work in people's lives when received by faith. It is a message that "cannot be bound," because of the power of the Spirit. When we today use the phrase to refer to the Bible as a whole, we should realize that we are using it in a more developed and different sense than the New Testament itself does. The positive side of our usage is to secure for the Bible a place under the category "word of God" that it deserves, as we will show. The negative side is that it can hamper and inhibit our use of the phrase "word of God" for the activities of proclaiming the gospel today in our own words, for when a person testifies to the saving grace of God, he or she is indeed speaking the word of God.

Content is an important facet of this phrase. The word of God is not a bare existential address but includes objective truths about the gospel and ourselves. Paul made it clear that the gospel he preached was a communication full of content, centering upon the vicarious death of Christ for sinners and on his bodily resurrection from the dead (1 Cor. 15:1–19). This goes directly against a strong tendency in modern theology to affirm revelation as a transforming experience but not to affirm a message full of content and truth given in intelligible speech and language—as if there were some kind of opposition between personal revelation and verbal communication. The New Testament knows of no such dichotomy; it stems from modern philosophical objections to cognitive revelation and an objective knowledge of God. However it is that these objections ought to be answered, revelation according to the New Testament is contentful and intelligible and speaks to human beings about subjects we are able to understand. The loss of confidence in revelation as cognitive led to a great crisis in theology, and it is important to recover this confidence if we hope to make an effective proclamation of the gospel in our generation.[26]

In brief, the Old Testament gives us a richly variegated pattern of revelation that sets forth Israel's convenant with God and anticipates further developments to come, whereas the New Testament focuses all its emphasis upon the fulfillment of that hope in Jesus Christ. At last the promise to Abraham, which was meant to encompass all nations on earth, has reached out to include them in Jesus Christ the incarnate Word.

Revelation and the Scripture Principle

But where does Scripture fit in to this pattern of revelation? Obviously, it has a place as documentation, as a collection of ancient texts mediating to us the formative insights that were reached or received long ago. But why consider it anything more than a human text or in any way consider it to have been miraculously produced? Warfield admitted that Christianity could be completely true without having any such thing as biblical inspiration.[27] Perhaps Scripture is just part of the tradition and not intended as revelation in the proper sense. Of course, we know that both Judaism and Christianity developed a Scripture principle early on. After the exile, the Jews needed a Torah to preserve their ethnic identity, and in the second century A.D., the Christians, feeling pressure from the likes of Marcion, followed the Judaic pattern and settled upon a New Testament canon of divinely inspired texts. But this development did not have to happen, and some would say ought not to have happened, at least in the case of Christianity. After all, a religion oriented to the living Christ and universal in scope does not want to be tied to a sacred text that would hamper its life in the Spirit.[28] Or as James Barr says, "It is not at all clear from the New Testament itself that Jesus or the earliest Christians intended Christianity to be a scriptural religion, a faith bound and controlled by its own scriptures and one in which such scriptures would have ultimate authoritative status: indeed, the New Testament seems to make it clear that they did not so intend."[29] What problems we could avoid if this appealing line of thought were true! The Bible could still be prized as the unique medium of revelation, but we would not have to be worried by the presence in it of slips and errors.

Whether we would have fewer problems were we to believe in a Christianity without the Scripture principle is certainly debatable, given the rather chaotic state of liberal theology, which does in fact operate without it. The fact is that the notion of inspired Scripture accompanying and attesting God's covenant with humanity is present in revelation reality as far back as we care to go (Moses is depicted as the writer of Scripture as well as the great prophet) and, most importantly, is integral to the thinking of Jesus and the apostles. On the basis of the evidence that I will present fully in the next chapter, there is a kind of symbiosis between revelation and its scriptural objectification that makes it impossible to separate them except as a thought experiment. "What advantage hath the Jew? Much in every way—to him has been entrusted the oracles of God" (Rom. 3:2). It was not merely that these writings bridged the generations from the time of revelation past to the present, but that God intended writings that would do so in a way that would carry his authority and fidelity. There is just too much testimony about the character of these documents for us to set it aside and pretend to examine revelation apart from it. It would seem that God gave us Holy Scripture along with the other products of his disclosure and intended us to receive them as his written Word. Scripture was not added on to biblical faith but is intrinsic to it. Salvation, as far as one can trace it, is supported by documentation in which the covenantal obligations are spelled out and sustained. From the way in which Christ and the apostles receive the Scripture principle from Judaism and regard it as a product generated by divine revelation itself, the issue is settled for Christianity in principle. It could no more get rid of that Jewish legacy than get rid of Jesus himself.[30] God had spoken to his people Israel in the past, and the Scriptures were seen to be an extension of this modality of divine speech, revelation cast into written form for the direction of the church.[31] Living in such a universe, it was natural for the early Christians to receive new covenant scriptures in much the same way and move in the direction of a full Christian Bible.

Inspired Scripture constitutes a term in the rich pattern of revelation given to humanity in Jesus Christ. It is a capstone and completion of it in the sense that it conveys in a reliable manner the freight and burden of revelation secured in an appropriate form by God's own action. We are not given to view this development as fortuitous and contingent but as a component of the revelational activity God was intending and performing. In no way does this fact affect the sheer centrality of Jesus Christ in revelation or hinder the ministry of the Spirit. The Bible is a witness, although the primary one, to the revelation of God in the face of Jesus Christ. Christology, not Bibliology, occupies center stage in Christianity. (It is otherwise with Muhammad and the Koran.) Holy Scripture is an important part of the picture but not the whole. It is one of the forms of the Word of God through which the light reaches us. But what a wonderful gift it is! A durable and objective record of the burden of divine revelation, engendered by the Spirit, and given to bring us to the saving knowledge of God. It would have been possible, of course, for God to have had the message passed under ordinary conditions, much the way our knowledge of Plato's thought depends on human authorship and transmission of texts. Here there is no in-spired vehicle required. But such a course of action opens the door to an undetermined amount of dilution, distortion, and corruption enter-ing in, and it pleased God to add to his gifts the benefit of Holy Scrip-ture, the literary objectification of his Word and revelation, so that we might have a light and a guide in matters of faith. Thus we can say with the psalmist: "More to be desired are they than gold, even much fine gold; sweeter also than honey and drippings of the honeycomb" (19:-10).

The Functions of Scripture

Just as revelation itself is many-sided, so the Bible has a number of functions in the life of believers. Most important of all, it is the medium of the Christian message. Like a telescope, it summons us to look through, not at, it and see the starry heavens. The most crucial ques-tion to ask is, Have you seen the stars? not, What do you think of the lens? Like a loudspeaker, the Bible invites us to hear the Word of God. What is urgent is to receive the Word that was given, not to conclude what to make of the background noise. Like a lamp, the Scriptures make it possible for us to see; like bread, they satisfy our appetite and nourish us. It is very important not to forget, when we are discussing the topic of biblical authority academically, that the Bible is a means to an end, not an end in itself. It is a God-given vehicle that puts us in touch with the Light of the world and the Bread that came down from heaven. It is proper to think of the Bible in sacramental terms—as Ru-pert of Deutz did in the eleventh century: "As often as the Holy Spirit opens the mouths of apostles and prophets and even doctors, to preach the word of salvation, to unveil the mysteries of the Scriptures, the Lord opens the gates of heaven to rain down manna for us to eat. We are fed in our minds by reading and hearing the Word of God, we are fed in our mouths by eating the bread of eternal life from the table of the Lord, and drinking the chalice of eternal salvation."[32] How barren it is to regard the Bible only as a study document, when from the the the divine storehouse it nourishes believers in every aspect of their being. The paper and the ink act as the outward and visible signs of an inward and invisible grace as faith toward God is invited and extended. Not only is it mistaken to treat the Bible as a merely human text, it is also wrong to treat it as a merely natural object, which will yield its treasures to the scholar and learned exegete. It is more appropriate to think of it as the context to stand in when you want to encounter God and have him address you. As Vatican II expressed it, "God is present in his Word, since it is he himself who speaks when the Holy Scriptures are read in church" (*Constitution on the Sacred Liturgy* 7). We wait patiently and prayerfully in the midst of the biblical witnesses, expecting God to teach and lead us.[33] If we do not hear his voice there, being assured that the medium of God's Word is perfect and flawless will not help us. The problem is deeper than one that can be addressed with apologetic arguments about the text. How God speaks to us and leads us through Scripture is a mystery wrapped up in the hidden operations of the Spirit in our hearts. The medium has to be empowered to deliver the message.

The Bible performs a number of other functions for us in addition to the basically religious function of leading us to the saving knowledge of God in Jesus Christ, and we need all of them to be performed. I will refer to three of them. First, there is its function as a witness to the saving deeds of God and their significance for us. Having this witness in the durable form of writing ensures that its impact continues to be felt. We recall Job's ironical words: "Oh that my words were written, oh that they were inscribed in a book" (19:23). Like John the Baptist, the Scriptures bear witness to Christ and keep the subject of God's gracious redemption ever before us. The Bible announces that light has come into the world, and human beings can walk in that light. When we say that the Bible is a witness (as Barth also stresses), we do not deny that it is part of the revelation it witnesses to but simply make it clear what the burden of the Bible as witness is.[34]

Second, as a deposit of revelational truth, the Bible provides the church with a kind of charter or constitution by which to measure her doctrine and practice. By setting forth a set of symbols, doctrinal commentary, and ethical instruction, the Scriptures reliably inform us on the basic issues that confront the church. It serves as a memory bank, reminding us continually of what God has said and done. As a psalmist said, "Let this be recorded for a generation to come, so that a people yet unborn may praise the Lord" (102:18). Because it is so easy to forget even basic principles that lead to salvation, the Bible exists to remind us of them, as Peter noted: "I intend to remind you of these things, though you know them and are established in the truth you have" (1 Pet. 1:12). The Scriptures, in effect, draw a circle around us, indicating the ground where it is spiritually and theologically safe to walk and the field where it is nourishing to feed. They do not answer every question we may wish to put to them, by any means, but they do establish a fundamental orientation and direction for the community. They indicate the basic symbolic structure and norms by which we ought to be living. God has willed the Bible to be a charter document that will help to prevent the church from being swept away into human philosophy and vain deceit (Col. 2:8). By being faithful to it, the church declares her desire to be rooted in the original and decisive revelation through Jesus Christ and the apostles that has been objectified in Holy Writ.[35]

Third, the Bible is the religious classic of Christianity. It uniquely embodies the style of faith and experience that characterizes Christians. Without in any way detracting from its other functions, the Bible enjoys pride of place in witnessing to the experience of the risen Lord, and as such, it illumines and transforms the lives of those who place themselves under its authority. Theologians of the experiential type are not wrong when they appeal to the Bible for inspiration and direction, for it does speak often of communion with God and encounter with God. But they are wrong insofar as they do not equally intend to receive the other aspects of biblical authority, such as its teaching, and when they construe "religious classic" to mean a merely human text with power to illumine experience.[36] But the Bible is our religious classic, and Christianity is inconceivable apart from it. It is preposterous to suppose that at this late date Christianity will be anything other than a scriptural religion.

Summing Up

The overall picture of revelation according to the Bible is quite clear. God is engaged in effecting the salvation of sinners and in pursuance of this goal has revealed himself and his plan. Revelational activity includes, as we have seen, a great variety of products, including historical events, verbal communication, the astounding event of incarnation, and the outpouring of the Spirit, and it has generated a scriptural witness, as well, to render effective in an ongoing way the revelation itself.[37] Rather than turning over the gospel truth to fallible human beings in its entirety, as he might have done, God has given the church the canonical Scriptures to help to ensure the integrity of our knowledge of God and to prevent the proclamation from being lost or twisted beyond recognition. It is not that Christianity rests upon the foundation of the Bible (its foundation is Jesus Christ) as much as that Christian truth comes in and through the medium of Scripture and brings a doctrine of inspiration with it. As Athanasius said, the Bible is "a holy school of the knowledge of God and the conduct of the soul" (*Incarnation of the Word* 12). In this manner, the objective side of revelation, whose subjective side is made actual through the Spirit, is secured by means of scriptural symbols and doctrines that set forth the shape of saving truth.

Is revelation only in the past, in the witness of the Bible, and in the present, in the leading of the Spirit, and altogether signed, sealed, and delivered? No, the New Testament indicates a mighty revelation that is to come ("the revelation of our Lord Jesus Christ") and a time when we shall know not only in part but fully (1 Cor. 1:7; 13:12). The Bible itself points forward to the full revelation when all flesh shall see the glory of the Lord (Isa. 40:5). At present, there are many questions that have to go unanswered, even though we have the norms of Scripture. We operate with a provisional revelation, a form of God's Word that, though valid and true, conceals as well as reveals and is destined to be replaced and supplanted by the fuller revelation that is coming. Although we look back for the gospel norms that bring us salvation, we also look forward to greater light and direction, both in this present age and in the age to come. Though loyal to the scriptural words from the past, we live and walk in the Spirit of God and anticipate being led into the full truth of Christ and to the coming of his kingdom.

If revelation has not been exhausted, even though normatively outlined in the Scriptures, then it is possible to hope that our understanding of the truth will grow and mature over the years. Now that we are in touch with world religions, for example, and in a position to learn what is true in their experience of the God who addresses everyone, it may be possible to sharpen our understanding of what God is intending in the Bible. In the mutual struggle and competition of religions we can all be stimulated and challenged to learn more of the divine mystery. This need not relativize the absolute truth given in Jesus Christ that is, we believe, the definitive revelation of God.

The Shift from Objective Content

The most pronounced feature of contemporary theology is the way it has moved away from the biblical and orthodox belief that revelation involves content (among other things). Not that the older view neglected to recognize the subjective side of revelation, but it did so in a balanced way, together with confidence in the message God gave through revelation. Indeed, revelation is such a prominent subject of discussion in the modern period, when it was not so before, because of a major shift and attempted reconstruction that goes strongly against the historic faith of the church in all its branches. As is so clear in Augustine or Aquinas, Calvin or Luther, God communicated truth about himself and his plan in the course of revealing himself. Admittedly, in scholastic theology, revelation was too closely identified with supernaturally given information and not sufficiently inclusive of symbolic and existential aspects, and it became narrowed down too much. But the conviction that God spoke to human beings as well as encountered them in revelation was almost a universal in Christian theology before the Enlightenment. John Baillie has taken note of the shift away from revelation as information to revelation as inner experience or encounter, a much vaguer concept and one more difficult to get hold of.[38] There are many modern views of revelation, but they all tend to share a reaction against content and opt for a more ethereal concept that leaves people free to develop their own content. Piously declaring that revelation is not something human beings can possess or control, this view has delivered it over to autonomous human beings to do precisely that. Instead of revelation coming from God in deed and word, yielding norms and doctrines to guide the church, the emphasis is on the human contribution and construction. Revelation wells up from human subjectivity, affecting the human spirit in some fashion but not issuing controls over what people think and what they ought to do.[39]

The deists were among the first to make the attack upon the historic view of revelation. They maintained that reason alone was competent in the realm of truth, and revelation ought to concern itself with questions of piety and obedience. Revelation can add nothing to what we can know by reason and does not offer valid information about the nature and purposes of God that are given with the creation. As Lessing went on to say, the truth of revelation is intended for the heart and not the mind. Religion must be kept within the limits of reason. Kant was prepared to say that practical reason can supply certain convictions about God, the soul, and immortality but agreed that we cannot claim to know anything about the noumenal, and therefore about God himself and God's Word. All human beings can do is respond to the ethical side of revelation as if it came from God, even though, strictly speaking, they cannot be sure that it did.

Schleiermacher, the father of modern theology, reared as a pietist, connected revelation to the experiences of the heart. We experience the feeling of absolute dependence, and this gives rise to the idea of God on whom we depend. Revelation does not break upon us from without but occurs as a transformation of human consciousness. All religions, not only Christianity, rest upon the same experiential base and can claim revelation in the same sense (though Schleiermacher would say that Christianity rests on a unique God-consciousness possessed by

Jesus). The main point is that revelation does not involve content given by God, though it leads to doctrinal formulations out of religious communion. But these formulations are human in nature and authority; thus, revelation really has no infallible substance of truth and content to offer. This is a radical departure from historic Christianity and a shift to revelation as inner experience. For Ritschl, too, although the emphasis is upon morality rather than experience, revelation involves no communication of information to be believed but only the manifestation of an ethical ideal to lure us on to moral maturity. With Hegel, the stress is upon philosophical theology, but the bottom line is the same: revelation bubbles up from below, offers only obsure symbolism, and needs to be supplemented by clear philosophical thought. The French liberal Auguste Sabatier is delightfully clear. He identifies revelation with religious experience and finds it in all religions, particularly in Jesus. For him, it is a revelatory experience that is important and by which one knows oneself to be a child of God; it is an inner, subjective experience and develops with the evolution of the race. Although a subjective element is part of the biblical and historic pattern of revelation, in effect this kind of modern position is totally opposed to the balanced picture and distorts it beyond recognition.[40]

Following World War I, a number of theologians, often called neo-orthodox or dialectical thinkers, made the same shift from the objective in revelation, but in a new way one might call neo-liberal. It consisted in thinking of revelation, not as a universal human capacity of mystical experience, but as an encounter with God and God's Word such that revelation can be captured neither in propositions, as in orthodoxy, nor in experience or rationality, as in liberalism. Utterly transcendent, God encounters the human subject when it pleases him by means of an experience of the "Word", which faith recognizes to be present. Kierkegaard began this way of thinking about revelation in reaction to Hegel's rational approach and maintained that the truths of revelation were existential and paradoxical and could by no means be made to seem plausible. Like the mature Barth, Kierkegaard did not intend his emphasis to work any substantial change in orthodox beliefs, but in Bultmann it is plain that the emphasis had very radical implications indeed. Believing that liberalism had neglected the otherness of God and revelation, Bultmann conceived of revelation as an eschatological event that encounters an individual in decision. In a famous paragraph in an essay on the concept of revelation, he says: "What then has been revealed? Nothing at all, as far as the question concerning revelation asks for doctrines . . . on the other hand, however, everything has been revealed, insofar as man's eyes are opened concerning his own existence and he is once again able to understand himself."[41] Revelation is taken to be personal and not at all propositional, and to involve nothing by way of the communication of infallible information. Therefore, Bultmann goes on to explore existential subjectivity rather than the content orthodoxy has always been interested in, and he cares not at all for the content of what the apostles teach or the history that the evangelists record. That simply does not matter except as it can be shown to relate to existential experience. The next logical step, of course, as critics like Buri have shown, is to eliminate Bultmann's conservative insistence upon the uniqueness of Christ in this wholly existential affair of revelation and dekerygmatize as well as demythologize the gospel.[42] Revelation, in such a view, belongs to a person's inner history and not to the outer realm of fact and truth.

The more typical way of abandoning the objectivity of revelation in our day is to think of it as expanding human consciousness in relation to what God is supposed to be doing in the secular movements of our time. God is not seen as the object of experience so much as mysteriously present in all human engagement in creative tasks. Revelation is correlated with the inner drive of the human spirit toward fuller awareness, raising these powers to a higher pitch of activity. It is present as direction and stimulus, not as truth and content, as transformation, not information. Somehow enlightened by God, the individual is enabled to speak with new confidence about the human situation and locate new solutions to its problems. Revelation serves to stimulate the imagination and enable us to break through to higher stages of human conciousness. Understandably, this way of thinking about revelation is not greatly impressed by an appeal to the actual teachings of the Bible where they are inconvenient to whatever secular insight is in vogue.[43]

In his recent book, *Models of Revelation*, Avery Dulles suggests that we think of revelation in terms of the rich set of symbols contained in the biblical documents, symbols like the cross and resurrection, which are richer than bare propositions in the way they reveal God and his plan. In saying this, it seems tolerably clear that Dulles does not mean to cut these symbols off from their historical and propositional anchors within biblical revelation but to see them as something more than facts and concepts, as indeed they are. Yet there remains a certain vagueness about the symbols. Are we bound to the event-symbols as actually occurring or to the truth-symbols as infallibly defined by the Scriptures? It seems as if Dulles wishes to leave it somewhat vague, thus avoiding controversy on questions of miracle, in the case of events, and literalism, in the case of the doctrinal content. If we extract the symbols from the Bible, and divorce them from their scriptural context, there is a real danger that they will be construed in arbitrary ways, undisciplined by the Bible itself. The cross becomes the symbol for all suffering poor, not of vicarious atonement; the resurrection comes to signify new life, not the bodily resurrection of Jesus. God is the symbol of the depth dimension in human life; he is not the living God who made heaven and earth—and so on. Though I appreciate the emphasis upon God-given metaphors and agree that they are richer than bare propositions, I am nervous when I see a theologian seem to back away from the factual and cognitive content of them, given the widespread retreat from content in the liberal movement. In our modern context we just cannot afford to be vague about what we mean by revelation. Nothing less than the clarity of the gospel is at stake here.

What has gone wrong in nonconservative modern theology across the board is the retreat from contentful revelation, with devastating results for dogmatic theology. Instead of seeing revelation—as the Bible invites us to and as historic theology always has—in terms of a balance between the objective and the subjective pole, the modern emphasis practically drops the objective side (*what* has been revealed) and leaves revelation as a subjective matter.

The Reason for the Shift Away from Content

One could explain the dramatic shift away from content by listing a series of factors that incline modern minds to resistance: the theistic model presupposed by taking the Bible as written revelation, the miracles accompanying the story of divine redemption, Kant's dogma that one can have no knowledge of the transcendent such as the Bible claims to deliver, numerous objections to one or another of the biblical concepts, the belief in the fallibility of the Bible as propounded by liberal criticism, and the imperialism of any claim that makes Jesus the only way of salvation. But when it comes right down to it, there is only one reason for the rejection of content in revelation: a lot of moderns are not willing to have dictated to them how they must think and how they must act. The idea that human beings must approach God on his terms, implied by the second commandment, not in ways they themselves define, is simply unacceptable to the autonomous people of today. We face such a resistance to what the Bible teaches today that the battle necessarily takes place around the issue of revelation and inspiration.

Without denying that there are some real problems to face, what accounts for the shift to the subjective in revelation is a simple reflection of the widespread unwillingness to bow to the God who speaks authoritatively in the Scriptures. The idea that the Bible has the right to limit human freedom of thought and action is a hated idea that must be crushed and eliminated. For the humanistic liberals it is subjective revelation or no revelation at all. The objective content is not simply overlooked and omitted—it is despised and rejected. Though it would be true to say that a balance is needed, it would be truer to say that conversion is what is needed. A large number of modern theologians are not prepared to accept the restriction (as they would see it) represented by full biblical authority and are passionately dedicated to denying it. It is the content rather than the fact of special revelation that is objectionable. For when the Bible says something pleasing to the ear of autonomous people, for example, that love is important or that Christians should be one and put aside all differences, they, like classical Christians, treat the Bible as an oracle. But when the content of it discloses such truths as vicarious atonement, a supernatural deity, miracles, prophecy, incarnation, resurrection, Satan, and other such beliefs out of favor with "modern people," then the Bible must be denounced, reinterpreted, or reconstructed, Bultmann, as usual, provides the easiest illustration of this because he is so honest and straightforward in his views. The New Testament teaches such notions as I (and he) have listed and that he (not I) deems mythical and incredible for "modern people," He believes that the only possible way to make any meaningful sense out of them is to existentially reinterpret the material. The content of the Biblical gospel, according to Bultmann, can be traced to the mythology of Jewish apocalyptic and proto-Gnosticism and is not credible to us today. We have to strip away the mythological framework and get down to the existential power of the myths that offer us salvation through an encounter with God who "acted" (whatever that means for Bultmann) in Christ.[44]

In order to show that Bultmann's general approach—which is in utter revolt against the biblically defined gospel—is representative rather than atypical, let me give a few other examples. Edward Farley is quite explicit in his third reason for rejecting the Scripture principle—that it is bound up to a theistic way of viewing reality that he finds unacceptable. The problem of evil and the reality of human freedom rule out the existence of a God such as is presupposed by the biblical concept of revelation and inspiration.[45] The school of process philosophy determines results from supposedly rational procedures and does not hesitate to deny Scripture if the text proves unsuitable.[46] In liberation theology, there is enthusiasm for the revolutionary, prophetic line of thinking uncovered from the exodus or from a way of reading the Jesus story, but there is little reluctance to reject and denounce those parts of the Bible that jeopardize the conclusions liberation theology wants. Norman Gottwald, for example, would celebrate the Mosaic liberation trajectory embodied in an early Israelite peasant revolt but be highly critical of the royal consolidation under David when all of this was suppressed and forgotton.[47] Paul D. Hanson is eager to see God as "dynamic transcendence," which means not tying him down to old scriptural pronouncements but leaving him free to be up to date and flexible.[48] The list can go on and on. The point is that the Bible teaches some awkward things that modern people have difficulty receiving, and some think the only way to deal with that is to qualify its authority and deny its infallibility. After all, how can we believe in creation and fall after Darwin? How can we accept the Bible's teachings concerning women and homosexuality? How can we take seriously the incarnation and salvation through the blood of Christ alone? The cleanest way to deal with all these difficulties at once is to retreat from the notion that God's revelation involves necessary content, and this is what has been done by a host of modern theologians. Though the cost is awfully high (the entire basis of doctrinal and ethical theology in any traditional sense disappears), it is considered worth paying by the liberal theologians. It leaves them free to pursue enticing doctrines of their own making and preference. The great roadblock, the full authority of the Bible, no longer stands in their way to keep their subjectivity in line. Construing revelation as an event without binding content, there is no real chance that one's own doctrinal inventions will be refuted or considered heretical, the basis for any such judgment having been destroyed.

My coming down hard in this way on what I see to be an unworthy retreat from God's truth does not mean that I am unsympathetic to the difficulties there are in our believing certain aspects of biblical and traditional teachings. I do not want people to think they must swallow down orthodox concepts just because they are traditional and come bearing authority. I believe that one must be intellectually honest, and that faith's honest questions ought to be sensitively addressed. What I oppose is handing over to autonomous human beings the right to specify the conditions of their faith in God. That right belongs to God, however fitting we may be able to show the content of his disclosure to be in relation to human existence.

A Return to Revelation

By shifting away from the objective content of revelation, liberal theology has given the church a migraine headache. The truth foundations of the gospel are swept away and the validity of the gospel cast in doubt. We face a dilemma not unlike the one Luther faced: is the gospel and salvation based upon the Word and work of God, or is it founded upon human wisdom and achievement? Is Christian theology a clear rendition of the Word of God given in the Scriptures, or is it the highest and best human opinion? Emphasizing the objective side of revelation and the authority of the Bible has nothing to do with bibliolatry or rationalism. It has to do with keeping the church securely founded upon the apostolic scriptural witness, which is essential to its life and work. The church is in danger when it no longer hears the authoritative message of the Bible. It soon forgets what it believes and what it is in the world for and is easy prey to whatever philosophy is dominant at the moment. Everthing becomes blurred when the prophets and apostles fall silent.[49]

Therefore, I call us back to the biblical pattern of revelation, which includes propositional communication as well as personal communion. It presents the acts of God and the response of faith, the words of God and the call to obedience, the objective and the subjective. It tells us about God, and it brings us to God. I have no interest in downplaying the subjective dimension of revelation. Quite the contrary, I consider the work of the Spirit absolutely crucial for recognizing and understanding revelation. What concerns me at present is the way in which so many modern theologians have walked away from the sure content of the gospel that saves sinners for reasons that do not convince. Revelation, according to the Bible and historic theology, is not merely subjective and existentialist but a meaningful disclosure of the gracious God who acts and speaks. It supplies us with crucial information about the character and purposes of God, given in creaturely modalities we can understand, that enables people to be reconciled to God. It enables us to become aquainted with God so that we might meet him and know him. It is critically important not to lose this conviction.

The Bible presupposes that God is able to reveal himself and truth about his plans to us. This he has done pre-eminently in Jesus Christ, and in forms of speech and historical action. There is every reason to include, not exclude, the Bible from the pattern of revelation as one particular form of it. Not only have countless Christians experienced the Bible to be a special vehicle of the knowledge of God, and the occasion of freshly encountering God and learning about him, but the pattern of revelation as presented in the Bible everywhere assumes that God has communicated to us in human speech, thus rendering the relationship between God and people fully personal. As Marshall puts it, "To say that God cannot make use of words and statements to reveal himself is to go against all that we know of persons and how they relate to one another."[50]

Verbal communication is the marvel of human existence. The capacity to give and receive meaning by means of language is a priceless gift. It enables us to encode what we want to communicate and express and makes possible rich cultural coopertion and development. That God might employ language in his revelation to us is something anyone would have to hope for. That God has actually done so is something Christians can only rejoice in and celebrate.

CHAPTER 2

The Biblical Witness

Having sketched in the pattern of revelation with broad strokes and suggested that it is proper to think of the Bible as a product of revelation and a component of God's revealing activity, I want now to focus in on the matter of the greatest interest to us in this book and to look in greater detail at the evidence that supports the concept of a Scripture principle. What sort of doctrine of inspiration is supported by the Bible's own witness, fairly assessed?

There are really two questions it is important for us to try to answer. The first, the more general one, has to do with the church's decision to accept the bipartite Christian Bible as a canon of inspired Scripture, a decision already reached in Irenaeus by A.D. 200. Was this momentous decision a sound and good one, and ought the church today affirm it? It could be argued that it was not appropriate for the Christian community to accept as Scripture the Old Testament, which suits the Jewish community far better in that it presupposes an ethnic group, not the universal community gathered around Jesus Christ. It may have been natural for the earlist Christians who were Jewish to accept the Old Testament as inspired Scripture, but it does not follow that the church nowadays ought to do so. Why would a faith community under grace want to place herself under the Old Testament as her law? Furthermore, what evidence is there that Jesus and the apostles anticipated a New Testament canon, or expected Christianity to become a religion of a book? Of course, there were historical factors that led the later generations of Christians to a bipartite Scripture principle, but that does not require us to follow suit. It may be that a Christianity that viewed the New Testament as a human kerygma collection and not an inspired canon would be in a better position to understand the gospel and proclaim it for our time. Can the Bible itself help us decide whether the church has been right to accept the Old and New Testaments as her Scripture principle?

The second question, following the first and more specific, relates to the kind of Scripture principle the Bible commits us to, if it does. Is the Christian idea of biblical inspiration and authority identical to the Judaic understanding, or different? Does it involve strict inerrancy of detail and leveling of all the material, or is it more flexible? All classical Christians agree on the validity and importance of the Scripture principle, but they do not agree with one another precisely as to what is entailed by it.

In order to find some answers to these questions, we will need to sift carefully through what the Bible teaches with regard to a Scripture principle. Because most of us who conduct such an investigation already have convictions about the Bible, the challenge will be to approach the data fairly and in an open manner. Sadly, it is common to feel that the liberals refuse to see the strong claims in the Bible in favor of the Scripture principle, whereas conservatives quote the Bible's claims in the interests of their own preset dogma of biblical inerrancy.[1] I will not attempt a technical presentation of the biblical witness but aim at a judicious grasp of the overall picture. I will also try to be quite scrupulous in noting what certain verses do and do not claim and observe where they occur in the unfolding and progressive development of the biblical account. Futher, I am interested in the use of Scripture as well as the doctrine of Scripture as displayed in the Bible. Too often the valuable evidence contained in the way the New Testament writers handle the Old Testament is passed over in this connection, as if all that needed to be consulted were the so-called doctrinal verses. But the evidence of use must not be passed over in this kind of study, because it fills out what the direct claims themselves were taken to mean by those who make them and prevents us from speculating about their meaning in the abstract and in the interests of our own systematic theology.[2]

The ground can best and most economically be covered by considering three areas of evidence: the Old Testament witness to "itself", the New Testament witness to the Old Testament, and the New Testament witness to "itself". (I put "itself" in quotes because I recognize that the Old Testament did not exist as a canon at the time its books bore the witness I am referring to—the same with the New Testament.)

The Old Testament Witness to Itself

What we find in the Old Testament are strong indications of a canonical process in motion. Various kinds of writings are surfacing and beginning to be shaped into a Scripture principle. Almost from the first, in the ministry of Moses and the Sinaitic covenant, a document is being formed that will serve as a vehicle of religious and social duration for Israel, people of God. Since this vehicle is something quite structural and not accidental, it was natural for the Jews of a later date to conclude that God had been giving them his Word in the form of written texts. Of course, there are many questions the books of the Old Testament do not answer for us: which books precisely? which text of it? what kind of authority? why anonymous? and so on. Nevertheless, the Scripture principle as we now know it is firmly rooted in this rudimentary way in the Old Testament.[3]

Of particular importance is the way the figure of Moses is presented in the Penteteuch as the prophet of God and mediator of the law of God. "With him I [God] speak mouth to mouth, clearly, not in dark speech" (Num. 12:8). Moses was God's prophet, by whom the Lord brought Israel out of Egypt (Hos. 12:13) and the first and most eminent spokesman in a series of prophets that would follow (Deut. 18:15–22). He is described as writing down the law of God in a book as a permanent testimony to Israel (Deut. 31:24–29). Through Moses, as Paul would later say, Israel received the oracles of God (Rom. 3:2). Moses was a mediator of revelation, and writing down the word of the Lord was an integral part of his office. At Sinai he wrote down the words of the Lord, called the book of the covenant, and made it the document attesting the treaty between God and Israel, as was the custom in the suzerainty treaties of the period.[4] This would seem plainly to be the root and origin of the later Scripture principle, which cannot be written off as a late and extraneous decision.

Later books in the Hebrew Bible refer to Moses as the author of written revelation. This is particularly true of the post-exilic books (Chronicles, Ezra, and Nehemiah), which appeal to the law or the book of Moses as a written text bearing divine authority. Psalm 119 is a lengthy eulogy to these Scriptures and breathes a spirit of joy and gratitude because of the gift of God in this respect. Pre-exilic historical books also refer to Moses, but less often to his literary activity, whereas the pre-exilic prophets never refer to it explicitly. Evidently the Penteteuch was formed over many centuries, and Moses, though not the author of it in its final form, was the instigator of the literary activity that produced it.[5] But it is not necessary for my purposes here to declare a firm opinion on the authorship of the Penteteuch, which is a matter of debate among Scripture specialists. It remains true in any case that Moses is seen to have mediated a revelation and a covenant that issued in an authoritative document, and this is witness to the fact that Israel was conscious of God giving written Scriptures to her. The Scripture principle, then, is native, not alien, to the basic nature of Israel's relationship with God, a point of utmost importance for us.

To this ought to be added that it does not follow that such a document is altogether immutable and inflexible. Treaty documents of the ancient world were authoritative for the circumstances but could be altered at the behest of the sovereign. The Lord, in this case, was free to revise or update his treaty provisions as need be.[6] We see that plainly in the two versions of the Decalogue and in the filling out of the Penteteuch over time as the original Mosaic nucleus was expanded. It is also implied by the manner in which the classical prophets interpreted the Mosaic material in fresh ways and applied it to new situations. Obviously, they did not consider the text closed to new points of signification arising from fresh reflections of their own. The Old Testament, in fact, does not support in every respect the Judaic Scripture principle, which involves rigid immutability. From the promise to Abraham to bless all the nations through the prophetic anticipation of new covenant and changes in the people's relationship with God in the messianic era, we have a forward-looking and revisable trajectory open to the future, not a closed text complete and sufficient in itself.

In the prophets of the Old Testament we encounter a group of people who see themselves, in the tradition of Moses, able to mediate God's Word to the people. They were conscious of having received a calling and commission from God and spoke out boldly the words he gave them. They were servants to whom the Lord had revealed his secrets (Amos 3:7). They believed that God had put his words in their mouths and that they stood in the counsel of the Lord (Jer. 1:9; 23:22). They spoke the very word of God to the house of Israel (Ezek. 2:1–7). They did not see themselves as radical innovators, but as ministers of the Mosaic covenant given much earlier, and their responsibility was to call the people back to the covenant agreement whose conditions they were forsaking. One could call them conservatives, concerned to call the people back to the original law of God (Hos. 4:1 f.). Surely, what we have here is a strong claim to verbal revelation, a claim that bears directly upon our subject.

Not to be carried away by this fact, let me mention a few qualifications that are in order. First of all, when Jeremiah claims that his message is of God, it is not fair to lift this claim out of context and apply it willy-nilly to another book, like Chronicles, that it does not have in view. Often, conservatives eager to enhance their belief use strong claims originally referring to prophetic oracles in reference to other texts. This is not responsible practice, Second, even though the prophets claim divine authority for their messages, a certain human element often appears in them as well. Micah predicted the fall of Jerusalem at the hands of the Assyrians (Mic. 3:12), but this was not to happen, because the Lord intervened to save the city (Isa. 37:35), a point noted later in the trials of Jeremiah (Jer. 26:19). Because of the freedom of God, even a clear prophecy can turn out to be void if God decides not to do the thing predicted. The prophets did not have so divine a viewpoint as to make their words absolute. Third, the claims that the prophets make refer primarily to their preached oracles, not to the texts we now have. They were preachers rather than writers, as far as we can tell. References to their written work are rare. We do not know exactly how the preaching of Amos or Hosea reached written form, whether they or others took responsibility for that. Isaiah instructs his disciples to preserve the testimony for a future time (8:16; 30:8). Jeremiah had Baruch write down his words on a scroll (Jer. 36:2, 4, 8), but the book of Jeremiah contains more than that, including connecting tissues in the form of historical narratives, as do Amos and Isaiah as well. It is impossible to avoid the conclusion that people other than the prophets themselves played a role in shaping the scriptural documents that incorporate the prophetic message, a role that would have included decisions about ordering the material and precise working to bring out the essential thrust. We know virtually nothing about these people who worked on Scripture. We can think of them as faithful disciples, perhaps, who wanted to be sure the burden of the prophets was remembered in the future. From internal evidence, it would seem likely, too, that they felt free to adapt some of the oracles to the new situation in their ordering and phrasing of the material. In any case, the prophetic claim to verbal inspiration does not apply directly to their important work, which must be considered in some other way. My own view is that the canonical momentum is clear enough to justify seeing their work in terms of the gift of God to Israel of anonymous scribes to shape and consolidate the texts. The popular idea that biblical books were normally the work of a single author writing under the inspiration of God does not fit the complexity of many biblical books, which seem to have multiple authorship. The way to think of this is to rid our minds of the notion that the scriptural writers wanted to make a name for themselves and wrote as individual authors rather than as representatives and servants of the community. Divine inspiration marshals more than a short list of famous writers we can name. It calls into service a whole company of gifted persons who contribute in different ways to the ultimate product and do so anonymously for the most part. Although it would make it easier for us apologetically if the anonymity were raised and we could say that only these acknowledged prophetic persons had anything to do with the Scriptures we now read, we are not able to say that and must be satisfied with a condition of lower visibility.[7]

These qualifications notwithstanding, the crucial point remains that in the Prophets we have a very strong claim to verbal revelation in human language and one that supports the Scripture principle in a very obvious, if not unlimited, way.

In the so-called writings of the Hebrew Bible, in books such as Psalms, Job, Proverbs, and Kings, there are far fewer claims of this kind, only occasional references at best (2 Sam. 23:2; Ps. 102:18). There is nothing to compare with the claims we saw in the Penteteuch and the Prophets. The author of Ecclesiastes considered himself a wise teacher, a writer of words of truth, but nothing more (12:9). Many readers have considered the book itself a product of secular experience at best—see even the original Scofield Bible notes. I think that the writer of Job would have been astonished to find his book later placed alongside the Law of Moses and the prophecies of Jeremiah, and I think that the sages of Proverbs would resist the suggestion that their aphorisms are legally binding in the way that the commandments are. They would not have considered their work revelation in the way in which the other writings are. The point is that in the Old Testament collection there are different kinds of literature, some that make a powerful claim and others that do not, some that stand on high ground of revelation and others that occupy a lower position. Conservatives in particular need to realize that not all Scripture is prophetic oracle or Decalogue. Many texts express the Word of God, but some are content to perform lowlier tasks, such as giving utterance to a spiritual struggle or expressing an honest doubt.

From the writings we can learn two lessons in regard to the Scripture principle. First, we have to admit that we do not know exactly why or how some of the books of the Old Testament came to be included in that canon. We can only assume that the canonical trajectory that is visible elsewhere in the Testament is at work here too and that God guided his people in the recognition of his Work. Second, we must be prepared to allow biblical books to retain their particular character and claim and not force them into another mold. It is proper to regard Ecclesiastes as God-given Scripture, but not to pretend in reading it that it is like Amos or Deuteronomy. We must assess from Ecclesiastes itself what claim the author wishes to make and read it accordingly. It does not assume the form of the divine command, and it must not be distorted in that direction. It is plain from reading Proverbs that the genre of the book is not to formulate divine commandments but to advance wise counsel for the practical living out of faith. Without doubt, the proverb writers and the psalm singers believe that their work conveyed truth about God and his will, and their preservation in the canon endorse this conviction. But the truth that calls us to dialogue and decision is a different kind of truth from the truth of command and demand. It is essential that we read the literature appropriately as it was actually intended and not try to change or improve it.

In summation, the Old Testament witness to itself yields several insights. First, a process of Scripture collection and formation is in motion from the very beginnings of Israel's existence that proves that the later Scripture principle is not a late distortion or misdevelopment but a predictable result of the momentum of her faith. It is irresponsible for modern scholars to disregard this fact and to refuse to take seriously that these documents are properly taken as the normative Scriptures of Israel, not just pieces of ancient literature. The claim for Scripture is as good as the claim for God revealing himself in the history and experience of Israel—if we accept one, we should accept the other as well. Israel's awareness of being called to be the people of the Lord is all of a piece with her awareness of being in possession—in her Scriptures—of the knowledge of the Lord's will for her. The Scripture principle is inherent in the faith of Israel. Second, just as the ways of God are in general untrackable (Rom. 11:35), so in the provision of Scripture there is much that cannot be observed by us now. The community played a role in shaping and defining the Old Testament. Many quite anonymous persons were active in its preparation. We cannot think of the inspiration of the text in simplistic terms. Its locus must have been much wider than just a special illumination of the final redactor. The formation of Scripture is almost indistinguishable from the formation of tradition in Israel, and its inspiration something that must have been a process involving a great many people and taking place over a longer span of time than we have been accustomed to thinking. To do justice to the text, we have to posit God's leading in the preparation of it in all sorts of ways that do not lie on the surface for easy viewing. The final composition, crucial though it is, was not the only important moment in the event of inspiration.

Third, given the diversity in claims we have noted, we have to distinguish between kinds and degrees of inspiration. The Old Testament tains within it many kinds of writing—poetry, proverb, law, oracle, story, parable, and prayer. They are not all alike and do not carry truth in exactly the same way. The speech of Deborah stands on a very different plane from the speeches of Ezekiel. In one text God may be the speaker; in another text human advice seems to be offered. The Bible, as the very term (*books*) implies, is a library, a God-given reader for the people of God. Inspiration does not secure only one kind of text, but many kinds. Out of respect for them all, we need to make proper distinctions and be careful how we read and listen. Like the church, the Bible resembles a body having many members, and not all of them are the same. They perform different functions, some humbler, some nobler. Our aim should be to take the record in its entirety, comparing one part with another, so as to come up with the truth in its fullness.

The New Testament Witness to the Old Testament

By the time of the New Testament, the Scripture principle was firmly established in Jewish minds and part of the symbolic universe of the early Christians. The writers of the New Testament cite the Old Testament as support and illustration of their own teachings hundreds of times. Their minds were steeped in the language and thought of the Scriptures, and they expressed the gospel in terms of them. What understanding of the Old Testament did they hold that led them to do this?

To answer this question exhaustively, one ought to examine each New Testament book critically, taking note of every nuance. There are differences in the way in which Matthew, Hebrews, Paul, and John use the text. But I think there is a common pattern underlying the whole Testament and that it is best for me to support and summarize what it is. It involves standing a little farther back from the text than the biblical specialists do and getting a view of the whole that is important for our purposes here.

When we look at what Jesus and the apostles say about Scripture and take account of how they use it, we see a clearly dialectical attitude. On the one hand, they endorse it as the written Word of God, and on the other hand, they read it as if it were a premessianic text coming to fulfillment in their time and they interpret it accordingly. We could say that they endorse the Old Testament in a messianically qualified way. This is nicely summarized in a saying of Jesus recorded by Matthew: "I did not come to destroy the law and the prophets but to fulfill them" (5:17). Being no heretic, Jesus endorsed the Scriptures of the covenant, but being also God's emissary of the new age, he explained what God was now doing through him as their fulfillment. As far as the genuineness of this text is concerned, I think it has excellent credentials, but even if it is doubted, I think one can say that it represents the dialectic everywhere evident.[8] As Jews, the earliest believers accepted the Old Testament as inspired Scripture, and as messianic Jews, in their use of it they qualified it in relation to the new phase of God's kingdom that had dawned. The Old Testament is the written Word of God intended to be read in the light of Jesus Christ.

This dialectic reveals why it is so important not to neglect either the doctrinal verses or the use to which the Old Testament text is put by the New Testament authors. If we look only at the "claims," we will end up thinking that Jesus is some kind of Pharisee in the rigidity of his attitude. But if, on the other hand, we examine only his use of the text, we may gain the impression that he is the first liberal Christian, critiquing and correcting the Bible at every turn. The fact is that Jesus and the New Testament writers respected the text enormously as God's written Word and qualified it in view of the new messianic situation. He is a "progressive-conservative" in a sense and should not be "used" by any modern church party in a dishonest way. Warfield uses Jesus to pitch the doctrine of inspiration too high, and Käsemann uses him to pitch it too low. To get it right, let us look at all the data.

The Endorsement of the Old Testament

Let us look first at the way in which Jesus and the apostles endorsed the divine authority of the Hebrew Scriptures. I do not see how anyone could deny that Jesus himself believed that the will of God was revealed in the Scriptures, which stood above all merely human tradition. He criticized the Pharisees harshly for making the written Word of God void through their traditions (Mark 7:1–13). He believed that the Scriptures must be fulfilled and that they were being fulfilled in his ministry (Luke 4:21). He parried the temptations of Satan by appealing to them and quoted from them as if God were speaking the very words (Matt. 4:4–7; 19:4 f.). That Jesus possessed a remarkable sense of his own authority under God only underlines the impressiveness of this attitude. It seems clear that he did not feign respect for Scripture because people in his day shared it but that it was an intimate conviction that he cherished.

Jesus used the Scriptures in many distinctive ways, just as we do today. There is an allusive use, in which he cited texts because they were so familiar to him and because they said what he wanted to say, like the echo of Isaiah 5 in his parable of the wicked tenants (Mark 12:1–12), or the allusion to Isaiah 35 and 61 in his answer to the disciples of John the Baptist (Matt. 11:5). Then there was a confirmatory use, by which he sought to show how things that were happening now fulfilled the Old Testament in some important way, as when the response to his parables evoked a reference to Isaiah's experience of the same blindness (Isaiah 6) or his sermon at Nazareth was a pointed reference to Isaiah 61. There was also an argumentative use of Scripture, where a text was used to prove a point, as in the temptation narratives, when Jesus quoted the Bible to refute Satan (Matthew 4), or when Jesus cited the law itself in order to answer the question about the greatest commandment (Matt. 22:37, 39). He also used the Old Testament in a challenging way, in polemical contexts, to force an issue of decision: "Have you not read? What do you think? What do you make of this?" (Mark 2:25; 12:10, 26). Jesus would use the Old Testament to turn the tables on his opponents. Always Jesus appealed to the Scriptures as the resource the Father had given Israel for a hearing of his Word.[9]

Though I do not wish to blunt the force of this point, recent polemics have distorted it in the direction either of denying it or exaggerating it. In reference to the latter tendency, I would like to add some points of clarification and caution here to guard against misusing the evidence. First, his quotations from the Old Testament do not reveal a concern for the original text but range widely over the available texts, suggesting that for Jesus it was the message conveyed rather than the precise wording that concerned him. Second, though grateful for what God had said to past generations in the Scriptures, he was also particularly excited about what God was doing and saying now. Anyone in the kingdom, he said, was greater than the greatest prophet of God in the past (Matt. 11:11). Third, although I do not believe Jesus ever broke the law or intended to, it was the case that he was more concerned to be loving than to be seen as strictly adhering to the letter of it. Healing on the Sabbath and letting his disciples pick a few ears of corn to eat on that holy day did not constitute breaking Sabbath for Jesus, but he certainly knew that it did mean that for others, who concentrated upon the details of legal observance. For him the Word of God was gospel, not legalistic code, and he resisted handling it in any other way. Fourth, the evidence does not permit calling upon Jesus of Nazareth to settle the modern debates over biblical inerrancy. These have to do with whether in the original autographs of Scripture any mistakes occur and involve discussions over what mistakes would qualify as errors.

Though I do not consider this a foolish debate in itself, I do object to the oft-repeated claim that Jesus taught the answer to it, as if he were on one side against the other. Of course Jesus had complete confidence in the Scriptures, and even appealed to them for such an obscure fact as Lot's wife's fate, but it is stretching the evidence to suggest that Jesus can be appealed to in order to settle a debate that entertains questions such as original autographs, authorial intention, the status of the New Testament—issues not directly addressed by him. These are questions that we have to deal with and that cannot be short-circuited by an anachronistic appeal to Jesus. Fifth, along similar lines, his authority cannot be captured by the conservative party in disputes over biblical criticism, though it is tempting to try. Because Jesus cites a psalm of David or a prophecy from the Book of Isaiah, it does not follow that he is placing his divine authority on the line for the precise literary authorship of those texts. In quoting them, Jesus always calls attention to what the Scriptures teach and not how they got to be written in the final redaction. It is an abuse of his authority to use it for partisan purposes of ours. It is more natural to think that when Jesus cites the Old Testament he does so according to the accepted conventions and not in order to refute some piece of higher critical guesswork. It is not that I have much use for theories about the anonymous prophet of the exile, the so-called Second Isaiah (how is it that the greatest of the prophets is unknown?), but, rather, I object to a misuse of Jesus' authority. The literary composition of Isaiah is an issue to be settled by Old Testament scholars weighing the evidence, not by a spurious appeal to Jesus.

One further mistake to avoid when making an appeal to Jesus' high view of the Old Testament is to reverse the proper relationship between them. Conservatives regularly use Christ to witness to the Scriptures as a kind of irrefutable proof of their position. "He said it—do you believe it?" As though Jesus were a kind of John the Baptist witnessing to something even higher than himself and wanted to be the key link in a chain of theological logic. In fact, it is the other way around. The Scriptures bear witness to Christ and derive their authority for Christians from that fact (John 5:39). Of course his view of the Bible is important for us when we try to ascertain what our own view should be, but it ought not to be used as an independent proof to establish objectively the authority of the Scriptures apart from faith in Jesus.[10]

Like Jesus, the apostles also make a clear endorsement of the Old Testament as God's Word, continually quoting from it as the Word of God. The Scriptures are "inspired by God" (2 Tim. 3:16) are called the "oracles of God" (Rom. 3:2) and "prophetic" (Rom. 1:2; 16:27). They can be represented as God speaking (Gal. 3:8) and the Spirit speaking (Heb: 3:7). At the same time, we must not exaggerate the evidence. Paul can write Romans and Galatians without bothering to discuss a doctrine of Scripture. And even in a text like 2 Timothy 3:16, there is no mention of original autographs or inerrancy or anything as theoretical as that. The whole emphasis is upon the practical profitability of the copies of the Old Testament Timothy was using. The comments are very low key and do nothing to prove the strict conservative view. Paul does not discuss the nature of inspiration or the degree to which the Scriptures are reliable in order to achieve their practical goal. He is simply not interested in our modern debates about inerrancy and sticks to the profitability of the Scriptures in the practical realm. The only way 2 Timothy 3:16 can be used as a proof text for the modern discussion is by first reading a modern view back into it.

To take another case, when Peter affirms that no prophecy originated in the human mind but from the impulse of the Spirit, he is referring to the prophecies uttered and then to the prophetic Scriptures, but not to Scripture in general, much of which is not prophetic. He is not making a judgment about the entire Old Testament here, and we have no right to twist his words to apply to the whole Christian Bible. Nor should we be too quick to conclude that when the phrase "it is written" is employed it necessarily means God is speaking. Paul uses the formula in 1 Corinthians 3:19 in citing from a speech of Eliphaz, one of Job's friends who did not always tell the truth. We need to be fair and accurate in our use of this material.

Misuse aside, it is of the utmost importance that we recognize that for Jesus and the apostles the Old Testament is God's written Word and we ought to acknowledge it. If Jesus' authority means anything to us, then it means something here.

The Messianic Qualification of the Old Testament

Looking at the other side of the dialectic, let us consider the messianic qualification that Jesus and the apostles placed upon the Old Testament. They saw the text structured around the promise of God that was in the process of being fulfilled. They viewed its authority, not as an unconditional work standing alone, but as a stage in God's revelation moving toward the coming of the Messiah and kingdom. In this way they identify themes of continuity, areas of fulfillment, and even points of negation. Jesus could do this because of his sense of unique sonship and the coming of the new age in which ears were blessed to hear what the prophets had longed for (Matt. 13:16 f.).

To take a few concrete examples of his messianic use of the Old Testament, Jesus knew what God's original intention for marriage was and felt free to declare null and void the Mosaic permission of divorce in Deuteronomy 24. He could say that Moses's Law was provisional and temporary and no longer in effect (Matt. 19:3–9). In his Nazareth sermon, Jesus dropped out the whole element of judgment in a text he was using (Isa. 61:1 f.) because it was the other half of the text that was relevant and true for that situation (Luke 4:18). He would not accept criticism of his Sabbath activities, because he was sure what God had in mind in ordaining the Sabbath and how he wanted it to be observed (Mark 2:27 f.). He said that anger was as bad as murder and that oaths were not to be used anymore. He seemed to critique the tradition of clean and unclean foods. Now, it is important not to misunderstand what Jesus is doing. It would be a travesty to depict him as anti-Torah in the slightest. He reinterpreted but did not break any of the commandments. He could distinguish between the greatest commandments and the slightest, and then say, "You ought to do the one without neglecting the other" (Matt. 23:23). Nevertheless, without ever denying that the Scriptures were the word of God when they were given, Jesus could say they were not the word of God to the present stiuation, in which the kingdom of God was coming near. He recognized a covenant relativity in relation to certain texts and thus shocked some of his hearers, who had no room for such a limitation.

What Jesus was doing was reading the Scriptures in the context of the dawning kingdom of God and seeing them in the light of this wonderful fulfillment. Divine revelation was being updated and advanced before people's eyes, and hidden depths of the Scriptures were coming to light. Such messianic exegesis was another way of raising the Christological question: "Who do you say that I am?" If people granted that he was the Coming One, they would see the new dimensions he was pointing to in the text, but if they did not, they would refuse both him and his exegesis. Though they knew the Scriptures well, certain Pharisees would not take his claim seriously, and could not see what the Scriptures were really saying (John 5:39 f.). Focused on the text as immutable object, they were not open to consider the possibility of a fulfillment that might transcend it. Jesus endorsed the Old Testament, but he did so in a messianically qualified way. He did not consider a text of the Old Testament to stand necessarily on the same plane as the message of the kingdom, and he did not think of them all having immutable truth value for all succeeding generations. In that sense, his Scripture principle was more flexible than the Scripture principle of orthodoxy often is. Fortunately, our practice is often better than our doctrine is.

It is important to notice that Jesus did not see himself "under" the Old Testament the way other Jews of his time did. In fact, he placed himself over it and saw it leading up to him and witnessing to him. He had messianic authority apart from the Scriptures and felt free to use it liberally. The text alone did not determine what he had to say at every point. Had Jesus and the apostles thought that everything the Old Testament taught was currently binding on them, there could have been no Christian gospel as we have it. If we disregard the messianic qualification that Jesus placed upon the Old Testament, we run the risk of Judaizing the church and her message. It is an insult to Jesus to say that he had the same view of the Old Testament that the unbelieving Pharisees did.

The Apostle Paul, too, was conscious of a divine call to minister in the new covenant in the service of Christ and was aware that this gave him freedom and authority to rethink the meaning of the Old Testament in the light of the new situation. From his encounter with the risen Lord, Paul could see that the Scriptures were a premessianic trajectory pointing forward to the age in which he was now living. He could say, "They were written for our instruction, upon whom the end of the ages has come" (1 Cor. 10:11). He could now see in them depths of meaning he had completely overlooked as a Jew. Christ had transformed everything for him, including his use of the Bible. Now, when reading the story of Moses placing a veil over his face, Paul could see the great contrast between age of law and the age of grace (2 Cor. 3:4–18). In the story of Hagar and Sarah, he saw a typology of Jew and Christian, law and grace; in Israel's wandering in the desert he could find lessons for the church. In the singular form of the collective noun "seed', he could see an intimation of Jesus Christ. In many cases the crucial meaning was provided not by the text itself but by the messianic fulfillment around which the text was adapted and fitted. Even more radically than Jesus, Paul would say that circumcision is no longer required for the people of God, and the Law of Moses has a different quality of authority than it did earlier. The seventh-day Sabbath was no longer insisted upon, and laws about clean and unclean foods were shelved in the gentile mission. Hebrews boldly asserts that the old covenant has become obsolete, and the sacrifices, in particular, are abolished (8:13; 10:9).

Just because they are familiar to us, we should not overlook the importance of these developments. These were practices clearly taught in the Scriptures and dear to the life of the biblical community, yet they were abandoned. The reason can only be that the coming of Jesus into the world relativized the Old Testament in certain respects and made parts of it no longer in effect as Word of God for Christians. Paul would certainly have rejected the charge that he was guilty of twisting the text when he interpreted it afresh in terms of Jesus. He would also have rejected the assumption underlying that charge, that the only meaning of a text is its exegetically established original meaning. It is obvious from his modes of interpretation and his selectivity and adaption of the texts he cited that he was concerned above all to preach Christ from the Old Testament. For him the text had collided with the messianic event, creating a host of new insights that he was breathless to share. The significance of this for Paul's doctrine of Scripture is that he did not simply equate the text with the Word of God for today or consider it to have an independent authority on its own. It had been promulgated in the period of redemption prior to the coming of the Messiah, which made it relative to gospel authority. Now it was free to function as the servant of the gospel and to be the occasion of some fresh themes. It should no longer be read just on its own, but correlated with the fulfillment of Christ.

It might be amusing to imagine a battle for the Bible in the first century, with the "conservatives" insisting on the final authority of the text in relation to, say, dress requirements and the "liberals" maintaining that the gospel has taken us beyond that. The Jews of that period found it shocking that the early Christians would dare to claim superior truth to that of Torah. Would today's conservatives be comfortable defending Saint Paul against the loyalists who held firmly to the infallibility of the Old Testament? It bears thinking about.

The New Testament, then, regarded the Old Testament as Scripture, as the Word of God given in the premessianic period, now to be read in the light of Jesus Christ. It was in every respect infallible and valid for the time when it was issued but had to be thought out as the Word of God for messianic believers in the present age. This conclusion ought to give just about everyone something to ponder. In the first place, religious liberals need to explain why they take a lower view of the Old Testament than Jesus and the apostles evidently did. It is a lame excuse to say it was appropriate for them because they were Jews but inappropriate for us because we are not. Something so close to the center of the original gospel cannot be so summarily dispensed with. Obviously, Christians will want to follow Jesus in this matter. But in the second place, conservatives will need to explain how they handle the messianic qualification of the Old Testament. They do not live like Jews; they do not heed much of the dietary and other ethnic instruction taught in the Jewish Scriptures. In fact, they orient themselves to Jesus Christ, not to the Old Testament independent of him. Thus it is not the Judaic Scripture principle that they accept but a Christian one in which the Old Testament is a premessianic trajectory finding fulfillment in the gospel and not possessing absolute and independent authority. Of course, each Old Testament provision was the Word of God in a histori-cal sense (God gave it to ancient Israel), but it is not necessarily a Word addressed to us. The text is "infallible" in this special sense for us, but not in the sense it is infallible for Jews, that is, literally and immutably. It is high time we evangelicals came clean on what we actually mean by our proud slogans.

If we take seriously the New Testament use of the Old Testament as well as its "doctrine" of it, another relevant point arises for conserva-tives. It must be proper to use the text the way the New Testament used it. How otherwise can we credibly claim to be following the New Testament counsel on Scripture? This must mean interpreting the Old Testament Christologically and not always sticking closely to the origi-nal meaning of the text. There are two exceptions that I think we ought to allow. First, rabbinic exegetical methods per se are not normative but historically relative.[11] In this case, we ought to note that Paul's use of a small detail like a grammatical singular in Galatians 3:16 is not proof of detailed inerrancy but evidence of precisely rabbinic practices. To press this kind of point would be to commit Christians to the whole gamut of rabbinic techniques to which we have not been sympathetic, at least since the Reformation. Second, and most important, Jesus and the apostles enjoyed an authority and position in divine revelation that gave them a freedom to declare in what respects the Old Testament was or was not valid and relevant. Their pesher exegesis depends upon a revelatory stance that was unique to them.[12] Of course, we should follow them in the interpretation of the Old Testament that they made, but we cannot initiate new criticisms of the Old Testament, and we certainly can not adopt a stance superior to the New Testament, the charter of our new covenant. But having made these exceptions, Christians today ought to follow the New Testament in seeking to discern what significance a text has for us now in the ongoing purposes of God. It may be that God will use the Scriptures in a way a little different from the original meaning as we are led by the Spirit. Believing that the text is God's written Word does not put us in a box as regards the truth God may use it to teach us. "The Word of God is not bound." The New Testament indicates to us by its use of Scripture that the text can give meaning on several levels and possesses a surplus of meaning potential that transcends the meaning it originally had. Our modern concern for "scientific" exegesis has impoverished our reading of the Bible, and we need to return to a "precritical" approach in which we are open to God's Word in more ways than one.[13]

The New Testament Witness to Itself

Even more crucial for the church is the question whether the decision, however early, to make the set of writings we call the New Testament part of the Scripture principle was sound and appropriate. Was this a legitimate development out of the intentions that Jesus and the apostles had for the Christian movement? We often mask this issue by assuming that a claim like 2 Timothy 3:16 applies to the New Testament as well as the Old Testament, when, of course, it does not. Where, then, is the evidence that New Testament Scriptures were supposed to come along and join in a bipartite Bible? Is not Christianity focused on the incarnation and the gift of the Spirit? Is it not sufficient that it be attested by a set of kerygmatic documents of human derivation? Just because we have always thought of the New Testament as inspired Scripture does not make it so. Perhaps it is important that we correct this tradition and go to work delving critically behind the documents to the more original layers, in this way capturing the gospel as it really was. Belief in the Scripture principle prevents us from doing this.[14]

The majority of Christians probably feel that it makes no sense to reopen a question that has been closed for eighteen hundred years and is for all practical purposes irreformable. Besides, have we not heard the Word of God from the New Testament all this time—has it not proven itself as Scripture? It is just intellectual honesty that requires some of us to ask the question. Why was it that the church decided to go beyond Jesus Christ as the canon of revelation and add a New Testament Scripture principle? And how did they know what books ought to be included in it?

There are several factors that support the ancient decision to receive New Testament writings as the canon of the church. One is the canonical process already in motion in the Old Testament and virtually in place by the time of Jesus. Another is the authority of Jesus himself and the apostolic structure put in place by the Lord. A third is the natural way in which the early Christians accepted the authority of the New Testament writings.

The underlying factor always to keep in mind is the canonical process that produced the Old Testament. Now that the quenched Spirit had returned through the ministry of Jesus, the expectation would be kindled of fresh revelation and the possibility of new inscripturation. The reason the New Testament Scriptures were so readily accepted in the primitive church, without there being any direct effort to achieve it, is that inspired writing had been the complement of revelation under the old covenant; the same factors at work in the new covenant occasioned no surprise. God had given his written Word to Israel in the context of their salvation history and was engaged, it could be assumed, in providing the written complement of new covenant revelation. Revelation, in the Judeo-Christian tradition, generates Scripture, and Christian minds were instinctively prepared and predisposed to receive it. Just as the Old Testament message called for fulfillment in the New, so Old Testament Scripture anticipated a written complement to itself should the need of generational passage arise, the purpose in each case being the maintenance and stability of the believing community. Given the delay of the return of Christ and the open-ended nature of church history, the importance of new covenant Scripture was as great or even greater as it had been in the premessianic period. Furthermore, the prophets and apostles in the New Testament church not only enjoyed equal status with their Old Testament counterparts but even greater dignity and authority on account of the surpassing splendor of the new covenant they were administering (Matt. 11:11; 2 Cor. 3:4–18). The emergence of New Testament Scripture was predictable by analogy with Old Testament experience and legitimated by the fresh flow of divine revelation. A resumption of the canonical process would be expected.

The initial intimation of this was the action of Jesus in calling the apostles and promising the Spirit for their enabling, thus providing the vehicles of continuity for the ongoing life of the church. By means of this eyewitness testimony, the faith "once delivered to the saints" can be handed down in purity and integrity. Indications are that Jesus anticipated and planned for a period after his death and resurrection during which the Supper would be observed, the gospel preached to the nations, and judgment visited upon Palestine. The apocalyptic interpretation of the New Testament, in which there is no room for a church age because the end is imminent, is incorrect. If anything, what the New Testament writers had to counter was precisely an overeager and false anticipation of the Parousia, which tended to frustrate the outworking of Jesus' gospel and the mission of the church. The kingdom has drawn near; the date of its consummation is not something human beings can know; therefore, get on with it! "Because the eschatological reality is present, the length of the interval until the consummation is of no crucial consequence."[15] Anticipating this period, then, Jesus in his lifetime trained disciples, of whom twelve in particular were given a place of special importance. He called them to follow him, appointed twelve to be with him in a special sense, gave them private instruction, ordained them with authority, and sent them out to preach and to heal (Mark 1:17; 3:14; 4:34; 5:37; 6:7). They knew that they were being trained for a world mission and that Jesus was preparing them for the time when he would no longer be with them. No doubt, like the rabbis, Jesus would have handed his teaching over to them and made it clear that it was their responsibility to hand it on to others. He spoke about the founding of this church or messianic congregation and the role of Peter and the apostles in its leadership and discipline (Matt. 16:18 f.; 18:17 f.) and, in the farewell speeches of John 14–17, prepared them for his withdrawal from the scene. After the resurrection, he sent them forth in the authority of the gospel to make disciples of all nations and to be special witnesses of all they had seen and learned (Luke 24:47 f.).

To help them in this ministry, Jesus promised the Spirit in power to enable them to be witnesses to the ends of the earth (Acts 1:8). He would help them know what to say in tight situations and help them to recall the instructions he had given them before his departure (Matt. 10:19 f.; Luke 12:12; John 14:26). Furthermore, the Spirit would lead them into all truth and enable them to explicate the gospel in new circumstances and in answer to new questions (John 16:12 f.). Though it is true that these promises do not explicitly refer to the writing of Scripture, "they provide in principle all that is required for the formation of such a canon, should that be God's purpose."[16] It is most natural to believe that these promises of remembrance and guidance into new truth have found their most far-reaching fulfillment in the New Testament Scriptures. I think it would be true to say that Jesus preauthenticated the New Testament canon as the Scripture of the church when he called the apostles to be with him and promised the Holy Spirit to guide them.[17]

The easiest place to see this being worked out and confirmed is in the writings of Paul, whose claims to authority are far-reaching and nuanced. Though not one of the Twelve, Paul was commissioned by the risen Lord and his apostleship accepted by the rest (Acts 26:16–18;

1 Cor. 9:1; 15:5–11). His understanding of this commission and the kind of authority entailed by it is most germane to our thesis. Significantly, the wording of his commission contains allusions to prophetic calls in the Old Testament to Ezekiel, Jeremiah, and Isaiah and gives some indication of the way he saw his ministry. Paul believed that the Lord had set him apart prior to his birth to be an apostle to the Gentiles, that the gospel that he preached was not human in origin but came by revelation of Jesus Christ, and that he had been graced with this calling (Gal. 1:11 f., 15 f.; 2:9). His task was to lay the foundations of the church and make the Word of God fully known (1 Cor. 3:10; Col. 1:25). He had received a stewardship of the grace of God to preach the un-searchable riches of Christ and could speak out boldly because of his office (Eph. 3:1–10; Rom. 15:15–21). The signs of a true apostle were evident in his ministry, and he had been given authority for the up-building of the churches (2 Cor. 12:12; 13:10). Paul saw himself, and was seen by others to be, standing in the circle of primary apostles specially called to proclaim the message of Jesus and the kingdom and could compare himself favorably with Moses as one who was mediator of even greater divine revelation (2 Cor. 3:5–18).

For this reason Paul expected people to heed his words and written communications. He felt competent to issue commands and expected them to be observed (1 Cor. 14:37), because they were instructions giv-en "through the Lord Jesus" (1 Thess. 4:2). He wanted believers to "stand firm and hold to the traditions which you were taught by us, either by word of mouth or by letter" (2 Thess. 2:15). His authority ought to be respected, whether mediated in person or by means of written communication: his letters were to be read in all the churches (Col. 4:16; 1 Thess. 5:27). It was natural, then, that the Pauline corpus would be revered and heeded as New Testament Scripture in subse-quent Christian generations and be placed alongside the Old Testament (2 Pet. 3:16). Our Lord's intention that there should be after his death authoritative persons to communicate the truth and spread the Word was abundantly fulfilled. The radical view that holds that this whole picture of apostolic authority is an invention of the church in the suba-postolic age to justify itself in controversies with Gnostics is itself imagi-nary.[18]

To get a clearer impression of how apostolic authority worked, let us consider the following points. First, Paul places an eschatological proviso over himself: "We know in part" (1 Cor. 13:12). He is conscious that not everything has been given to him to know. Exhaustive knowledge and comprehensive infallibility belong to the future age after the Parousia. Therefore, there are times when he can only issue some advice based on what he acknowledges to be his opinion (1 Cor. 7:25, 40). He has no word of the Lord on this matter and no special insight from above to give. In reply to criticisms of him, he is content to leave the matter with God, the righteous judge who will make everything clear (1 Cor. 4:4 f.). Referring to some who disagreed with him, he expresses the hope that in time they will see it differently (Phil. 3:15). This is not the picture of the apostle one often encounters, a man dogmatically sure about everything. Of course, he is not suggesting that for this reason the truth value of his plain teachings is in doubt, only that there is a partiality and fragility to what we are grasping even in Paul himself. His modest attitude allows us, his readers, to argue controversial matters with him and not feel guilty. I think he would welcome that, as long as our attitude is modest and respectful.

Second, Paul was frank and open about his human weaknesses and did not try to hide them behind his apostolic office. He knew himself to be a frail earthen vessel and not a superman, as some of his opponents imagined they were (2 Cor. 11:5). He experienced the weakness of the cross and the grace of God in that context (2 Cor. 11:30; 12:9 f.). Jesus made use of weak people, who were often unbelieving and full of misunderstanding, in order to praise the power of God in and through them (2 Cor. 4:7). This dimension of human weakness can be seen as a factor in his writings as well. We hear one side of a conversation when we read Galatians or Corinthians and have to think hard to figure out what Paul is teaching and what, in our context, we should be learning. Sometimes there can be a question whether Paul or his opponents said something (1 Cor. 7:1) or what he meant in a verse like 1 Corinthians 4:6 or 1 Timothy 2:15. How we would like to ask him if he thought hairstyles would always be a sign of the male-female distinction (1 Cor. 11:4 f.) or if he meant that a woman should never be the main pastoral leader (1 Tim. 2:12). The epistles of Paul do not resemble Scriptures sent directly from heaven but are more human than that. His authority as an apostle speaks to us through the weakness of human flesh, and we must not be ashamed of this or try to cover this up.

Third, Paul does not exercise his authority in an authoritarian manner very often. He much prefers to exhort rather than command. Of course, he has authority he can use, and will do so where the gospel is at stake, but often we find him quite conciliatory and collegial. It is rather typical of Paul to say, "I say this not as a command" (2 Cor. 8:8). More than twenty times in the letters, Paul exhorts people to do things rather than commanding them to. "We might have made demands as apostles, but we were gentle among you" (1 Thess. 2:6 f.). This says something about Paul's desire to have people respond to him as equals and not subordinates. He does not want "to lord it over your faith," as he put it (2 Cor. 1:24). As his sisters and brothers, believers were not slaves of his but mature sons and daughters of God who ought not to fall back into slavery—even to him. He wanted people like Philemon to act freely out of their own faith resources, and for that he had to woo, not threaten, them. "I prefer to do nothing without your consent in order that your goodness might not be by compulsion but of your own free will" (Philemon 14).

Paul wanted Timothy to observe his teaching and conduct and learn from them as an example but to be his own man in the ministry (2 Tim. 3:10 f.). He wanted believers to have the mind of Christ and be able to discern the will of God for themselves—after all, they would not always have him around to ask. He did not want people to be under him as Jews were under Moses. There is a liberty in Christ they needed to be experiencing, and one way of doing so was to take up the theological and ethical subject matter and think it through for themselves. I do not think Paul would be pleased if people were to interpret him legalistically rather than engage him in dialogue.[19]

Fully half of the New Testament, however, the four Gospels and the Book of Acts, contains almost no direct claim to apostolic authority, even though these books are absolutely crucial to the apostolic criterion. Have we been mistaken to consider them Scripture, if all they appear to be is human testimony?

What we confront is fascinating. On the one hand, the Gospels, like John the Baptist, are content to bear witness to Christ and do not feel the need to call attention to themselves as apostolic witnesses. On the other hand, also like John the Baptist, their credentials to do so are in fact exceptionally good. As Jesus said of him, there was none greater in the old covenant than him, being greater than any prophet (Matt. 11:9, 11). When pushed to defend himself, John chose to identify himself with the voice crying in the wilderness preparing the way of the Lord (John 1:23), not that modest a claim in itself. What seems clear is that the material concern of the four Gospels is to let the authority and light of Jesus shine out of their pages and not to complicate the issue by making claims for themselves. We can assume that in the age when they were written, about A.D. 70, it was the authority of Jesus people were concerned with; the authority of the four Gospels as texts was not the subject of controversy. But with the rise of false Gospels in the second century, both issues were crucial.

What emerges from reading the Gospels is a strong claim for the authority of Jesus Christ. The records wish to confront us with the one whose word will never pass away (Matt. 24:35) and whose authority is on a plane with God's own (Matt. 7:38 f.). The four Gospels in their setting are not concerned to prove their authority as texts but to make known Christ's authority and saving power. It is his authority that grounds the authority of the New Testament, not the reverse—it is Jesus whom we receive and honor when we receive and respect these apostolic writings. As Jesus said to the disciples, "He who receives you receives me, and he who receives me receives him who sent me" (Matt. 10:40). The basic aim of the Gospel writers is to put people in touch with reality of the risen Lord by telling of his earthly career, not to blow their own horns. As far as internal evidence goes, we are not told the identity of any writer or to regard them as apostolic Scriptures. Though their identities may have been well known, they remain modest on that score and give prominence only to Christ himself. But the way Matthew begins his Gospel, "the book of the genealogy [genesis] of Jesus Christ," and the way he structures his book around great blocks of teaching and actions, ending with the solemn commission and command "teaching them to observe all things I have commanded you," have a certain "scriptural" ring. It sounds as if he wanted his readers to regard his book as Christian Scripture—as, in fact, Christians have always done. The authority of Mark commends itself by means of a great vividness of style that strongly suggests the writer is giving us eyewitness testimony of the drama recorded. The writer of Luke-Acts, too, seems to know the history firsthand—the "we" passages in Acts suggest he was Paul's traveling companion, and he claims to have used eyewitness sources for the life of Christ (Luke 1:1–4). Whoever wrote John must have been, as Westcott put it a century ago, a Jew of Palestine, an eyewitness of what he describes, and very likely the Beloved Disciple and Apostle John.[20]

On the other hand, the same four Gospels that display such reticence in defending their own authority as texts could likely have done so decisively had they been forced to by controversy. A strong case can be made that two of them are apostolic in the strict sense, and two indirectly apostolic. In the case of Matthew, not only is the ascription "according to Matthew" present in all existing texts of the gospel, but the testimony of Papias, dating from early in the second century, refers to Matthew as the writer of a Gospel. The main objection to this strong external evidence is the conjecture that Matthew the Apostle would not have used Mark's gospel as a main source, assuming he did so. But this objection would not hold if the Gospel of Mark was based upon Peter's teaching, as Papias says, and if Matthew admired Mark's Gospel as a worthy statement. Robert H. Gundry has recently defended the apostolic claim of the First Gospel.[21] As for Mark, the early witnesses agree both on Mark as its author and on his association with Peter in the production of the Gospel. We know a number of things about Mark from the New Testament, one particulary interesting item being that John Mark was "servant" to Paul and Barnabas (Acts 13:5), a term that often means a person who handles documents (Luke 4:20). To such "servants" Luke himself makes reference (Luke 1:2) in relation to his own eyewitness sources.

Luke, for his part, was no eyewitness of the earthly ministry of Jesus but claims to have had access to narratives written by those who were. The early external testimony identifies Luke as the author, and the evidence of Acts itself suggests it was Luke the companion of Paul who composed it. The silence of Acts on the death of Paul and the destruction of Jerusalem strongly support Luke's authorship of it in the earlier 60s of the first century.

As for the Gospel of John, J. A. T. Robinson has recently argued at length for the evangelist being the Beloved Disciple and Apostle John. The Fourth Gospel, contrary to prejudice, is as good a historical source as the Synoptics are, and sometimes much better.[22]

The formation of the New Testament canon, then, was a natural and gradual process, as books like the epistles of Paul and the four Gospels were accepted and used. We should not think of canon as a list of books in a formal document (obviously, this is something that comes later) but as a process during which the various books came to be read and used and found to be of scriptural substance. We can see this happening in the New Testament itself and immediately after. In Timothy 5:18, a text from the Old Testament and a saying of the Lord's now found in Luke's Gospel are placed side by side and introduced by the phrase "the Scripture says". In 2 Peter 3:16, the epistles of Paul are mentioned in the same breath with Old Testament Scriptures and equated with them. The Didache quotes from the words of Jesus, apparently from a written Gospel, placing them on a level with Old Testament texts. In such references we see the beginnings of the New Testament canon, even though this is not yet the way it is spoken about. "By 170 A.D (at the latest) not only was the concept of New Testament Scripture firmly established, but the main contents of the new canon were undisputed: four gospels, Acts, thirteen letters of Paul, 1 Peter, 1 John. Complete unanimity had not yet been reached about the other books, but there was no doubt as to the existence and main contents of an extended canon."[23] The early church was, as Luke describes it, "devoted to the apostles' teaching" (Acts 2:42), not only at first but also in the subapostolic period. What we call the New Testament canon was the final result and crystallization of the process in which the early Christians recognized the authority of apostolic writings.[24]

Of course, it is true that the process is not altogether clear. We see the general pattern, but not much of the detail. But we can surely conclude, against Harnack, that the creation of the New Testament was a proper, not an improper, development, which proceeded naturally and gradually and appropriately from the apostolic essence of original Christianity. The move from apostolic authority to recognition in local churches to wider recognition of the canon is smooth, even though it took time and cannot be traced in the detail one might like. The evidence, though good and sufficient for reasonable people is not overpowering and coercive, and it compels us to refer to the leading of the Spirit and the providence of God. There are, on the one hand, the objective factors I have referred to, the Scripture principle manifest in the Old Testament and the structure of authority set in motion by Jesus and the calling of apostles to be ministers of the Word. And there is the subjective factor in the process, whereby the Christian communities evaluated the documents they received and listened for the voice of the Shepherd in them. In this way a de facto New Testament was formed, and the rise of heresies in the second century hastened along Christian thinking about canon, since it was now important to make explicit what had been only implicit in the practice of the churches. Christian experience did not create the canon, which had been set in motion by the objective factors I have mentioned, but it did confirm it and give it communal backing. Calvin wrote profoundly when he taught that there are "sufficiently firm proofs" at hand to establish the credibility of Scripture, but that, in the last analysis, the witness of the Holy Spirit in believers is stronger than any proof and gives the kind of firm confidence in the Bible that has always characterized Christians (*Institutes* I, chaps. 7–8). Even if we were less sure than I think we can be about the apostolic authorship of some of the New Testament books, we can still trust God to have overseen the provision of an adequate foundational record of his revelation through Jesus. The experience of truth and reality in the Scriptures in the context of worship and devotion can help us by confirming that God has in fact provided for us in this way.[25]

But why, if the Spirit dwells within us and the law is being written on our hearts, do we need an external letter such as a New Testament canon to guide us? It is because of the now and the not-yet of the kingdom of God. Until the coming of the Lord, the Scripture principle is needed to keep us on track theologically and ethically, and this is why it is incorporated into God's dealings with us in both the old covenant and the new. It helps to ensure the integrity of the categorical structure of the faith and prevent it from being distorted so that it cannot function effectively. True, the process was spurred on by the challenge of Marcion in the second century, but that crisis did not create the canonical process, which was happening already and well advanced.[26]

Some Conclusions About Inspiration and Authority

The Bible does not give us a doctrine of its own inspiration and authority that answers all the various questions we might like to ask. Its witness on this subject is unsystematic and somewhat fragmentary and enables us to reach important but modest conclusions. It does support the central place of the Scripture principle in Christianity. The evidence suggests that it was God's will that written revelation in the form of Scripture should emerge out of the traditions of Israel and church to preserve the substance of the faith for posterity and make it available to believers. This appears most clearly in the way Jesus and the New Testament writers handle the Old Testament as the Word of God, and in the way the apostles describe themselves as heralds and witnesses of the Word. What has been given is trustworthy and ought to be received obediently in a spirit of faith.[27] Religious liberals cannot successfully deny what classical Christians have always believed concerning the divine gift of Holy Scripture as the inspired Word of God. Christianity without a Scripture principle is a figment of the liberal imagination, something that has never existed and was not meant to exist. The idea that the Bible is a collection of fallible human documents whose authority is on a par with other sources of information is a modern idea out of keeping with the nature of the texts themselves and the way they have always been seen.[28] Without belaboring the issue, the Bible itself supports the view that Scripture is a product of divine revelation and to be gratefully received.[29]

A second conclusion the evidence leads us to is the practical purpose of the Bible as a book that testifies to salvation in Jesus Christ. As the thirty-nine Articles say, the Bible gives us "all things necessary" to the life of faith: "Holy Scripture contains all things necessary to salvation, so that whatsoever is not read therein, nor may be proved thereby, is not to be required of any man, that it should be believed as an article of the faith, or be thought requisite or necessary to salvation" (VI). The Bible is basically a covenant document designed to lead people to know and love God. As such, it has a focused purpose and concentration. This is the kind of truth it urges us to seek in it, and this is the context in which its truth claims ought to be measured. Even though our Bibles in their present form are not flawless, and there are many things in them that are puzzling and admit of no obvious solution, the Bible is not prevented from carrying out its designated purpose. The Bible was "written for our instruction, that by steadfastness and by the encouragement of the Scriptures we might have hope" (Rom. 15:4). Their treasure and their wisdom are oriented to presenting Jesus Christ, the wisdom and the power of God. We should never define biblical authority apart from this stated purpose or apply to it standards of measurement that are inappropriate. God speaks through the Bible, not to make us scholars and scientists, but to put us in a right relationship with God and to give us such a religious understanding of the world and history that we can grasp everything else better. Citing 2 Timothy 3:16–17, the Second Vatican Council was wise in asserting that the Scriptures teach "firmly, faithfully, and without error that truth which God wanted put into the sacred writings for the sake of our salvation" (*Dogmatic Constitution on Divine Revelation*, chap. 3).

The importance of grasping the purpose of the Bible is obvious once we consider that the interpreting of any book depends upon the kind of book it is, whether a novel or a cookbook or a dictionary. If the Bible is the covenant book of the people of God, then it exists for them and for their religious (in the broad sense) needs, not primarily for literary critics, historians, geologists, and text critics. It is the witness to the agreement we have with God through Christ. What we expect to learn from it is "teaching, reproof, correction, and instruction in righteousness" to make us the kind of mature disciples and servants of the Lord we want to be. Knowing how inspiration happened or whether the original texts were or were not free from what someone might regard as a flaw is not necessary for us, and the Bible does not tell us these things. What it does do is confront us with the living God and involve us in a relationship with him through our faith. About this, the Scriptures are clear and plain, and their profitability for the life of faith evident and empirical.[30]

Another conclusion the evidence points to is the complex character of the Bible as the Word of God. It contains many kinds of literature and several levels of claim to authority. The truth appropriate in a psalm or a proverb, in situated command or a parable, is discerned by reference to the genre in question. We will want to notice whether the author claims to be delivering a prophetic oracle or a piece of advice, an apostolic commandment or an agonized question. Although God is the ultimate origin, we might say author, of the whole Bible, he is not the speaker of every line in it except in an ultimate sense, so that we must give thought to what he is saying to us in each place. What is God saying through the psalmist crying out in this way, or through the scribe arranging the narrative in this manner, or through Ecclesiastes giving expression to his doubts the way he does? We need to avoid being too simplistic when we utter slogans like "what the Bible says, God says," when a glance at almost any page will show how unsimple such a conviction is in practice. The simple thing we can say about the Bible from the testimony is that it is the text in which the Word of God can be heard and the will of God discerned. What is not simple is cashing in on this assurance. We have to take the portion we are reading in relation to the organic structure of revelation it is a part of and observe the kind of claim it is making on us.

A conclusion we can draw from the New Testament use of the Old Testament that has great bearing upon hermeneutics and the interpretation of Scripture is the dynamic nature of our encounter with the text. Jesus and the apostles did not feel limited to every jot and tittle of the text as laid down. They accorded utmost respect to the smallest detail, but they also read the text in relation to the present context and sought for the will of God in the interaction between the text and their own situation. We saw how Jesus would drop out part of a text that did not apply to his hearers (in his use of Isaiah 61 in Luke 4:18–19). Obviously, he did not just place himself "under" the text but considered whether and how the text applied to his present circumstances. We cannot use Jesus to prove that one ought to subject onself at all times to whatever the Scripture text says. Even in the case of Jesus' own words, the Gospel writers take some liberties, when they rephrase what he said and place his words in new contexts to bring out fresh meaning. It is not that the authority of the original is being denied in any way, but that the text means something different in the new context. The key point to learn is this: the Word of God is not to be found simply by staring at the text of the Bible or by searching one's own religious consciousness, but in the interaction between the two, from the coming together of revelation past and revelation present. There is a freedom permitted us in our reading of Scripture that was lacking in the Pharisaic and in the fundamentalist doctrine. God's Word is related to the situation to which it was addressed, and to understand it properly, we need to search through it for the will of God for our own situation. God does not say exactly the same thing to every historical context, and we muzzle the power of Scripture when we refuse to ask how the Lord wants to use this Scripture in our hearing now. God has spoken in the Scriptures, but he also speaks through them today in ways that the original writer may not have intended. In saying this, we are simply confessing our faith in the Spirit as alive and active in bringing out from the Bible the ever-relevant Word of the Lord. Therefore, we study the text with the greatest care and also open our minds prayerfully to God's particular Word to us. In this way we do not exalt the letter over the Spirit or eliminate the written norms in favor of subjectivity but allow the Word of the Spirit to function together.[31]

Finally, what does the Bible teach in regard to the vexed question of errorlessness so vehemently debated, at least in North America? If God be the author of the Bible, does it not follow that the text must be free from any flaw and from all error? Can God lie? Did not Jesus use the Old Testament with such a total trust as to imply the total perfection of it? The argument from the nature of God linked to the evidence of the New Testament doctrine of inspiration appear to settle the issue decisively.[32]

But the case for biblical errorlessness is not as good as it looks. Of course God cannot lie, but that is not the issue. God gave the Bible, not by mechanically dictating it (as all in this debate agree), but by transmitting through all manner of secondary authors. We cannot determine ahead of time what kind of text God would give in this way. We have to inquire into what it claims and what was produced. The orthodox Lutherans thought that the vowel points in the Masoretic text must have been inspired but were proven wrong by such an inquiry. God could have produced an errorless Bible, but we have to look and see if this is what he willed to do. What we might expect God to do is never as important as what he actually does. We might hope God would reveal the list of canonical books, or ensure the perfect transmission of the text, or give us a pope to make the meaning of the Bible plain—but he did not perform according to human expectations. From the affirmation of the inspiration of the Bible, we cannot deduce what the Bible must be like in detail.[33]

This leaves us with the question, Does the New Testament, did Jesus, teach the perfect errorlessness of the Scriptures? No, not in plain terms. Harrison made the point a quarter century ago: "One must grant that the Bible itself, in advancing its own claim of inspiration, says nothing precisely about inerrancy. This remains a conclusion to which devout minds have come because of the divine character of Scripture.[34] It is not just that the term *inerrancy* is not used in the Bible. That would not settle anything. The point to remember is that the category of inerrancy as used today is quite a technical one and difficult to define exactly. It is postulated of the original texts of Scripture not now extant; it is held not to apply to round numbers, grammatical structures, incidental details in texts; it is held to be unfalsifiable except by some indisputable argument. Once we recall how complex a hypothesis inerrancy is, it is obvious that the Bible teaches no such thing explicitly. What it claims, as we have seen, is divine inspiration and a general reliability, with a distinct concentration upon the covenantal revelation of God. And when we examine the text in detail and note how the Gospels differ from one another, how freely the New Testament quotes from the Old Testament, and how boldly the chronicler changes what lay before him in Kings, this impression is strongly confirmed. Why, then, do scholars insist that the Bible does claim total inerrancy? I can only answer for myself, as one who argued in this way a few years ago. I claimed that the Bible taught total inerrancy because I hoped that it did—I wanted it to. How would it be possible to maintain a firm stand against religious liberalism unless one held firmly to total inerrancy? Factors in the contemporary situation accounted for the claim, at least in my case. All I had to do was tighten up the case for inspiration one can find in the Bible and extend it just a little further than it goes itself. The logic of inspiration coupled with the demands of faith today were quite enough to convince me. Looking at the actual biblical evidence today, I have to conclude the case for total inerrancy just isn't there. At the very most, one could say only that it is implicit and could be drawn out by careful argument—but this is disputable and not the basis for the dogmatic claims one hears for inerrancy. In the last analysis, the inerrancy theory is a logical deduction not well supported exegetically. Those who press it hard are elevating reason over Scripture at that point.

A major reason evangelicals have experienced difficulty following inductive, and avoiding deductive, thinking on the subject of inspiration is that Warfield, to whom they all look, also did. His own position gave rise to both the approaches, which seem divergent to us today. On the one hand, Warfield claimed to follow the inductive approach in arriving at his doctrine of Scripture and disowned a priori conceptions, but then, when he sought to define inspiration, he lapsed into strongly deductive arguments to prove why something that was inspired would have to be perfectly errorless. His powerful desire to see the Bible in a certain way overpowered the empirical support for his favored view. This inconsistency of his surfaces again and again in his theological followers. The deductive tendency that would see inerrancy as a necessary corollary of inspiration works against honestly facing up to the data, both in the case of the claims themselves and in respect of many of the phenomena of the text. What we have to say, instead, is that inerrancy is not precisely claimed by the Bible for itself and must be regarded as a possible implication on which sincere persons disagree. Being an inference of great complexity and difficulty, inerrancy is also a belief to be handled with sensitivity and not used as a battering ram to injure fellow Christians with.

When I say that the inerrancy hypothesis lacks exegetical foundations, I am not closed to the possibility that it has other foundations. If Scripture does not explicitly affirm inerrancy, neither does it deny it in so many words. The whole question is a matter given over to the theological judgment of the church. In an age when theologians boldly deny the Scriptures, can we afford to allow a doctrine of Scripture that falls short of the strictest specifications? Is the experience of the trustworthiness of Scripture in bringing us to know and love God not sufficient to cause us to trust Scripture in every detail without limit? Where can you draw the line clearly between what the Bible faithfully teaches and what is errant in it unless you simply assert total reliability? These are the sorts of considerations that move people to a view of the Bible "higher" than its own view of itself. A desire for religious certainty, the need for solid defenses, the logic of inspiration, the experience of God's reliability in the Bible—all of these move us to tighten up the doctrine of Scripture beyond what is written.

So what must be done? There ought to be as much goodwill and cooperation as possible between those who believe that the strict view of inerrancy is important to hold and those who think the more lenient view is truer and wiser. Exegesis will not, I believe, take us beyond the lenient view. Therefore, it is a question of theological and pastoral wisdom. It may be that in certain contexts the strict view will be the wisest to maintain, and in others, the lenient view.[35] For my part, to go beyond the biblical requirements to a strict position of total errorlessness only brings to the forefront the perplexing features of the Bible that no one can completely explain and overshadows those wonderful certainties of salvation in Christ that ought to be front and center. It makes us into sitting ducks for the liberal critics like James Barr and postpones our ability to be certain about the Bible to that remote time when the experts will be able to say, "At last we have proved the Bible in every respect." Much wiser, in my opinion, would be to stick with the more modest biblical claims and be able to shelve those perplexing biblical difficulties and not have to worry about them so much. We all work with an imperfect Bible, whatever translation we use, and we do not forsake our confidence in it because of some implausible number in the Chronicles. All of us live with uncertainty, so why even give the impression that some proven defect could bring the whole house of authority down? The Bible in the power of the Spirit has been true enough to bring us to know and love God in Christ. If this is what it claims and this is what it has done, then it ought to be enough for us.

It is common for special interest groups in the church to make the Bible say more about their distinctive convictions than it really wants to. In this case, practically the whole church, being committed to the divine inspiration of Holy Scripture, has a stake in the doctrine of inspiration being very precise and very tight. Yet we must permit the biblical testimony to be what it is, namely, "obviously fragmentary and unsystematic."[36] I will have to return to this topic again in the course of the book and say more about it. It may be that a moderately phrased category of inerrancy is the best operating principle, given the theological atmosphere we find ourselves in. But at this point, we can only say that the biblical proof for any strict view of inerrancy is indirect and fragmentary. Conclusions based upon such evidence must therefore be modest and cautious. They cannot enjoy the degree of authority of doctrines based upon clear and direct statements of Scripture.

CHAPTER 3

Inspiration and Authority

The task before us now, having surveyed the spectrum of revelation and the specific biblical witness to inspiration, is to explore some dimensions of a Christian doctrine of Scripture. What model of biblical authority is authorized by the testimony we have?

The first point to make is that the Scripture principle is inherent in and integral to the faith of Israel and the church such that it cannot be severed without great damage to the total organism. It is not something incidental or tacked on anachronistically but belongs to the dynamic of salvation history. The saving divine action has created not only a community of the faithful but also a reliable written witness to teach and guide them. It would seem reasonable to either accept the whole of salvation history with the Scripture principle or reject the whole, but not to try and hold onto remnants or separated limbs of the organism. If salvation history is credible, so is the Scripture principle. If it is not credible, neither is biblical authority. But the two do go together. Farley is clear about this; he sees the connection and rejects them both.[1] The plan of God for the salvation of sinners, from the evidence we have, includes the provision of a reliable written testimony to this redemption that is more than a product of merely human wisdom. It participates in the finally effective divine action on behalf of sinners. The person who can embrace the truth of salvation history will find it possible also to accept the gift of the Holy Scriptures. It is a gift that provides the message with sound epistemological foundations. First, God supplied the old covenant with authoritative documentation, and then the new covenant, with apostolic Scriptures to carry forward a true witness to the gospel. Had he left the message uninscripturated, it might have become irretrievably distorted and damaged. As it is, the truth has been enshrined in God-breathed Scriptures that ensure that the message will function effectively unto the salvation of the nations.

The second point follows upon this and brings out what a Scripture principle means. It means that there is a locus of the Word of God in a humanly accessible form available to us. It means that the Bible is regarded as a creaturely text that is at the same time God's own written Word, and that we can consult his Word, which reveals his mind, and seek to know his will in it. It means that God has communicated authoritatively to us on those subjects about which Scripture teaches, whether doctrinal, ethical, or spiritual, and that we believers willingly subject ourselves to this rule of faith. More than merely human tradition and merely existential address, the Bible is the informative Word of God to the church. The text is not reduced to an expression of human experience and tradition, as in liberalism, but is a contentful language deposit that addresses, as it decides, with the authority of God.[2] Deciding what functions the Bible shall have in the church is not ours to do; it belongs to the authority of Scripture to lay whatever burden on us, heavy or light that it decides.[3]

Ernst Käsemann is right when he passionately says, "Indeed—and whatever contradiction and annoyance I may cause by saying this—not everything that is in the Bible is God's Word. In the last resort the contemporary controversy is about the truth or falsehood of this proposition"[4] He has placed a finger directly upon the issue. In saying that not everything in the Bible is God's Word, one rejects the whole idea of the Scripture principle, which guarantees precisely that, and creates a crisis for classical Christian theology. Käsemann cares a great deal for the critical reading of the text; what we ought to care most about is what God is teaching us in and through the text, not the technology and speculative guesswork of that art. The battle line, if I mistake not, falls right here.

The Scripture principle proper to Christianity, however, is not just identical to the Judaic Scripture principle. Most importantly, the bipartite Bible is structured in such a way as to identify the Old Testament as prefiguring narrative, not the last word on the purposes of God. The messianic age has dawned in Jesus the Christ, and the revelation associated with that age takes precedence over the premessianic material. Scripture, thus, is not leveled in the way it is in the Judaic Scripture principle but is searched and interpreted in terms of a Christological presupposition. Naive rhetoric about biblical infallibility could easily lead to a tragic Judaizing of the Christian faith. In other ways, too, there is a liberty built into the principle. The existence of real differences of emphasis in the canon, say between Job and the Proverbs, prevents the Scriptures from becoming an authority for a petrified orthodoxy,[5] and the work of the Spirit opens up the text so that is can serve the church in very new ways to meet the challenges of today.[6]

What Is Inspiration?

For all the talk about inspiration, the term occurs only once in the Bible (2 Tim. 3:16), and even then without a definition. Warfield argued that the term itself means "breathed out by God," but the context of the verse also suggests a spiritual power possessed by the text that is what makes it so effective in the ways specified. Some have suggested that it means God dictated the words to the scribes of Scripture, whereas others propose thinking in terms of flashes of insight and religious genius.

What kind of divine activity is inspiration? A valuable clue can be found in the diverse products of inspiration in the phenomena of the Bible. Many kinds of divine activity seem to have been involved. One kind of inspiration was prophetic and enabled the prophet to speak the word of the Lord with great authority and assurance. Another kind of inspiration was scribal and supported writers in the researching and composition of their work. Another lies behind the wisdom literature, and another behind the poetic utterances. The obvious lesson to learn about inspiration from seeing what it produced is that inspiration is not one single activity but a broader superintendence over a process of Scripture making that is not simple but complex. It was wrong of Athenagoras to suggest that God used the biblical writers as a musician uses his flute. Mechanical analogies of this kind derive more from Hellenistic ideas of inspiration than from the Bible's picture of it, and they pose a danger to the real humanity of the Bible.[7] There is pressure to think of inspiration in mechanical terms because of the natural desire to have God speak directly in the Bible. There is the temptation to construe the whole text as if it were prophecy so that one might consider every verse in it as if it were an oracle from on high. But this overlooks the simple fact that the Bible is more than prophecy, and although direct divine speech is part of the record, there are many other kinds of communication as well, some of them more indirect and ambiguous.[8]

It is probably best to think of inspiration as a divine activity accompanying the preparation and production of the Scriptures. We are not privileged to observe how in hidden and mysterious ways the Spirit worked alongside the human agents in the creative literary work, but we can plainly see what was done. We have a book like Genesis that refers to the sources it used in composition: "these are the generations of" (2:4; 6:9, etc.). In Jeremiah we encounter a book that contains not only the oracles of his preaching but a good deal of narrative stitching the book together. The historical books are completely anonymous and were likely the work of a large number of scribes and historians making a contribution toward the final redaction. One does not get the impression that inspiration is a sudden activity in the isolated life of some famous writer known to us all. It seems to have been a quieter and more long-term affair, as traditions were shaped and texts brought to final form. We may speak of the social character of inspiration and of the complexity of its execution, involving the work and gifts of many people, most of them unnamed but doing their part under the care of the Spirit to achieve the desired result. Inspiration cannot be reserved for the final redactor but ought to be seen as occurring over a long time as a charism of the people of God.[9] God was at work in the community to produce a normative text for the community to serve as its constitution.

I suggest that we think of inspiration in broader terms than is customary—less as a punctilinear enlightenment of a few elect persons and more as a long-term divine activity operating within the whole history of revelation. Inspiration means that God gave us the Scriptures, but it does not dictate how we must think of the individual units being produced. Scripture exists because of the will of God and is a result of his ultimate causality, but it comes into existence through many gifts of prophecy, insight, imagination, and wisdom that the Spirit gives as he wills. The all-important point is that everything taught in the Scriptures is meant to be heard and heeded, because it is divinely intended. Every segment is inspired by God, though not in the same way, and the result is a richly variegated teacher, richer for all its diversity. The very differences are what enables the Bible to speak with power and relevance to so many different people in so many different settings, and to address the many-sidedness of the human condition.

The Proper Use of the Bible

Before one actually considers the rules for the interpretation of the Bible, there is a prior attitude to deal with. Something needs to be said about the use of the Bible that is appropriate to the Scripture principle, about the preunderstanding that is the foundation of good hermeneutics. First, we may mention a spirit of openness to the text. For if the Bible is no merely human product but has an identity with the Word of God, without exhausting it, then it follows that the believer will choose to accept the discipline of its teachings and seek to walk in the light of its statutes. Of course, the text can be studied in the academy too, from a scientific point of view that endeavors to evaluate the various claims the text makes in a somewhat objective way. There is a place for an uninvolved as well as an involved approach to the Bible. Nevertheless, the Christian will want to move beyond what can be known by reason to the level of hearing God's Word in the text. For the Bible is not merely the product of Near Eastern culture but the written Word of God and canon of the church. Therefore, it ought to be approached in a spirit of faith, in the context of the believing community, and received as a reliable witness to God and his relationship with us. For the church to be apostolic means for it to live under the discipline of the normative Word of God.[10]

This attitude brings one into conflict with the pretensions of a good deal of biblical criticism, which often operates under an attitude of suspicion of the text and is prepared to overthrow it in the name of critical freedom. Magisterial criticism is excluded when it lords it over the text instead of submitting humbly to it and serving it. It very easily becomes a technology of deconstruction that exalts the judgment of the scholar and demeans the authority of the Scriptures. Criticism is useful when it illumines the meaning of the Bible, but it is harmful and useless when it seeks to overthrow what the text was given to tell us. No one can be wiser than the Bible. It owes its origin to the activity of God, and in its most obscure corners his Word can be found. As a divinely willed language deposit, the Scriptures are the place to stand in order to hear God speak and the chief means of grace in the life of faith. They can be effective only when the reader approaches them in a spirit of openness and faith. A correct formulation of the Scripture principle is not the crucial thing but a determination to know and love and serve God under the authority of his Word.

Critically speaking, the proper attitude also means being concerned about the text both in the stages of its preparation, insofar as these can be exposed, and in the final form of the text as well. It could be that delving into the state of the tradition before it was brought into its canonical form might shed some light on the meaning of the final redaction. But since inspiration eventually secured the text in a canonical collection and in a stable text, the greatest attention must be given to the final shape of the Bible. We might speculate about the original parable as Jesus gave it, but when it comes down to it, what we have to read and preach is the parable in the redaction of a particular Gospel where, in the wisdom of God, it came to rest. It is this text that we trust, not any speculative reconstruction of a "better" form of the text. There is value in looking at the possible sources of the text, because God was active at every stage in the process of Scripture making, but it

is the final text that the Spirit ultimately gave us and where final authority resides. Placing the authority, as Ogden does, in a more primitive layer of tradition than the New Testament itself, as he, with the
help of Willi Marxsen, reconstructs it, really disowns the Bible as our
authority and enthrones the human expert with all his or her biases as
the last word.[11] Inspiration means that the proper place of a biblical text
is in the canonical collection and that it be read in this context. Though
Childs might not admit it, Barr has a valid point when he suspects that
this commitment to the canonical text really lowers our estimation of the
value of the critical work done on the earlier stages. It does in fact lower
it and make it much less important than he would like to pretend that
it is. What is implied is that religious authority does not attach to the
guesswork of critics but remains where God intended it to lie, in the Bible
unaffected by criticism.[12] Belief in inspiration is indeed hostile to all forms
of criticism that refuse to submit to the text and that prefer a reconstructed text to the text evidently intended by inspiration.

The appropriate use of Scripture, then, is that we approach it as our
God-given norm, the rule of faith and practice. This is the Protestant
principle. God has left the church with a body of normative tradition in
an objective language deposit for the sake of the people he is forming
for himself. Therefore, we look to the Scriptures to provide the definitive Word that can enliven and shape us. In this glass we can see who
we are and learn more about what our calling means. No other norm
can do this for us. Biblical revelation is the criterion of Christian
thought and action, a safeguard against human self-will, and it stands
ever as a witness for us or against us to keep our feet in the orbit of
God's will. It is not enough just to say that the Bible mediates an encounter with God and in it we hear an echo of his voice.[13] The Bible is,
in fact, the inscripturation of God's Word and is a self-determining
authority over the church. How it rules is not decided by the readers'
taste but by the claims of the text itself.

Unfortunately, there is a body of opinion that wants to retain the
freedom to critique Scripture and does not want to submit to its authority without reservation. Members of this body are prepared to use it as
a source of information about the way in which people thought of God
and themselves, but not as a source of divine truth. How, they ask, can
we believe a text that presents notions foreign to our understanding
and lacking in credibility for us? They are not prepared to humble
themselves and be instructed by the text on the assumption that it
knows better. They insist on retaining the right to say that on this

matter Scripture is only human and falls into error. To illustrate how tempting it can be to take this view under pressure, Paul K. Jewett, a thoroughly orthodox Protestant theologian in every other respect, when faced with texts in Paul that seem to contradict his own convictions about feminism, rejects certain texts as representing only a human opinion of Paul and rabbi, suggesting that some verses in the Bible are not divinely intended and not binding on us.[14] The logic of this approach to the Bible, of course, removes the basis for appealing to it on behalf of any conviction, including feminism. What Jewett should have done, to follow the normal orthodox method, would have been to respect the divine authority even of a situationally limited Word, and to ask what it may signify, if anything, for us.[15]

This example alerts us to the complexity of the norm of Scripture. It is not always easy to know how to appeal to the Bible, which can easily be used carnally to serve our own selfish purposes. For example, as we already noted, biblical revelation is progressive in character, moving from premessianic to messianic revelation, and therefore it is imperative to take careful note where a text occurs in the organism of Scripture. An Old Testament text may have been the Word of God to ancient Israel and not be God's Word to us now. We run the risk of Judaizing the church if we forget this. Then there are other sorts of complexity. For example, there are various levels of authority from one passage to another. There are commands and exhortations, parables and poetry, pieces of advice and expressions of ecstasy. Each of these carries an appropriate authority in a distinctive way, and we need to attend to this fact. Some passages aim to instruct us in doctrinal truth. Other passages want to transform our lives by challenging us to the quick. Still others exhort us to get moving toward discipleship. The Bible does all these things and many more. It tells truth in every case, but not the same kind of truth. We must be alert to picking out the kind of truth claim each passage makes on us. To take a couple of examples of a provocative kind, it is not necessary to understand the story of the fall of Adam as a historical, eyewitness account, which it could not have been. Even though the historical character must be preserved (Rom. 5:12), the story itself in Genesis 2–3 is probably an etiological inference drawn from human experience of guilt and salvation in history and presented in the form of what must have happened in the beginning to bring this about. The visual appearance of the incident need not be thought of as the heart of what is being asserted in the passage. The form of the narrative seems saga like, which is, of course, a perfectly legitimate way of presenting such a universal truth about all human beings. Our whole history is determined by the decision to rebel against God, and thus is presented in terms of the fall of "Man." Similarly, in regard to eschatological assertions, belief in their absolute authority does not commit the reader to the interpretation of them as anticipatory, eyewitness accounts of what the future shall be. This, in fact, lands us in the nest of problems we associate with date setting and prophetic crystal ball–gazing in premillennialism today. Rather, these assertions about the future are oriented to the present as well and are designed to bring out the opening up of the future in a symbolic way. Sitting at table in the kingdom of God has a much more than literal meaning. Statements about hell, too, say more about the dread possibility of finally deciding against God than they do about the high temperature of that region.

We also need to keep an eye on the wholeness of the biblical reader, so as not to take a passage out of its canonical context. Biblical study has often focused too much upon small units in the text and failed to examine the meaning of them in relation to the broader picture. Jonah, for instance, should not be read as an isolated book but viewed in relation to the later New Testament Scriptures that reflect upon its meaning as a prophecy of Christ. Deuteronomy should be read in dialogue with Job and Ecclesiastes, which force us to see the whole question of wealth and piety in a deeper way. Of course, passages must be studied first in their own right, but eventually they ought to be placed in the framework of the whole revelation of God. This was the way of the older exegetical tradition, which operated out of a firm conviction about biblical inspiration.[16]

Theological Reasoning in the Mode of Authority

If there is an identity between Scripture and the Word of God, then the data for theology will be sought in the vehicle of revelation first of all. Reason certainly has a role to play. It enters into the decision to appeal to Scripture initially, when the critical decision is made to accept the Scripture principle. It comes into play when we evaluate what the Bible teaches and when we consider how the truth can be intelligibly conveyed to searching minds. But it does not have the competence to overthrow biblical teachings once they have been established. They cannot be ruled out just because they seem unreasonable, if in fact they are exegetically well supported. Theological thinking is not done in the context of perfectly free inquiry but continually goes back to consult and to cite from the Book. In this it differs from ordinary sciences. It locates the primary evidence for its judgments in the vehicle of revelation. The fact that the Bible teaches about angels is enough to establish this reality, even if there were no other reason to believe they existed.[17] The hymn captures the mode of theological reasoning when it says, "Jesus loves me, this I know, for the Bible tells me so." We do not come to the Bible wondering if it will tell the truth. We already trust it to tell the truth, and we come to discover what the truth is. Theology makes doctrinal houses from the bricks and mortar of biblical texts, and reason seeks for the consistency between them.[18]

But has not such a view been a hindrance to the advance in knowledge? Does not Galileo symbolize the suppression of scientific ideas because they came into conflict with scriptural notions? Does it not require one to believe that Methuselah lived for nine hundred sixty-nine years, even though it seems absurd? Science in different modes *has* forced us to reconsider traditional interpretations of the Bible. Christianity provided the presuppositions necessary for the rise of science and does not stand in the way of advancing scientific knowledge. Science poses questions to theology and compels us to consider or reconsider what we believe theology to be saying. This is all to the good. And of particular importance is the focused purpose of the Bible we referred to earlier. Its purpose to lead us to know and love God in Christ and to grow to maturity in him, not to be a textbook giving scientific particulars that can be found by empirical research. It is a religious classic, operating in a specialized area, and not running competition to the sciences. But it would be true that, if the Bible asserts as a fact or truth some fact or truth controverted by some scientific theory, the believer would have no other choice than to side with the Scriptures against the scientist. Such is the mode of theological thinking in the house of authority.[19]

The Coherence and Reliability of the Bible

Most people would agree that inspiration would mean very little if it could not guarantee a basic coherence in the Bible's teaching and a solid reliability in the Bible's narrative. Broken would be the authority of a norm that could not rule. We surely have a right to expect coherence and reliability. The Scripture principle would be overthrown should the Bible turn out to be self-contradictory and fallacious. We have a right to expect such a coherence and reliability as the Scriptures claim to be able to deliver, focused as its purpose is according to 2 Timothy 3:15–17.

This would mean a coherence in the teachings pertaining to the covenant purposes of God and a reliability in the narration of the history of salvation germane to the purpose in view. It would, of course, be important to consider what kind of truth a given passage is wanting to convey, and the cultural differences in the standard of measurement appropriate to apply. Essentially, we would want to be open to the Bible's freedom to be true in the ways that it chooses.[20]

The issue we are grappling with here has to do with the perfection of the Bible. Is it perfectly coherent in such a way that there are not any conceptual incoherences at all? Is it perfectly inerrant so that there are no factual discrepancies at all? Because of their belief in the divine inspiration of the Bible, Christians have from very ancient times felt that it must be so, that inspiration entails such a prediction even before reading the text. The difficulty is that today both these inferences have been radically questioned and need to be examined.

Addressing ourselves first to the unity and coherence of biblical teaching, we have to face the challenge posed by a widely held current opinion that biblical theology is pluralistic and full of radical diversity such that the Bible cannot be used as our teacher in the ordinary sense. In the past, of course, the unity of the Scriptures was assumed, and drawing out the systematic message of the Bible was the theologian's task. The contents of Scripture were believed to have flowed from God's mind ultimately, and with patience and hard work they would prove to yield consistent doctrines. All this was implied by the fact of divine inspiration. When Luther concluded that James was out of line with Pauline teaching on justificatio, his immediate reaction was to deny Scripture status to one of them. If Scripture is our inspired teacher, making us wise unto salvation, then we expect it not to confuse us or tell us lies but to communicate intelligibly with us. This is implied by the Scripture principle, and the implication has always been drawn. The result has been that texts were read in the light of one another and never set in opposition to one another, and what is obscure is secondary considered in relation to what is clear and central.[21]

But nowadays there is a strong emphasis on the diversity of Scripture. With the increased stress upon the human character of the text comes a vision of it as a developing human witness full of complex ideas. The Bible is believed to include the most diverse material and therefore cannot be appealed to in any hope of achieving a coherent picture in a conceptual sense. The present trend goes back to the influential book by Walter Bauer *Orthodoxy and Heresy in Earliest Christianity*, in which he maintained that the early church tolerated highly diverse and mutually exclusive beliefs and that a clear sense of orthodoxy did not arise for several centuries.[22] More recently, the book by James D. G. Dunn, *Unity and Diversity in the New Testament*, extended the thesis into the earliest period and contended that the New Testament itself presents several different kerygmas and doctrines, denying the existence of a normative Christianity in it.[23] The result is that we can hardly appeal to the Bible anymore to establish Christian doctrines and norms, leaving the whole exercise of theology in a hopeless muddle. The bottom line, in fact, is that the method of classical theology, which involved piecing together the information supplied in various texts in order to construct a coherent theology, lies in ruins. No longer is it possible to arrive at truth by consulting the Bible, since it is as confused on all these questions as we are. The manner in which an Augustine or a Calvin did theology is forever closed to us now, and the results they reached are mainly of historical interest.[24] Small wonder classical Christians tremble in the presence of biblical criticism, which is most threatening when it attacks the assumption that the Bible can be appealed to as a norm for faith and practice.[25]

At the outset, it is important to ascertain just how radical the diversity is. Obviously, if the Bible presents a series of plain contradictions, the point is made, and orthodoxy had better pack its bags. But it is not as simple or devastating as that. Despite a degree of diversity, there is, after all, a tremendous unity in the Bible. Even though it was written over centuries, it yields a compelling set of doctrines that have occupied the minds of people unceasingly. Donald Guthrie, author of a massive New Testament theology, sees no evidence to show that there were several gospels in the New Testament, or that the variations in emphasis were anything more than that. He is impressed by the deep unity of biblical thought and sees the rich variety as contributing to it.[26] In other words, part of the problem is one of exaggeration. H. E. W. Turner showed in the Bampton Lectures for 1954 that Bauer's work was full of misjudgments regarding theological positions in the early church. Trinitarian orthodoxy is much earlier than the Nicene formulary.[27] As for the New Testament, nothing requires us to follow Dunn in concluding that the kerygma of the Synoptic Gospels is contradictory with the kerygma of Paul or John. Similarly, in Christology, though there is certainly a difference in emphasis in Acts as compared with John, it is not obvious that they do not complement one another.[28]

Exaggerations aside, there is rich diversity in biblical teaching, which adds to its profundity. Differences surface for most people when there is a dispute in interpretation on some interesting question. On a controversial question, such as war, one will notice the opposing sides quoting different texts to support their opinions. One side will resort to Old Testament statements that seem to support the right to defend one's country militarily, whereas the other side will appeal to the Sermon on the Mount to deny it. Quite apart from the misuse of texts, there seems to be a variety of teaching on issues like war, forcing the reader to ask how the Bible as a whole should be understood and applied. Tight consistency is not what we find when we read the Bible. It is like listening to an orchestra rather than a single solo instrument, or a large choir rather than a solo voice. This arises from several features of the Bible. One is that it is a progressive account of revelation given bit by bit over a long period of time, not all at once. In it we can trace the development of the promise of God as it was given to Abraham and then unfolded in stages, leading to its fulfillment in Jesus Christ.[29] Both unity and diversity are evident in the outworking of the divine plan of salvation. This becomes more apparent in the New Testament, where the old covenant is seen to have become "obsolete" in a certain sense and replaced by a new convenant (Heb. 8:13). Though it is not a contradiction that circumcision was called for in the Old Testament but not in the New, it does remind us that the unity of the Bible is not just simple and obvious, but makes room for changes. This means that we must assess the meaning of each part in relation to the whole and not lift passages out of context. Another feature of the Bible that gives rise to diversity is the dialogue that often arises between witnesses in the text. As we noted, some real diversity exists between the several New Testament writers as regards the person and work of Christ, and we have no right to force one writer to say what another says. We have to respect the distinctiveness of each witness.[30] Everyone is familiar with the tension in the Bible between divine sovereignty and human freedom, pairs of truth that seem to stand alongside one another, defying resolution.[31] The Bible is like that. It does not suppress differences of emphasis or angles of vision and does not force them onto a single plane. It would seem to be the will of God that the Bible should set forth its truth in a richly textured way, and our duty not to corrupt this policy by harmonizing the differences inappropriately.[32]

Yet another feature of the Bible that yields diversity is the situational orientation of much of the material. It is easy to pit one book against another when each was written to meet a particular need, but it is not necessary to do so. It is more likely to suppose that each of Paul's letters, for example, represent contingent expressions of his coherent position. Diversity is bound to arise when the gospel is being applied to different situations and cultures by different people with their own peculiarities and personal styles.

In this matter of the unity of the Bible one is not forced to choose between accepting contradictions, on the one hand, and striving feverishly to harmonize differences in a tight consistency, on the other. There is a third alternative—and that is complementarity. As Lonergan has pointed out, two authors may bring out some very different points and still be in basic agreement on the central issues.[33] Matthew and Paul certainly say some very different things about the Law of God, but what they say is compatible if we take into account the points of reference involved.[34] Rahner recognizes differences in ecclesiology on the part of the New Testament writers but concludes that it is a unity amid diversity. The differences are rooted in the practical problems facing the various early churches that produced the documents.[35]

But are we being honest when we adopt a complementary model, arising, as it obviously does, from a belief in the Scripture principle and saving it from being proved false? There can be no doubt that this conviction has in the past influenced and does even now influence Christians to seek for positive internal relations between texts and to reject outright contradiction between them. I would not want to deny that belief in inspiration supplies a hermeneutical guideline for me and makes me tend to deny the reality of apparent contradictions. It causes me to look for the underlying unity beneath every case of surface contradiction. But it is not just a case of presuppositions, as though one's hoped-for unity had to coexist with a surging mass of obvious contradictions. It just does not seem to be the case, from an empirical standpoint, that because we have four Gospels that paint a different portrait of the Christ we therefore have four frames that could not be dealing with the same person. Nor does the fact that in Paul and John and the author to the Hebrews we have three theologians with their distinctive vocabularies and categories lead me to conclude that we are dealing with three truth systems that do not dovetail and complement one another. So long as we do not exaggerate the differences in the Bible, but take account of the purposes and pastoral settings involved, I have never felt to be convincing any charge I have heard of that the Bible is contradictory at some point. Even in the extreme cases, it does not seem sensible to pit Jesus against Moses or Paul against James. Why does Bultmann say that belief in the virgin birth in Luke is incompatible with belief in the incarnation in John, when no such thing is required? The church has always believed them both, and not found them contradictory.[36] Why does Dunn assume that Paul could not have consented to what James said about justification? Of course there is a contradiction in surface terminology, but not in theology deeper down.[37] If there are real contradictions in the Bible, it is not very obvious to me what they are.

A final consideration that counsels caution against rushing to conclusions and patience in the presence of perplexing features in the text has to do with God's purpose in the polyphony of Scripture. What impresses me is the shallowness of the two extremes. Confronted with two seemingly contradictory texts, one person will declare a contradiction whereas another will claim a harmony, but neither one really pauses in the presence of the dialectic to see what God may be teaching through it precisely. Puzzling features are always found in great works of art, and it always wise to wait until the deeper nuances that explain them reveal themselves. The Bible is not coherent and unified in the way we might choose, but in the way God has chosen. And I think we can be sure that the paradox and tensions that are there are meant to lead us deeper into hidden theological riches. Cutting the Gordian knot by declaring contradiction or by rushing to harmonize tends to cut us off from the deeper teachings that come as we wrestle with the problems of unitive exegesis. There will always be some who propose that we drop one or another voice out of the biblical choir because they are not pleased with its contribution. But the church must always refuse to follow the suggestion, trusting, rather, that each voice was meant to be there and meant to add to the total effect of the treasury of the Word of God.

At the same time, we have no right to impose upon the Bible the sort of coherence that may suit us and no right to force the text into a greater coherence than it has chosen to display. God himself does not seem over concerned about tight coherence when he introduces quite significant changes into the new covenant as compared with the old. It would not be right to pretend that Ecclesiastes did not deny the hope of life after death in order to bring him into line with New Testament writers. It does not follow that the apostolic directive in Acts 15 pertaining to dietary practices should be considered binding upon us. The Bible is marked by diversity as well as unity, and this is part of the rich package God has given us.

The Factual Reliability of the Bible

Belief in the Scripture principle certainly predisposes one to trust the Bible and expect it to teach the truth. It is instinctive for Christians when they encounter perplexing features in the Bible to hope for some explanation or resolution. In this they are in line with the trustful spirit we see in the biblical writers themselves and with the historic confidence Christians have displayed toward the Scriptures over the centuries. It is even logical in a certain sense, not in the sense that whatever God gave by way of inspiration must be inerrant in some way prescribed by us—we are not in a position to tell God what he has to do—but in the sense that, if there are mistakes in the Bible, how can we appeal to it as the source of truth? Finding an error in the Bible would not discredit all its assertions, but it would create some uncertainty about the Bible as consistently truthful. It is not hard to understand why there would be discussion about biblical inerrancy, especially in an age when the suspicion is abroad that the Bible is not trustworthy.[38]

At the same time, we must recall from the last chapter that the Bible itself does not teach a doctrine of inerrancy in so many words. Though we might grant that it teaches a broad and untechnical kind of inerrancy, it does not teach a technical and strict version of it. Therefore, we ought to proceed with caution on this subject. Inerrancy as Warfield understood it was a good deal more precise than the sort of reliability the Bible proposes. The Bible's emphasis tends to be upon the saving truth of its message and its supreme profitability in the life of faith and discipleship. It does not really inform us how we ought to handle perplexing features in the text.

That the New Testament does not clarify this issue is plain in that people today cannot agree on the definition of the term *inerrancy*. Much of our bickering stems from this inability to define it effectively. Some make it a strict category, which necessitates a good deal of special pleading to show that minor discrepancies of one kind or another are not really so, whereas others find a great deal of room to move under this rubric. This latter view, in turn, turns still others off, on the grounds that as ambiguous and difficult a term as this surely can be dispensed with. Sticking with the simpler, less problematic language of the New Testament seems wiser to them than the present bickering over a word. If it is not clear even to those who use it what inerrancy means, why impose it as some kind of shibboleth? It is obviously not the ideal term and should not be used to divide the Christian community.

What, then, should we say about the reliability of the Bible and this question of inerrancy? First, we must proceed more carefully and stop being so dogmatic about it. We all agree that the Bible is trustworthy in the fundamental sense. In telling us what God has said and done, it brings us to a saving knowledge of him and builds us up in our holy faith. Further, we are all aware of certain perplexing features in the Bible that resist easy answers and desire wisdom in knowing how to handle them. But wisdom has seemed to be in short supply among us, perhaps because of the pressure we feel from Bible deniers.

On one side, we have people claiming that unless the Bible is perfectly inerrant in quite a strict sense it cannot be trusted. Actually, they do not mean our present texts of the Bible are inerrant, but the original autographs given long ago and not now extant. What must an ordinary Christian think of such an approach? They are being told in effect that they cannot trust their Bible because it contains potential errors. It forces them to place their trust instead in the scholars at work to show why each of the hundreds of apparent errors are not real errors. Should they take it seriously and think about it, it actually threatens the confidence in the Bible they now have because of its effectiveness in bringing them to God and substitutes for it a confidence that may one day be warranted when the scholars have finished their work—if indeed they ever do. Surely it would be an exaggeration to call this a "high" view of Scripture, since it does not warrant us to trust the only Bible we have and possibly ever will have. And at the same time, our belief in the clarity of Scripture is also placed in jeopardy, because we are told that texts that apparently say one thing in actual fact may not when all is known. And all the while we live in fear that a single point should prove inexplicable and threaten to bring the whole of Christianity down on its head. There is not much wisdom here.

On the other side, too, wisdom is in short supply. What is gained by going around claiming to have found so many biblical errors? What message is that calculated to give? And how sure are we that we want to call them errors, anyhow? Dogma is not appropriate, either, when it comes to declaring the Bible errant. For one thing, it is well accepted that something formerly thought to be an error can, upon further research and reflection, turn out to be nothing of the sort. And besides, the question of error is so tied into the language game being played by the text that it seldom comes up in actual exegesis. The numbers of chariots may not line up, but that does not prove there was no truth on another level in the numbers given. The person who announces the discovery that the Bible errs on the basis of a list of errors uncovered is not likely to accomplish much except to forfeit the trust of Christians in his or her teaching, since their instinct to trust the Bible is greater than their instinct to trust such a teacher. Warfield was right to say one does not need to rush to negative conclusions, but ought to wait patiently for the text to reveal itself. Biblical scholars are sometimes tempted to declare, in reaction to the fundamentalists, that the Bible makes mistakes and we have to be honest about that. But wisdom would counsel them to be careful of the way they speak in this regard. It is far wiser to delve into the purpose of the text and reason for the anomaly than to come across in a negative way. Errancy dogmatism, too, is foolish and immature, and creates only problems. Worst of all, it raises suspicions about those very scholars who may in fact have a lot of positive things to contribute.

The way of wisdom here would seem to be to concentrate upon the focused authority of the Bible, which is concerned to bring us the gospel and reconcile us to God, and not to allow the marginal difficulties to cause us so much anxiety. We have all come to a vital confidence in Scripture on the basis of Bibles less than perfect in their present state, and we must never forget that simple fact. It did not require a perfectly errorless Bible to give us the certainty we all enjoy and share. This fact ought to lower the pressure we feel and enable us to approach the problem of apparent errors in a calmer and more settled way. A great deal, perhaps most, of biblical interpretation can make progress without ever raising or answering this issue. Indeed, it is likely that evangelicals have spent too much time arguing about it, causing them to fall behind in productive scholarship. All difficulties do not have to be resolved for us to advance in our understanding of God's Word. Certainly, because of inspiration, we are right to expect a high degree of ordinary reliability from the Bible. But we are not in a position to know precisely what degree of inerrancy, according to our modern understanding of it, God has willed to actualize in the Scriptures. All we can do is trust the Bible and look to see what is there. When we encounter some perplexing detail in the text, we inquire into it to see if it will yield its meaning. If not, we will let it stand, refusing to cover up the difficulty by jesuitical ingenuity. The Bible has never in any age lacked these features, and we can count on it to do its effective work in spite of them.

Second, in relation to biblical inerrancy, it might be best to adopt an inerrancy expectation as an operational policy. Although the New Testament does not teach a strict doctrine of inerrancy, it might be said to encourage a trusting attitude, which inerrancy in a more lenient definition does signify. The fact is that inerrancy is a very flexible term in and of itself. All those who use it qualify it in various ways in response to the perceived phenomena of the text. We are told by inerrantists that the Bible, in order to be inerrant, need not always give numbers exactly or spell everything just right or make precise references to things. It is not an intrinsically narrow term just because some use it that way. Given that inerrancy expresses a sturdy confidence in the trustworthiness of the Bible in a day when we need it and also, when fairly interpreted, allows a great deal of latitude in application, I think it would be wise to retain and employ the term. Bloesch is surely right when he says: "I am not among those who wish to give up inerrancy and infallibility when applied to Scripture, but I believe we need to be much more circumspect in our use of these and related terms. Scripture is without error in a fundamental sense, but we need to explore what this sense is."[39]

Inerrancy simply means that the Bible can be trusted in what it teaches and affirms. The inerrant truth of a parable is of course parabolic, and the inerrant truth of a fable is fabulous. If Matthew gives us some fictional midrash, then it is inerrant according to the demands of this genre. All this means is that inerrancy is relative to the intention of the text. If it could be shown that the chronicler inflates some of the numbers he uses for his didactic purpose, he would be completely within his rights and not at variance with inerrancy. The term possesses a nice combination of strength with flexibility that make it usable even in relation to hard biblical difficulties, and that it also enjoys wide acceptance in our day as symbolizing the trustworthiness of the Bible makes it practically irresistible. Indeed, my prediction would be that many will flock to its use in the coming days, forcing the strict conservatives to give up the term themselves, just as they have given up the term *evangelical*, for much the same reason.

Inerrancy is not, to be quite frank, an ideal term to say what needs to be said. This is chiefly because it connotes in many people's minds a modern, scientific precision that the Bible does not display. But a moment's attention to some of the phenomena of Scripture is enough to cure anyone of such an expectation, and it is relatively easy to indicate why the term requires a nuanced, flexible definition. Of course, ridiculous contortions will be performed by those who wish to show the Bible is inerrant in the strict sense. But once people see what is involved, this approach is not likely to carry many intelligent people with it. A moderate definition of inerrancy is likely to carry the day and come to express the deep confidence we ought to have in the Bible. What legitimate objection could any Christian have to Erickson's definition of inerrancy? "The Bible, when correctly interpreted in the light of the level to which culture and the means of communication had developed at the time it was written, and in view of the purposes for which it was given, is fully truthful in all that it affirms."[40] Does it not convey the strong respect we are seeking as well as giving us all the room we could possibly need for handling the biblical difficulties?

Scripture and Church Authority

It must be amusing for Catholic observers of Protestant theology to notice how they will point in delight to Augustine's doctrine of Scripture (which was undoubtedly high) and ignore the fact that it was tied in with two other beliefs of his, namely, belief in creeds and in church authority. We must not leave this issue unexamined.

The same impulse that led the early church to define the canon of Scripture also led it to other conclusions. Underlying the logic of the Scripture principle is the belief that God will see to it that his truth will not perish but be reliably transmitted. But this logic requires more than a Bible, because new questions arise and people wonder how the text should be interpreted. What if the message were not secured by the Bible alone but were still in some doubt? It was this kind of concern that led the church corporately to move toward doctrinal definitions in the form of creed and dogma in order to spell out just what the message essentially was. Judaism had done much the same thing in her extensive commentaries upon the sacred text. Such authoritative commentary was particularly urgent when the church was confronted with religious pluralism and theological heresy. And beyond that, a further safeguard was located in church authority. Christians began to think in terms of an authoritative institution that would not be subject to human failings and would be able to guarantee the truth year in and year out. Thus the expectation underlying the Scripture principle itself resulted in other products as well, especially creeds and church authority. The catholic tradition has believed that the truth is best served in this way. How, when the message is complex and the Bible's teaching less than self-evident, can we avoid moving along this logical path? We need more than the Bible to ensure that the saving truth will be passed along in its purity. The development of the church in a catholic direction from very early on is quite understandable.[41]

Protestants like to think they are different, but they really are not. The Reformers accepted the creeds of the early church and drew up extensive confessions of their own, as if a "canon beyond the canon" were needed to clarify what the Bible teaches, in case any Lutheran or Calvinist missed it. Even the Baptists, who think they are free from such formularies, have always drawn up similar statements of faith in response to the same pressures. There is admittedly less tendency to accept institutional authority in Protestant groups, but even here, some pious things are said about God calling together this church assembly and God guiding this church declaration. When this happens, the differences between Protestant and Catholic in the area of authority look very faint indeed. And of course the same process is visible today. In response to the attacks on biblical authority, many believe that we ought to define the doctrine of Scripture with great precision and then go on to specify the rules of its interpretation and the limits of critical study. Such documents as the ones produced by the Chicago group for biblical inerrancy are like hedges around the Torah and are designed to prevent readers of the Bible from getting the wrong ideas. For all our talk about "*sola scriptura*," the Bible is seldom left "alone." It is a wonderful irony that in order to remain evangelical today we find it necessary to be more catholic! The fact is that evangelicalism is theologically catholic without knowing it. Why would we appeal back to Calvin or Luther or Augustine on the doctrine of Scripture if we did not think tradition were important? Today's call for a "catholic evangelicalism" should not surprise anyone, even though it sounds odd.

For myself, I think that the logic that sees God providing Scripture to convey his Word and then raising up church leaders to further protect and define the message is good and scriptural. The idea surfaces in the Pastoral Epistles and is well articulated in 1 Timothy 3:15: "The church of the living God, the pillar and bulwark of the truth." Not only in the postapostolic church, but in the New Testament period itself, false teachers arose trying to pervert the truth, and action had to be taken against them. Paul warned the elders of Ephesus about the problem of heresy and instructed them to keep a close watch over the flock of God (Acts 20:28–31). He told young Timothy to be sure to pass the message deposit along to faithful persons who could do the same for others (2 Tim. 1:14; 2:2; 4:1–6). The Bible needs the church as its bulwark. How else will it be preserved, translated, interpreted, and proclaimed? How else will its message be protected against attempts to distort it? There is a link between the authority of the Bible and the work of the Spirit in the community. As the Preacher put it: "A threefold cord is not easily broken" (Eccles. 4:12). The Bible is the church's book and does its work in the ecclesial context. Insofar as our faith has content, we are dependent upon definitions and delineations. We need to have abbreviated statements of the faith once delivered. We need polemical demarcations of what is and is not Christian when false teachers propose their imaginative novelties. Sometimes it is necessary to define doctrines in the face of a serious challenge.[42] Where, then, is the Protestant any different from the Catholic in this area?

The difference came about through historical necessity. It would have been so much better if the threefold structure of authority had remained intact and the church of Jesus Christ with it. But the sad and regrettable fact is that it could not. For it came about that the message of salvation became seriously distorted in the tradition and had to be reclaimed. Luthers's protest had to be made, even though the effect of it was traumatic to the church. Scripture had to be separated somewhat from the too-close embrace of the institutional church so that it could be free to re-establish its liberating message. As in Jesus' own day, the tradition that so often serves the Word of God well became a hindrance and had to be corrected. The tragedy was that the correction was resisted and the path of schism taken. Protestantism stands for the freedom of the Word of God to critique church traditions and to bring them back into line with the gospel. It means abandoning traditions, if necessary, to get back on track. Ideally, Scripture would be a norm along with tradition and church—but as it happened, Scripture had to be put over tradition to bring about a reformation. What came to light was a keener awareness that, though the Bible is an infallible rule, the tradition is not. We may speak, as Hans Küng does, of the indefectibility of the church, of God's promise not to let her fall irretrievably into error and fail in her whole mission, but we may not speak of her infallibility, of any inability to go wrong and never to require reformation.[43] The catholic tradition tends to take the logic of God preserving his Word one step further than Protestants do, to the point of declaring the church magisterium itself infallible. Though understandable in terms of logic, it seems to be unwarranted scripturally and in view of historical developments. Tying up the package of authority so tightly in this way binds the Word of God more to the creaturely realm than it wants to be and permits the message to come under too great a degree of human control. Luther saw that we must give Scripture the focus of our greatest attention and let it have a free ministry and the primary authority.

All this seems to be implied in the notion of canon itself, which suggests a unique normativity over the ongoing developing traditions. Otherwise, the Bible would just melt into human traditions and lose its capacity to bring about change and reform. In opting for the canon, the church seemed to say that the criteria of truth lay outside herself in a text that stood over her and at times even against her. By accepting the norm of Scripture, the church declared that there was a standard outside herself to which she intended to be subject for all time. Being the

Word of God in this special sense, the Bible could measure the other authorities and be the foundation for Christian hermeneutic. The church can fall into error and needs the Bible to measure herself by. In turn, the church serves the canon by continuing in the truth and faithfully proclaiming the Word of God.[44]

Part II

IN HUMAN LANGUAGE

CHAPTER 4

Incarnation and Accommodation

Thus far we have concentrated upon the first duty in regard to the Bible, namely, to treat it as the written Word of God given to the church. Now we want to begin to speak about a second duty—the responsibility of accepting that God gave his word in human language. If we are going to grasp what God is saying to us through the Bible, we will have to understand these documents as historically and concretely as possible, in all their particularity. We will have to take note of the vocabulary, the literary forms, the character of the propositions, and the cultural background in order to pick up the nuances of teaching in the Scriptures. The Bible is God's Word in human language—the two aspects cannot be disassociated. God has willed the human characteristics of the text as much as he willed the poverty of the manger and the hard wood of the cross. In the present chapter, we will consider the humanity of the Bible in general terms; in the next chapter, we will look at a host of textual phenomena that give flesh to this humanity; and in Chapter 6, we will examine the problem of biblical criticism.

Looking at the humanity of the Scriptures ought not to give us anxiety, because it is part of God's will for the Bible and because the Bible has proven its effectiveness in carrying out its religious purpose in Christian experience. The Bible was not given as an end in itself but as a medium through which one can come to know and love God, just as eyeglasses are not purchased to be an object of examination but to help us see better. Ordinarily, the wearer of glasses is not conscious of having them on. The main thing is that they enable him or her to see reality out there. Of course, glasses can be removed and inspected if the wearer wants to, and this is what we are doing when we talk about the humanity of Scripture. Anxiety ought to arise in this context only when the biblical medium is not functioning well, and if that is the case, the problem lies at a much more basic level than specks on the lens, as it were. No one who has come to know and love God through the good news of the Bible is likely to feel threatened by some supposed flaw on the periphery of the medium through which this knowledge has come (unless, of course, some rationalistic theologian comes along and suggest that he or she ought to!). Such a believer will more likely be puzzled by it and curious about it, and want to obtain some information on the matter. We examine the humanity of the text, not because it poses a threat to the divine character of the medium of the Word of God, which has already been settled for the Christian, but to facilitate its proper interpretation.

The Form of the Human

When we are open to receive the human form of the text in which God was pleased to give us the Bible, we honor the divine way of wisdom in this matter. God himself has chosen to communicate with us using the resources of human literary composition, which belong to the creaturely realm. Therefore, it is foolishness and impiety for us to disregard this decision. It would be comparable to despising the bread and the wine in the Lord's Supper or, even worse, to demeaning the true humanity of our Lord Jesus in the interests of exalting his true divinity. This latter tendency in orthodox religion we call Docetism, and it is a heresy that crops up also in the doctrine of Scripture, and for the same reason. We are a little reluctant to face up fully to the reality of the human in the case of Christ and the Bible, for fear of obscuring the divine authority, and even the divine essence, of them both. One recalls the occasion when Dorothy Sayer's play *The Man Born to Be King* was first performed on the BBC in 1941 and the strong protests it aroused because of the way she presented Jesus as a man among men. The listeners were unwilling to believe that Christ actually laughed and said good morning and were shocked by her depiction of the crucifixion scene in the eleventh installment. The belief that Jesus is God incarnate tends to cause us to neglect any real sense of his being also truly human. What is at stake in Christology, and here in Bibliology, is whether we are prepared to honor the manner in which God has chosen to reveal himself to us.[1] God's will, evidently, is to reveal himself to us in forms of the creaturely realm, in which the human is a fundamental element that cannot be scorned or ignored safely. It is unbelief to be afraid of the divinely chosen mode of revelation. To use an analogy of Luther's, we should no more take offense at the plain, even vulgar, forms of expression in the Bible than at the humble circumstances of the birth of Jesus. For in both cases, beneath the unimpressive exterior lies a treasure more valuable than all the world. God's Word comes to us in human words and human thoughts that are not transubstantiated, as it were, into divine words and divine thoughts. Earthly modalities are what have been chosen to convey the freight of divine revelation, and this must suffice. We have looked at the Bible "from above"; it is now time to look at it "from below" and consider the human dimension. There is no point in trying to save the Bible from its humanity.

There is a very practical reason, as well, why we should honor the divine decision to employ the human in revelation. It is that, if God has joined content to form in this way, we can only understand the content in relation to the form. "What God hath joined together, let not man put asunder." If we are to "rightly divide the word of truth" (2 Tim. 2:15), we must pay the closest attention to the way in which the Word has been given. Neglecting the human flavor of the communication is bound to lead to misunderstanding. Only by taking careful notice of the human shape of the text will we be able to pick out its distinctive truth claim and receive God's Word. If we were having to explain the parable of the Pharisee and the publican, for example, we would need to understand what Pharisees and publicans were like in the first century and how people regarded them and would have to guard against modern presuppositions about them being read back into the parable. In particular, we would have to remember that the Pharisee was a much-respected member of the community and not the social pariah that the name suggests to us today. If we do not know this, or forget it, the parable will not register with the force it did when first told. It is terribly important to let the text speak authentically, and in order for that to happen, we the readers must give attention to the human form and situation.[2] These texts in the Bible were oriented to another world than ours, and this must be taken into account if we hope to understand them. We will not understand revelation if we refuse to take into account the historical and cultural dynamics at work in it. Had Paul's letter to the Galatians been received by the Corinthians instead, how hard it would have been for them to understand it! Texts like Paul's epistles were written to specific communities and exemplify distinctive emphases. The more we can discover about these settings, the better our interpretation of these texts will become. Revelation comes to us embedded in history, and therefore, we must attend to both revelation and history. The human and the divine components cannot be separated but, as in the incarnation, dwell together in unity. The divine Word and the human form are both present in every place, and both call for recognition.

Let it not be said, then, that the reason we ought to attend to the humanity of Scripture is to win favor with negative critics, who like nothing more than to point out how very human the Bible is. No, we do it in order to understand the Scriptures better. Unless we pay due attention to the form in which God's Word comes to us, we will not be able to grasp what that Word is. Instead, we will tend to twist the text and make it say what our context wants to hear. For if we replace the original sense by superimposing upon the text our modern set of assumptions, we will abuse the Bible as surely as if we had denied its authority and declared independence from its rule. It is not only the modernist, after all, who twists the Bible. We all do it whenever we skip over the historical integrity of the text and choose the interpretation that our own situation calls for. If the Bible is our authority, then we must be committed to historical hermeneutics, which means we must view the text in its context and not as if it were floating above history.[3]

This, in turn, will mean that we resist a certain tendency in orthodoxy to place the whole Bible on the same level of absolute assertion. Once the church has identified the whole Bible as the Word of God, the temptation is enormous to forget about the original historical situation and to regard every verse as a kind of oracle for us. This is the danger reflected in Augustine's expression "What the Bible says, God says." Then we no longer hear the precise word spoken to people by the text in the first instance, but construe it as a universally valid logion independent of context. Thus a text may no longer have a merely provincial meaning but must have a universal application. The tendency is to dehistoricize the vehicle of revelation and to make each text an immutable and inerrant proposition. Since God (in Hellenistic thinking) does not change in any way at all, neither can God's Word signify anything different for one community at a certain point in history than for another. Progressive revelation is thus lost sight of, and the Bible becomes a rigid, legalistic tool. Even though God in the Bible narrative obviously does command one thing for one group and something else for another (the Jewish and Christian communities, for example), there is an impetus at work in the doctrine of Scripture to minimize this feature of the text. The Bible must always be valid, even in changing circumstances—and in exhaustive detail. Such is the extension in logic that the doctrine of inspiration always tempts us to make. The remedy for such precarious deductions is, of course, due attention to the human form of the text.[4]

The Positive Side of Biblical Criticism

The positive value of the close scholarly study of the text often called (correctly or not) biblical criticism is the way in which it focuses on the text as a past object and helps us to see it as it really is in a distanced way. It helps us to see the text in itself and not as an image from our own self-projection. Criticism tries to bracket the reader's prejudices as far as possible and allow Scripture to be heard on its own terms. It asks about the date of the composition, the historical setting of the text, the function in the community, the type of literature it is, how it relates to other similar texts. By distancing the text from the reader, criticism allows the Bible to register its own message and stand over our biases and preconceptions about these matters. Its inability to tell how to apply the text to our context does not overshadow or negate its ability to shed light on the original meaning of the text, which is the starting point, if not the end point, of hermeneutics. It has suceeded brilliantly in vastly expanding our knowledge of the historical, cultural, and linguistic backgrounds of the Bible. It has put into much sharper focus the distinctiveness of Israel's faith, the origin of the Synoptic Gospels, the religious environment of Paul's mission and message, and so on. Thus, biblical criticism is a permanent feature of the church's ongoing task of ascertaining the meaning of the Scriptures.[5] It is legitimated by the human character of the Bible, which does not come to us in a supernatural form raised above all human weakness but in the form of language that has to be translated, evaluated, and interpreted.

The subject of biblical criticism is burdened by the fact that one of the results of the fundamentalist-modernist debates of the 1920s was that theological conservatives came to distrust biblical criticism as a tool of Bible-denying influences. They were so alarmed by the anti-Christian presuppositions that so often cropped up in criticism that they refused to see the good fruit that also came from scholarly study of the Bible. Although the suspicion has by no means disappeared, we are in a better position today to appreciate the fruitfulness of criticism when it performs unaffected by negative presuppositions. Indeed, we have come to the place where we can insist on the necessity of biblical scholarship as something that the Bible as a human medium requires us to employ. As George Ladd puts it, "Because it is history, the Bible must be studied critically and historically; but because it is revelatory history, the critical method must make room for this supra-historical dimension of the divine activity in relevation and redemption. A methodology which recognizes both the historical and the revelatory aspects of the Bible is what we mean by an evangelical criticism."[6] It does not imply that we sit in judgment upon the Scriptures, but that we take the historical nature of revelation seriously and ask intelligent questions of the text in terms of its history, philology, text, composition, and the like. The term *criticism* derives from a Greek word that means making judgments, and criticism as an art means asking questions of the text so as to learn more about it. In this sense, anyone who asks these questions is a critic, and the opposite approach is to be unthinking in our use of the Bible.

In the last analysis, the question is whether we are willing to accept the Bible as it is, or demand that it be something else. Curiously enough, in their different ways both liberals and conservatives insist on a Bible different from the one that is given to us. The liberals criticize the Bible when it does not teach what they would like, but the orthodox sometimes want to save the Bible from itself when its humanity is uncomfortably obvious. Coming upon a difficulty or a hard saying, we will resort to some desperate expedient to get around it and not have to face up to the divinely willed form of the text. However we do it, twisting the text to make it more acceptable to our convictions—whether liberal or conservative—is not something we ought to be doing. We are not in any position to prescribe for God how he must give his Word, but only to ask how he did so. And if it appears he did it in some surprising way, we must conclude that it is possible. What exists must be possible.[7] Moses felt he was not the kind of prophet God needed, and we may feel the Bible is not the kind of text he ought to have given. But ultimately we have to defer to God's will in this matter as revealed by the results. After all, we are not so competent in knowing what is best for us, so it is risky to try and prescribe what God should do. It lies within his freedom to do what he wills, and the wise course on our part is to receive gratefully what he did. We have no right to determine in advance what the text must be like. What we must do is to look and see.

A Threat to Biblical Authority

At the same time, we must be wary when we stress the importance of the human, not because we fear what God has done, but because in the modern world people will take the human to have swallowed up the divine. In the past, of course, the idea of divine revelation tended, as we have noted, to obscure the processes of human composition. God's initiative was very much to the fore. But nowadays it is human work, human traditions, and human response that threaten revelation and inspiration. *Revelation* is being used as a word to refer to human insight that emerges out of tradition. It sounds as if it is God-given but, in fact, is a product of the human mind.[8] In place of orthodox Docetism, we have liberal Ebionitism, which surrenders the divine authority of the text in favor of the human.

As Thielicke has also pointed out, emphasis on the human dimension can swiftly lead to a radical questioning of the position of Scripture as norm and rule over us. What may begin as an effort to study the human factor alongside the divine often spreads out to cover the whole territory. The integration of divine and human is lost, now in the opposite way.[9] The authority of the Bible is made relative, and its teachings are viewed in the context of transient human thought and time-bound cultural perspectives. The Bible is seen as a response to revelation, perhaps, but not itself revelation or a divinely inspired product of it. As Langdon Gilkey says, the Scriptures are human, not divine, bearing witness to God but themselves full of errors and mistakes, a means of grace but no true witness in terms of content.[10] In this way, the divine is displaced by the human, and we are forced to regard the Bible as fallible human utterance.[11]

The reasoning behind this shift to the solely human sounds plausible. Modern consciousness tells us that any statement will be conditioned by its historical context and will share the biases and limitations of that time. There is no definitive culture. Every community is in continuity with every other one in the flux and change of human development. Every utterance—including those of the Bible, it is natural for modern persons to think—will be part of the time-bound, transient human situation, part of a network of fallible, human meanings. To think that the Bible is one enormous exception to this modern perception strains credibility. Thus, the deepest problem facing biblical authority is not whether there are errors in the text but whether the text in any way can be viewed at any point as anything more than a reflection of its time and place. How could it have escaped the relativity that hangs over all things human? The Scripture principle seems to violate the assumptions of modern historical consciousness.[12] This would mean, as Tracy observes, that even "the theistic self-understanding of Christianity may be as time-bound and indeed erroneous as other of its once-cherished beliefs."[13] Even Barth was prepared to admit that the biblical writers were not only capable of making mistakes but actually did so. "The men whom we hear as witnesses speak as fallible, erring men like ourselves." Of course, he turned away at the last minute from the dire implications of this statement for his own theology by appealing to the miracle of religious encounter and by questioning human competence to judge error in any given case.[14] But he was obviously very close to the precipice.

But before we jump on this way of thinking as a clear example of lack of belief in the claims of the Bible, we ought to admit what a serious question it raises for any thinking person. As human, the Bible does exist in a network of history that can be examined. How can it be a divine Word unless it was dictated (a theory that has always attracted some conservatives because it solves this problem)? How did the work of ancient biblical writers escape the historical relativity that is the human condition? No wonder classical Christians almost instinctively shy away from too close an examination of the human aspects of the Bible. They feel in their bones the danger of the human devouring the divine. Grant Wacker has pointed out what a powerful effect the modern historical consciousness has had upon contemporary theologians. William N. Clarke, a leading nineteenth-century liberal in North America, started out believing in the inerrancy of the Bible but because of his increasing awareness of the historicity of all things human, moved gradually to the view that it was humanly fallible. And more troubling still for an evangelical, the great conservative A. H. Strong was greatly troubled by the same factor. He felt torn between the timeless certainties of the old theology and the historical relativity recognized by the new theology. The two dwelled together in his mind and never did become resolved.[15]

To make matters worse for conservative theology, do we not, in fact, admit the cultural limitations in the Bible quite often? Not many of us insist on women wearing veils in church, even though we believe Paul commanded it (1 Cor. 11:5). Whether this is what Paul meant by "covering" in this passage does not affect my point. I have not noticed Christian women refraining from braiding their hair or from wearing jewelry and robes, in line with Peter's instruction (1 Pet. 3:3). Even though people are often described as being demon-possessed in the Gospels, very seldom do we resort to this explanation to account for strange behavior when we see it. We seem to have no difficulty transferring what Paul said about slaves being obedient to the modern context, in which we hold to abolitionism as self-evident. We readily accept references such as Philippians 2:10 as culture-bound, prescientific allusions. In other words, almost without thinking about it, we seem to acknowledge the liberal contention that there are culturally conditioned elements in the text that do not carry over authoritatively into the modern world. We seem to practice naturally the kind of demythologizing that we denounce when liberals speak openly of it. And we never explain what it is we are doing, even to ourselves and to our communities.[16]

How might we explain it, then? Because we believe in the humanity of the Bible as the mode of God's revelation to us, we are not opposed to recognizing culturally conditioned aspects of the text, *if* that is what they are. We gladly admit that, in order to convey his Word to the church, God uses forms of expression that are culturally authentic and meaningful to the time they are given. But we do not deny the infallibility of the Word he is conveying, and we do not arbitrarily decide which material is culturally conditioned and which is not. On the contrary, we try to discern the claim that the text is making upon us and submit ourselves to it. We search out diligently the intended assertions of the text and commit ourselves to them. In doing so, we keep in mind the covenantal purpose of the Bible, and in difficult cases we compare one Scripture with another. And in everything, we seek the mind of the Lord and recall the wisdom of the past. Admittedly, it is not always clear-cut how we should handle the text. Should we perhaps wash one another's feet? Ought we not to take the possibility of demon possession more seriously than secular culture does? We should never pass by any declaration simply because it offends modern opinion. It is natural for a modern person to feel that, when it calls God "father," the Bible is reflecting the assumptions of a patriarchal age and that we are free to adopt nonsexist language. But our respect for the reliability particularly of Jesus' usage of the term makes me, at least, hesitate to dispense with it. It makes me ask what the difference would be had the Bible spoken of God as mother instead and whether that difference does not still hold true.[17] But these are not matters in which dogmatism is called for, and they illustrate the careful caution that is appropriate. We strive to be biblical people, but we must not pretend that there are no difficulties in knowing how to do so.

The real threat comes, not from relatively unimportant questions like foot washing and hair styles, but from the attempt to use the presence of culturally conditioned communication to evade and deny what the Scriptures most certainly do teach. Because of his thoroughgoing radicalism, Bultmann illustrates what we must oppose. Starting with the assumption that the New Testament is basically a kerygma collection not intended to teach objective truth about God or deliver authoritative information about anything, Bultmann labels as mythological practically the whole of the New Testament message. Modern persons cannot believe in the incarnation or the atonement or the Parousia or the resurrection or the Holy Spirit or the fall of Adam or miracles or Satan or sacraments! All this he tells us in two brief pages. The result is not entirely negative for Bultmann himself, because somehow he exempts God from the list of unacceptable beliefs and because he sees value in the existential thrust of the New Testament, which is certainly part of its teaching. But he supplies an apt illustration of what can happen when the divine authority of the text itself is lost.

The answer to this kind of Bible denial lies in the fact that the New Testament, contrary to Bultmann's assumptions, most certainly does want to teach us truth about God and salvation and is not limited to giving a vague existential address. It is nonsense to say that Paul did not intend to communicate objective truth when he said that Christ died for our sins, or to suggest that the New Testament writers were not interested in the bodily resurrection when they proclaimed Jesus Christ risen from the dead. Of course such assertions have a bearing upon my existence. But they possess relevance because they are true apart from it. As Paul put it, "If Christ be not raised, your faith is vain" (1 Cor.15:14). Before a redemptive fact can be existentially meaningful, it must first be a fact. Before we can safely trust the atonement as taking away our guilt, there must have been the shedding of blood. Of course the writers use pictorial and analogical language in speaking about God —they had to. We cannot speak about God literally without falling into idolatry. But they were referring to transcendent realities when they used the imagery. They did mean to tell us truth about what concerns us ultimately. The similarity between what Bultmann does and what Bible-believing Christians do when they seek to discern the meaning of the Bible for today is superficial and not profound. They seek to submit themselves to the Bible's teachings once they have determined what these teachings are, whereas Bultmann has no intention of doing so, having determined that the Bible is a fallible human book, not reliable in what it says except in a very limited sphere.[18]

But what of the larger question of the modern historical consciousness? How could the Bible, even in part, be free of the nexus that seems to exist in all things human and that prevents any human utterance from being considered a Word of God? In the last analysis, this is a question about God and his freedom. The modern scientific approach is atheistic methodologically, as it should be. It is fitted for investigating the mundane creaturely realm. But it cannot rule out the possibility of an absolute creator on whom the contingent world depends. Indeed, it seems most probably that belief in God is necessary if the world is to be rationally accounted for. Christian theology, in any event, presupposes such a Person and therefore is not beyond its epistemic rights in claiming that God has reliably revealed himself and his will in a set of creaturely modalities. It is under no obligation to explain how it could be, because it frankly confesses the mysteriousness of God and his activities. So long as the God of the gospel is believed in, the Bible itself is no conundrum. It can be God's infallible Word in exactly the way that it claims to be his Word and the product of God's revelational activity. If Jesus Christ was raised from the dead (and the evidence for believing that is strong), then the process of revelation and its products that center upon the Christ are vindicated and validated along with him. How can the Bible transcend the causal nexus of the total human situation? It can do so because the nexus is not a closed one, but a pattern of causality created by God and fit to be the theater of his self-communication. To deny this is not simply to lose hold upon an infallible Bible but to give up the message of which it is part. The liberals have chosen such a path, and the logical implications of traveling down it are plain, but let it not be said that there is no other road to choose.

The Bible does stand over our culture and is the critic of the thoughts and intents of the human heart (Heb. 4:12). We recognize that the culture of today is very different from that of the Near East millennia ago and admit that in interpreting the Bible we have to take the distance between these two worlds into account. But by no means need we grant that the message the Bible presents about the living God who sent the Son to be the Savior of the world is uncommunicable today and lacking in authority. Exactly in the way in which that same message challenged the polytheism and magic of the ancient world, it can today undercut the presuppositions of atheism and pantheism that underlie these objections to biblical authority.[19]

The Accommodation of Revelation

There are at least three categories we can use to bring out the human dimension of the Bible, categories drawn from Scripture itself and appropriate to our subject. The first category is accommodation. It is a familiar one from the history of theology. Many of the older theologians, like Origen and Calvin, spoke of God stooping to our human condition and lisping in his speech with us as a parent might lisp in speaking to small children.[20] In order for God to communicate with us, the infinite with the finite, if we are to understand his Word, God is compelled to employ the symbols of earthly speech and experience. Perhaps we ought to think of these symbols as created by God in order to make his self-communication possible. At any rate, cross-cultural communication on this scale certainly requires God to accommodate his revelation to our creaturely condition so that we might be able to receive it. Selecting analogies from our universe of discourse, and framing his message in the cultural forms we understand, God effectively revealed himself to us.[21] Immersed as we are in culture, this was really the only way to proceed. Revelation comes in the form of a servant like the Lord himself. Because of the humility of God, Jesus was willing to partake of all sorts of human weaknesses, and the Bible, too, bears the marks of its true humanity. In choosing to inspire a literature, God took up a human vehicle and adapted his revelation to the categories of understanding our minds are fitted to employ.[22] For this reason it is important that we the readers take careful note of the communication model of accommodation and make a serious effort to understand what is being conveyed by this means. It will be crucial to inquire what the text would have meant in the cultural world in which it was first given before deciding what it ought to mean in our own. If we do not do this, we will be in danger of imposing on the text the expectations of our cultural circumstances and very likely missing the point.

But speaking of accommodation can make us feel very uneasy. If revelation is not above the human and the Bible not unmistakably divine, how far is it free from human taint, and how far can it be trusted? For this reason, some hesitate to use the category of accommodation at all, particularly because it seems to imply error in incidental details of the text, and this would make God a liar (so it is said).[23] But this is surely overreaction. Jesus, when he wanted to use an analogy of a seed for the kingdom of God, mentioned the mustard seed as the smallest seed. It was not scientifically the smallest seed in existence, but in the Jewish world of the day it was considered the smallest seed of all. God gives his Word to us authentically in ways that we understand, in ways that are culturally specific and able to be understood by those who come later. Revelation comes to us as an earthly event, bearing the marks of humanity, in the forms of culture, without being swallowed up by them. As for those phenomena in the text we all call "apparent errors," they have been allowed to exist in the Bible. It may help some to be able to say to themselves that The Bible once was free of these, but they have never seen such a Bible and cannot prove from its claims that such a Bible ever existed. What we all have to deal with is a Bible with apparent errors in it whose exact status we cannot precisely know. Whether in his inspiration or in his providence, God has permitted them to exist. From this we may suppose that flaws such as these are not meant to make us stumble or divide the body.

The second category is incarnation, the prime example of accommodation in revelation. Unlike the God of Judaism and Islam, the God of the gospel does not stay in his safe sphere free of contact with the lowly creation, but moves out of heaven and dwells with us in the God-man Jesus Christ. At one stroke is smashed the almost universal stereotype of God as one who stays far away. God is prepared to communicate to us, not only in personal, creaturely terms, but actually through a human life not protected against weakness and death. The pre-existent Son did not cling to his rights as God, but laid aside his glory and took upon himself the form of a servant (Phil. 2:6–9). In this manner God could reveal things about himself that could be shown in no other way. All the books in the world, as the evangelist said, could not contain the riches and depth of this disclosure (John 21:25). Paul, too, experienced the weakness that is intrinsic to human life. The body, as he said, is sown in weakness, raised in power (1 Cor. 15:43). The apostle was not ashamed to admit that he felt his human limitations keenly, just as prophets like Moses and Jeremiah had much earlier. He claimed to be no super-apostle but, rather, an earthen vessel entering into the sufferings of Jesus. He even boasted in his weaknesses, because God could be glorified even through them (2 Cor. 12:10).

It is natural to see an analogy between the incarnational character of revelation and the Bible. As the Logos was enfleshed in the life of Jesus, so God's Word is enlettered in the script of the Bible. In both cases there is some kind of mysterious union of the divine and the human, though of course not the same kind. But in each case both the divine and the human are truly present. The analogy helps us to defend the true humanity of the Bible against Docetism and to defend its divine authority against the Ebionitism of liberal theology.[24]

Two other points should be mentioned in this connection. First, just as Jesus' sonship was both hidden and revealed, so that some people saw it and others did not, so it is with the Scriptures. They look like ordinary writings; they are interpreted in ordinary ways. Though they shine with glory to the eye of faith, they seem quite unspectacular to unbelief. We must take care in our defense of the Scriptures not to give the impression that we are able to prove the perfection of them in such a way as to make belief in them inescapable. God's revelation leaves room for our cognitive freedom and does not welcome such apologetics as might try to rip away the veil. Second, in a related matter, the analogy between Christ and the Scriptures is often used in the following way: just as Jesus though human was free from sin, so the Bible though human is free from error. Is this a legitimate argument? Though the parallel is rhythmic and pleasing, it is not exact. For sin and error need not be equated so closely. Jesus himself did not know all things, by his own admission, and therefore spoke in terms that belonged to the first century. In this he did not sin, but acted as a man of his times. He claimed truth for that which he taught but made no such claims for what he had not received from the Father (Mark 13:32; John 12:49). By analogy, we cannot conclude that the Bible never makes any mistakes at all, should these not affect what the Bible was truly teaching us. In other words, this issue cannot be settled by appealing to this analogy as a shortcut.

The third category is human weakness. As we have just noticed, Jesus was crucified in weakness, and Paul gloried in his weaknesses. "The weakness of God is stronger than men" (1 Cor. 1:25). Revelation has not come to us in the unmistakable forms of glory but in the midst of human weakness. This is something to exult in rather than shrink from or be ashamed of. But some of our behavior as regards Scripture suggests a reluctance to embrace this truth. Our exaggerated concern about what to do about perplexing features in the text strongly suggests that we fear people will not believe in Christ unless we remove all trace of weakness from the record, even that we ourselves may inwardly take offense at the givenness of revelation. We would not be the first to draw back from the unexpected mode in which God approaches us. But we must say with Peter, "Lord, to whom shall we go? You have the words of eternal life" (John 6:68). We must not take offense at the Bible because it partakes of human weakness any more than at Jesus or Paul. Is not the quest for an errorless Bible that once was but is no longer an indication of disordered priorities? The preaching of Paul and the message of the Bible bring human beings to Christ, despite their being weak—is that not enough for us?

But in what way does the Bible show marks of this weakness? There are many details we can mention. For one thing, propositions fall short of expressing exactly what a speaker would wish. There seems always to be a gap between what I want to say and what I do say, and this leads to misunderstanding and the need for further clarification. Words possess a range of meaning, and with the best will in the world, one cannot prevent misunderstandings. Difficulties increase when the meaning has to be carried over from one language to another. Some of the nuances cannot be expressed well in the receiving tongue, because forms of expression are not universal. Furthermore, language is in constant motion, the language of both text and reader. Sentences can change their meaning in a new situation and become quite unintelligible. When we ignore such factors, texts can become weapons in our own ideology as we make them serve our private ends. Moreover, the Bible is a literature that no one would claim always excells in rhetoric and grammar. Its linguistic forms were not perfected but used in their ordinary human ways. There is often a strangeness in its manner and mode of expression.

I have no desire at all to malign the Bible, but simply to point out that God, in giving us a literary vehicle of his Word, accepted a definite limitation upon himself. He shows himself willing to speak to us within the limits of human language and to accept the risks that belong to that decision. Barth was right to speak about a distance between the Word of God and the text of the Bible.[25] The medium is limited in many ways. But message given through it overcomes these restrictions and triumphs gloriously. For language, though imperfect, is nonetheless a marvelous instrument of communication, so that in spite of all the background noise that is present the truth about God's saving plan is effectively stated. This has been our Christian experience, and it is the promise of God to keep his church in the truth.

In reaction to the Roman claim of infallibility and out of fear of modern secularism, we have exaggerated the perfection of the Bible and made it appear as though God were the real author and the human writers mere phantoms and penmen. We have tended to shy away from any thought of human weakness attaching to the sacred text. The slightest flaw, we have said, would have to be charged to the Spirit and would bring the authority of the Bible crashing down. It is high time that we stopped denying the humanity of Scripture in this way. The Bible does not claim to be free of all deviations from a modern standard of truth, and a close study of the text proves that it is not. Mark says that it was under the high priest Abiathar that David entered the house of God and ate the loaves of offering, whereas 1 Samuel says it was under Ahimelech, not Abiathar, that it happened (Mark 2:26; 1 Sam. 21:1–6). In Matthew, the fulfillment of a prophecy from Jeremiah is reported that in fact comes from Zechariah (Matt. 27:9; Zech. 11:12). Of course some explanation can be devised to make such examples fit with strict perfection, but it is not necessary or proper to seek them. The Bible does not attempt to give the impression that it is flawless in historical or scientific ways. God uses writers with weaknesses and still teaches the truth of revelation through them. It is irresponsible to claim that in doing so God himself makes a mistake. What God aims to do through inspiration is to stir up faith in the gospel through the word of Scripture, which remains a human text beset by normal weaknesses. Thus God achieves his ends without doing violence to the human through human weakness and historicity. As Küng says, "Through all human fragility and the whole historical relativity and limitation of the biblical authors, who are often able to speak only stammeringly and with inadequate conceptual means, it happens that God's call as it finally sounded out in Jesus is truthfully heard, believed, and realized."[26] The Bible is not a book like the Koran, consisting of nothing but perfectly infallible propositions, a book that should not be translated or commented upon for fear of corrupting the incorruptible. The Bible did not fall from heaven. We do not need to wash our hands before picking it up. Inspiration did not make the writers superhuman. It did not cancel out their historicity and weaknesses, but guaranteed that through them the true testimony to Jesus Christ should come that would have lasting normativity and authority in the church. We place our trust ultimately in Jesus Christ, not in the Bible. He alone is the foundation and ground of our faith. What the Scriptures do is to present a sound and reliable testimony to who he is and what God has done for us. The marvel of it is that he has done it, not through angels, but through ordinary human beings, with all their limitations.

The Interplay Between Human and Divine

A great mystery is involved whenever the divine and the human come into some kind of union. In the case of the Bible, it is natural to ask how the inspiration of God caused the human writing of the Scriptures. Though a speculative question, it has practical implications, too. Were we to think of God dictating the Bible, we would certainly fall into the docetic error of denying its true humanity; if we put all the emphasis upon the literary freedom of human authorship, we might end up denying inspiration entirely, except in a nominal sense.

The traditional doctrine of inspiration has certainly employed images of inspiration that suggest total divine control. The Fathers were fond of the image of musical instruments, thinking of God playing out a tune upon a flute. In plainer terms, they thought of God as the author of the text and the human writers as his instruments. The recognition of these writers as truly authors themselves surfaces only occasionally (in Jerome, for example), and then only sporadically and inconsistently. In Scholastic theology, the Aristotelian category of efficient causality was brought into use. God effects his goal of an inspired Scripture by employing human beings as one might use a piece of chalk. The human agents were manipulated by the divine Author to realize his aim. It is easy to see how unsatisfactory this would sound to one who cared about free human authorship.[27] In the modern period, most conservatives wish to avoid giving the impression that God dictated the text word for word, but they still want to hold on to the results of such a dictation. "Whether God speaks directly to people, through the lips of his spokesmen, or through written words, He is viewed as the sovereign Lord of human language who is able to use it however he wills to accomplish his purposes."[28] A text that is word for word what God wanted in the first place might as well have been dictated, for all the room it leaves for human agency. This is the kind of thinking behind the militant inerrancy position. God is taken to be the Author of the Bible in such a way that he controlled the writers and every detail of what they wrote. Were we to allow that they made any kind of slip in the smallest detail, this would have to be attributed to God himself, which is impossible. Therefore, any appearance of such slips must be judged to be unreal, and an explanation must be sought that will prove no slip occurred. Inerrancy thinking is deductive thinking rooted in the assumption of total divine control. Needless to say, it has a wide appeal for ordinary believers who have not looked closely at the human dimension of the text and who see it as a simple way of preventing Bible denials of all kinds. Unfortunately, it also gets one into great difficulties with the actual phenomena of the text and stakes the entire truth of Christianity upon not finding any slips in the whole Bible.[29]

In short, although it is true that few modern conservatives would admit to believing in the mechanical dictation of the Bible (there is usually a ritual denial of it in their books), they often talk as if they did. Materially they believe in it, but not formally. To hold that God predestined and controlled every detail of the text makes nonsense of human authorship and is tantamount to saying God dictated the text. It is quibbling over words to deny it so vigorously.[30]

The willingness of many modern conservatives to think in terms of total divine control, thus inviting the charge that they believe in dictation, stems from the Calvinistic orthodoxy underlying so much of the modern movement. The theology of a Warfield or a Packer, which posits a firm divine control over everything that happens in the world, is very well suited to explain a verbally inspired Bible. Not only the words of the Scriptures, but those of the *New York Times* as well, are predestined in God's immutable decrees and cannot be other than they are. As the Westminster Confession puts it, "God from all eternity did, by the most wise and holy counsel of his own will, freely and unchangeably ordain *whatsoever* comes to pass" (chap. III). The divine initiative in such a theology is so powerful and irresistible that it can determine the human response. Human beings can be said to choose, but what they choose was never in any doubt and cannot be other than what God predestined. Applied to inspiration, this means that the text down to the smallest detail is what God ordained it to be and nothing else. It was easy for Warfield to say that God could make a Paul to write exactly what he did write just as a builder could get rose-colored light in his church by installing rose-colored panes of glass. People can be manipulated, according to this mentality, just as tools and materials can.[31] It is sometimes called divine monergism, which means God's actions are the only ones that really count.

Two qualifications are in order. First, there are some in the Reformed tradition who, like Barth and Berkouwer, would not endorse the high Calvinism I have described. Still holding to divine sovereignty, they would not use it to deny human freedom, as rationality would invite one to do, but leave the two in tension and unresolved. Similarly, there are many who do not think systematically and limit their Calvinism to this one subject. After all, victorious divine sovereignty that is able to secure a perfect Bible has strong appeal to a broad conservative constituency that has little taste for other implications of predestinarian thinking. My difficulty with both these groups is that they think opportunistically. They want to be able to appeal to strong divine causality when it suits them (e.g., to secure a perfect Bible) but not when it doesn't (e.g., when a madman blows up an airplane). But one can only be permitted to do this if one admits that thinking consistently is not very important.

For a great many Christians, the idea of God being in total control of all things in general and of the Scriptures in particular is very disturbing. If God really is in total control of all things, then he must have willed all the tragedies and atrocities that have happened throughout history. He must have wanted them to happen to serve some higher purpose of his. Repeating the disclaimer that predestination does not make God the author of evil cannot change the fact that it surely does so. God is the one responsible for everything that happens if he willed it so completely, and he must take the blame. This is the kind of theology that makes atheists. The only way around it is to posit a degree of creaturely autonomy and divine self-limitation. There is a dimension of creaturely freedom alongside divine sovereignty that accounts for the events that go contrary to God's will. God brought a significant universe into existence outside of himself, and established a dynamic interaction between himself and it that Calvinism cannot account for. In terms of our subject, inspiration, it makes nonsense of genuine human authorship to say that God is in total control of the Bible's composition. It leads directly to Docetism, which reduces the human aspect to merely nominal.

What is the alternative, then? How can God achieve his will in the world and with the Bible if his sovereignty is not all-victorious? Surely, what inspiration means is that these humanly chosen words are also divinely willed. If they were not, would the Bible not be a mixture of truth and error? How can one see it other than in a Calvinistic way?

At the level of worldview, we ought to conceive of God's will as including all things within its scope but not determining all things. As Paul says, "God works all things together for good to those who love him" (Rom. 8:28). It is not that he predestines everything to happen just as it does, but that he is able to overrule negative factors that come against his will and bring about a good result. God is not yet in full control of a world in rebellion against him (we pray, "thy kingdom come"), but he neither intends nor is he forced to let that frustrate his purpose to save the world. He permits many things that displease and even anger him but is wise enough and powerful enough to weave them into the tapestry of his unfolding plan. One might think of the master chess player who does not have to control his opponents to win a victory. He wins it through simple skill. Or, to use a more positive illustration (since humanity is not God's opponent in a game but the object of his love), God is like the bridegroom able to make the marriage work, or like a wise parent able to raise the child in the way it should go. The point is that God is not manipulating puppets on a string but dealing with personal agents whom he created to resemble himself. God does not take away freedom from the creature in order to force and enforce his will and gain his ends. On the contrary, God is everywhere at work in the creation upholding the structures of created causality, not working to undo them.

In relation to Scripture, we want to avoid both the idea that the Bible is the product of mere human genius and the idea it came about through mechanical dictation. The *via media* lies in the direction of a dynamic personal model that upholds both the divine initiative and the human response. We want to allow for a human element in the composition of Scripture, but also a strong role for the Spirit to ensure that the truth is not distorted by the human receptors. God is active in overseeing and directing the process of inspiration, and human beings are active and alive in responding to his initiative. The prophet feels a fire in his bones and has to declare the divine message. The writer of wisdom and narrative feels no such action of the Spirit but proceeds to work under a quieter influence of the Spirit. They work "in many and various ways." Variety and multiplicity characterizes the results. One writer will come across as intellectual, and another as emotional. One will patiently carry forward the tradition, another will practice literary artistry. Some are nonconformists; others speak for the people. In all these dynamically different ways, the Spirit is active, inciting and superintending and drawing out the work. God is present, not normally in the mode of control, but in the way of stimulation and guidance. The writers really are what they seem, truly human beings expressing themselves. God did not negate the gift of freedom when he inspired the Bible but worked alongside human beings in order to achieve by wisdom and patience the goal of a Bible that expresses his will for our salvation.

If what we were after were a perfectly errorless Bible, this would not be enough. Such a text would have to be more strongly determined. The whole mental activity of the writers would have to be overruled in order to produce a text that was a divine utterance in each and every detail. But this is not what the Bible claims to be. What it claims to be is an adequate and sufficient testimony to God's saving revelation, which culminated in Christ. A higher degree of perfection would no doubt require Calvinistic cosmology and material dictation, but this is not something the Bible aspires to. The authority of the Bible in faith and practice does not rule out the possibility of an occasionally uncertain text, differences in details as between the Gospels, a lack of precision in the chronology of events recorded in the Books of Kings and Chronicles, a prescientific description of the world, and the like.[32]

The Bible claims to be God-given Scripture, but not to be inerrantly dictated. Therefore, we are free to go back and check what is actually there in the text. Though expecting only truth, we can be open to diversity, to various genres, to perplexing features, to intents of different kinds, all the while keeping our eyes on the basic thrust the Scriptures were given to deliver. This means that we can be more open to the human factors in the text. We will not have to panic when we meet some intractable difficulty. The Bible will seem reliable enough in terms of its soteric purpose, and the perplexing features on its margins will not strike fear into our hearts and minds. In the end this is what the mass of evangelical believers need—not the rationalistic ideal of a perfect Book that is no more, but the trustworthiness of a Bible with truth where it counts, truth that is not so easily threatened by scholarly problems.

Classical Christians are not likely to be impressed by the objection that the Scripture principle is not basic to authentic Christianity, when the evidence is so strong that it is integral to it. Nor will they be much moved by the claim that the concepts of the Bible make it impossible for a modern person to accept its authority. We are not even much affected by the observation that the Bible's being human makes it impossible to regard it as divinely authoritative as well. If God made the world for his own self-communication to it, then it should not be too difficult to believe it is the kind of world in which revelation must be possible. But this last objection concerning the humanity of the Bible puts its finger on a weak spot and a neglected area in the classical theology of Scripture, in that we have tended to ignore the human side. This was not true only of the early theologians but especially of modern conservatives caught in a deadly struggle with religious liberalism. What we have, in effect, is a struggle between two kinds of Monophysite heresy in this area: between conservatives who tend to think of revelation as being all divine, handed down from heaven, virtually unmediated, and liberals who tend to think of revelation in very human terms, historically relative and open to continual change. In this debate it is clear that we must be willing to grant the human reality of revelation ungrudgingly and willingly. Revelation does not simply come to us from above but is mediated through the human. We ought to face up to that, and were we to do so, we would find fewer difficulties in the Bible and be less defensive in facing up to the phenomena of the text.

Inspiration should be seen as a dynamic work of God. In it, God does not decide every word that is used, one by one but works in the writers in such a way that they make full use of their own skills and vocabulary while giving expression to the divinely inspired message being communicated to them and through them.

CHAPTER 5

The Human Dimension

Thus far we have considered the human aspect of the Bible in a general way. The moment has come to examine some of the specifics that fill in the category. We want to ask exactly what God has done in accommodating his Word to human language. What is involved in confessing the humanity of the Scriptures?

As in Christology, it is important to approach the subject both "from above" and "from below." We need to look at the Bible from the standpoint of its claims to be the canonical Scripture of the church and from the vantage point afforded by the phenomena of the text themselves. The claims give us a framework in which to operate, whereas the phenomena add specificity to our understanding. The two factors are dialectically linked, and we need to travel back and forth between them. To ignore the claims leaves us without any overall perspective, and to bypass the phenomena leaves the doctrine of Scripture empty of detail and in danger of distortion by the observer, who will add his or her own expectations derived from modernity to fill in the gap.

Our respect for the Bible as the Word of God means at the outset that we will be open to allowing the text to declare itself and will resist seeking to change the literary vehicle to suit our own expectations. We will not try to be more biblical than the Bible! It would not be a good witness on our part to be found tampering with the text in order to deal with some awkward detail. The Bible must be allowed its distance, and this means not trying to overcome its strangeness by dubious means. Alongside this ought to go a feeling for the morality of knowledge, which involves a willingness to face up to the facts whatever they are. Belief in biblical inspiration commits us to respecting the concrete forms in which God gave us his Word.

When we inquire into the "difficulties" of the text, we are touching upon a pastoral and apologetic issue. Christians can be disturbed by what they read in the Bible, and it is part of our care of souls to try and relieve their minds. But non-Christians can see difficulties as a barrier to faith and demand answers. Sometimes these two demands can pull us in opposite directions. In order to assure believers we may be tempted to offer answers of a strict and safe kind, whereas to outsiders we may try creative solutions to make it easier for them. But the two needs are not really at odds. Believers deserve the same kind of solid and honest answers that unbelievers may demand. Ministry to the former includes ministry to their minds, and the answers for the latter must go beyond the merely intellectual to the challenge to decide about God's offer of salvation. Dealing with Bible difficulties is an aspect of our ministry of the Word of God.[1] For whatever reasons, a modern reader of the Bible will find difficulties in the material he or she is reading, and we are required to face up to the reader's problem.

Before actually beginning to categorize these textual problems, it might be good to remind ourselves that, to quite a large extent, "difficulties" exist in the eyes of the beholder. For example, a person with a modern scientific worldview might take exception to premodern Hebraic expressions in the Bible and find them difficult. A person of Catholic or Calvinist persuasion will run into some text or other that will sound problematic in his or her ears. Someone who expects absolute perfection of detail will stumble at the smallest slip, whereas another will be able to take such minutiae in stride. It is important, therefore, to consider whether a given difficulty exists in the Bible itself, or whether —possibly—it is created in the field of vision of a reader who balks at something in the text. After all, the Calvinist's proof texts are the difficulties of the Wesleyan, and the other way around.

Human Modes of Thought and Expression

At the level of minimum difficulty, we notice that the biblical writers employ the linguistic resources available to them. They have to make use of the vocabulary stocks, the semantic ranges of meaning, the peculiar forms of expression, the conventions, even the styles of thinking and of argument. In all of this they are not lifted off the earth or out of culture and are allowed to function in their own contexts.[2]

The language of the New Testament, for example, is Koine Greek, which differs in grammar and vocabulary from classical Greek. Thanks to archaeology and the bringing to light of first-century papyri, we understand much better the New Testament writings. Along with the language, we have to pay attention to the style of teaching and argument employed. Using Semitic hyperbole, Jesus can speak of cutting off a hand, and in a rabbinic manner, Paul can write about Mount Sinai and Hagar in an allegorical way (Matt. 5:30; Gal. 4:21–31). In the various books, the personalities of the writers shine through also, so that we gain quite a vivid impression of what Jeremiah or Amos must have been like by the way they choose freely to write. Evidently the Spirit did not force himself upon them in such a way as to obliterate that. Paul was a real man, beset by deep concerns and a universal vision, and spoke to specific situations in a directly relevant manner.

What I want to bring out is the necessity of paying close attention to the language that is used if we hope to excavate the precious truth that is embedded in the Bible. Even translation is a tricky business. Words change their meaning over time, as even an Old Testament writer reminds us, when he says, "What is nowadays called a prophet used to be called a seer" (1 Sam. 9:9). A word can broaden or narrow its scope, or shift to what was once only a marginal nuance of its meaning. It can be frustrating to try and find the best equivalents to the biblical phrases in our modern receiving languages. The writer of Ecclesiasticus understood this when he remarked, "You are urged therefore to read with good will and attention, and to be indulgent in cases where, despite our diligent labor in translating, we may seem to have rendered some phrases imperfectly. For what was originally expressed Hebrew does not have exactly the same sense when translated into another language. Not only this work, but even the law itself, the prophecies, and the rest of the books differ not a little as originally expressed" (Prologue). In order to get at what was originally intended by the Bible, we have to look very closely at the tools and media of communication, and also stay modest in judging the efforts of others in interpretation, seeing how difficult the task can be.

Of slightly greater difficulty is that the writers bring along with them a set of cultural assumptions that can create difficulties for readers of other times and places. Examples of these are not difficult to see. The Bible measures time, not by atomic clocks, but by the monthly cycles of the moon and the yearly turn of the seasons. When it wants to make psychological remarks, the Bible will refer to the heart, the bowels, or the liver. When it wishes to describe the physical universe, it will do so in ways that correspond to Hebrew beliefs. The writer may refer to the Septuagint, the pre Christian Greek translation of the Old Testament, to make the theological point he has in mind, even though this may make us a little nervous (Heb. 11:21). In other ways, too, the sacred writers were much less concerned than we are to be precise when they quote texts and report events. Even more striking is the way they feel free to make use of beliefs that were traditional but not necessarily asserted by the writer. For example, Job, as well as other writers in the Old Testament, refers to the great serpent Leviathan that God defeated at the dawn of creation (Job 3:8; Ps. 74:14; Isa. 27:1). Baal defeats him in the texts from Ugarit, and he appears in the Bible as Satan the great serpent. In a different example, Jude refers to the apocryphal Book of Enoch in his epistle, probably because it was a respected source among his own readers and expressed a valid insight on the point at issue (Jude 14).

In cases such as these, the difficulties can be resolved by observing that the detail in question enters into the formulation of the text but does not constitute the burden of its teaching. In themselves, they are certainly not transculturally inerrant in an abstract sense. They belong and remain part of the furniture of the vehicle bearing the freight of revelation to us, but they do not constitute the revelation itself. They illustrate how God elects to speak to people in the ways to which they are accustomed. It would be wrong to denounce these expressions as errors, but also wrong to defend them as not culturebound. They are merely the means by which God gave his truth to us, not truth specifying for us in our context.

The question, obviously, is how we distinguish between what is normative in the text and what is only cultural. There is no simple rule of thumb. We have to learn to be able to discern what a text is asserting through experience interpreting texts. It is a skill that comes with experience, and one not limited to reading the Bible. Ramm makes a wise comment: "In reading Plato, Aristotle, Augustine, and Aquinas, we frequently find items that are purely of the culture of the time. But this does not prevent us from laying bare the essential metaphysics of Plato or Aquinas; nor do these purely local, temporal, cultural items disqualify the basic metaphysics of these great thinkers. By taking as our guide those clear transcultural statements of Greek and Medieval authors, and adding to this a knowledge of the culture of their times, we can readily thread our way through their writings to determine what is essential metaphysics and what is not. There is no clear and precise rule for the classicist to tell what is cultural and what is transcultural. That is an art, and a skill developed from his learning."[3] The truth can still shine through in spite of some difficulty getting hold of it. The rule would be to go after the intended teaching of the passage in question, noting what is incidental to that meaning, and also to consider the matter in the light of the purpose of the Bible as a whole. Accommodation is risky, but it is the price of good communication.

The risk becomes concrete when we encounter religious liberals who desire to eliminate some feature of the text and resort to some principle such as this one to do so. For example, they may wish to deny that Paul taught a substitutionary atonement, and try to escape by saying that the belief in blood atonement was a cultural assumption and not meant to be carried over into modern theology. Or it might be claimed that "holy war" or Jesus' remarks concerning hell belong to the incidental and the culturally conditioned aspects of the text and should be passed by. The question must always be, Is this truly incidental to the text, or simply objectionable to the reader? We have no right to exaggerate the quantity of what is cultural merely to accommodate our own hermeneutical difficulties. Such are not really difficulties in the Bible, but only in our own minds. We must resist a misuse of the principle of cultural relatedness as a cloak to evade what the Scriptures really want to teach.

Of greatest difficulty in the area of human thought and expression are those theological and ethical assumptions that are linked to language and culture. To what extent do such beliefs affect biblical teaching? Was the destruction of the Canaanites and the practice of polygamy and the institution of slavery Israel's way of thinking, not God's commandment, even though represented as God's will in the Bible? These difficulties are much more sensitive because they seem to enter into what the Bible does want to teach, and thus cannot be labeled incidental to it. Should matters in the actual teaching content of the Scriptures be taken to be fallible, is that not the end of the Scripture principle? Does it not place a question mark over the competence and authority of the Bible to be our guide? Would it not land us in the dilemma posed by Saint James: "If you judge the law, you are not a doer but a judge?"

Everyone would grant that God took a people for his name and service where he found them. He did not insist that they be perfect; nor did God make them perfect all at once. Israel may have been delivered from Egypt, but she was not yet completely delivered from sin. The Old Testament makes no attempt to gloss over the sins of even its main figures—Noah, Abraham, Jacob, David—all behaved disgracefully on occasion, and this is not covered up. We are not meant to imitate them but to learn lessons of another kind.[4]

It is also clear that God engaged Israel in a process of education that was meant to take them from a lower to a higher plane of religion and morality. It is very important in interpreting the Bible to recognize the principle of progressive revelation. God's truth is not given all at once. The light begins dimly and grows brighter. Seeds are planted early that grow into mature trees. Revelation takes human beings where it finds them and does with them what it can. The old covenant was replaced by a new covenant. The promise was met with fulfillment. Values relating to power and wealth expressed in the Old Testament were sharpened and deepened in the New Testament. Jesus introduced changes in Old Testament Sabbath law, whereas Paul declared circumcision not to be binding upon Christians. In the soil of Old Testament texts God laid down principles that would flower into a more perfect disclosure of his will[5]

But let us not skirt around the crucial question: Does progressive revelation go from false to true, from fallibility to infallibility? Certain difficulties in the Bible tempt us to think so, but the implications for the Scripture principle would be very serious. We are fortunate to find that Jesus speaks to an issue of this kind and provides us with a model for proceeding. It comes in his pronouncements on the subject of divorce. Having been asked about the Mosaic statute that gave limited permission to the male to divorce his wife, Jesus replied: "For the hardness of your heart Moses allowed you to divorce your wives, but from the beginning it was not so" (Matt. 19:8). In his reply, we are given several valuable principles to use in thinking about progressive revelation. First of all, Jesus granted that God really did grant such a permission to Moses in that time and for that dispensation. So there is no question of it being a mistake or a merely human idea of Israel's. It is very important for us when reading the Bible to ask whether a given command is meant for us, and if it is, whether in the same form or in some other. God gave many commandments to Israel; some of them do not apply to us at all, and others apply to us differently. We have to take our stand within the circle of messianic revelation, as Christ did, to find out. Second, Jesus identified it as a subideal commandment, given for the hardness of their hearts. It was not God's highest and best command but the one he had to give to them in their moral and spiritual condition. It even fell short, as he pointed out, of the creational purpose of God, not to say the messianic. Jesus did not see the command as a mistake or an error but as a culturally directed and subideal value that had validity when it was given but now was being transcended in the gospel. Evidently, there are texts in the Bible that are not as relevant and adequate as others for Christian purposes, and we need to be alert in reading them. In a certain sense, there is a canon within the canon, insofar as the Bible inself indicates a certain weighting of the material by messianically directed revelation. In the most obvious case of it, the New Testament must be taken as the key for interpreting the Old Testament.[6]

To see if this paradigm will work, let us apply it to a few of the greatest difficulties, those in which the severity of God is shown. Saint Paul refers to the "goodness and severity of God" as two facets of the divine action in the world (Rom. 11:22). Though it is easy for us to credit a revelation of God's grace and salvation, it is harder to credit examples of God's wrath and judgment. But if we wish to try and approach the Bible as Jesus did and in line with the Scripture principle, then it will be necessary to search out the truth and wisdom even in these passages and to avoid rushing to negative judgment. Patience and openness will be needed if we are to hope that God's wisdom will become visible to us and our own prejudices corrected. Where the Bible differs from our modern attitudes may be precisely the place we need to listen most carefully to it. We must not regard our own opinions as absolute when we read the Bible, for it is wiser than any of us.

Many Bible readers have great difficulty with God's command to Israel to slay the Canaanites and to spare no one. In terms of "holy war," they were expected to devote the whole population and its goods to the Lord by destruction. It would be bad enough if it were Israel's idea, but the text presents it as God's command through his servants. "Joshua utterly destroyed all that breathed, as the Lord God of Israel commanded" (Josh. 10:40). What a temptation to put this down to human sinfulness and deny the teaching of the Bible at that point!

Three comments are in order: First, this command has to viewed in its context. It was directed to the destruction of an exceedingly wicked people. It did not become the policy of Israel in later centuries. At a later date, the prophets often counsel surrender rather than all-out warfare. We have to see the command to exterminate the Canaanites in relation to their own sinfulness and the threat they posed to Israel in her relation to God in those early days of covenant life. Texts from Ugarit have revealed some details of Canaanite religion and culture (child sacrifice, religious prostitution) that suggest these people were ripe for destruction, as the Scriptures say (Gen. 15:16). The Lord is a holy God and does not indefinitely tolerate human abominations. Second, history is the record of the destruction of civilizations, which have fallen because of their corruptions. I suppose what bothers us here is that Israel, rather than, say, Sumer, was used as God's instrument of judgment. Indeed, this is the only time God used his people in this way. The fact is that, through the providence of God, nations come and go in every age. It is not pleasant to be the executioner or to view the process in action, but it is certainly just and even merciful when viewed in the larger context. Third, Jesus more than anyone else warned of a divine judgment to come that would be more universal and terrible than any before it. So it is difficult to make the case that New Testament revelation judges "holy war" in the Old Testament to have been morally illicit. If anything, the severity of God is brought out more strongly in the gospel than in the law. It may be that we have to ask ourselves whose assumptions need correcting, the Old Testament's, or our own.[7]

The so-called imprecatory psalms, along with other examples of the divine curse being pronounced upon the wicked, are another example of this divine severity that grates upon our modern minds. We may recall that C. S. Lewis felt it necessary to judge such sentiments unacceptable to the Christian mind. How can we sympathetically understand a writer who wants babies to be dashed against a rock? Even when we allow for an example of human frustration in the face of gross evil, how can we countenance such sentiments?

Again, we have to be receptive and view the issue in the broader biblical context. Blessings and curses are a basic part of God's covenant with Israel. God blesses those who love and obey him, and curses those who disobey his commandments (Deuteronomy 27–28). The prophets bring out very plainly God's intention to curse those who do abominable things. Ezekiel and Jeremiah are full of oracles of divine judgment, which is the proper response to wickedness. These difficult texts belong to a larger doctrine of divine justice and should not be viewed in isolation. Things do not alter when we enter the New Testament. Jesus himself declares to some, "Depart from me, you cursed, into the eternal fire" (Matt. 25:41). He speaks of whole communities being destroyed on the day of judgment (Matt. 11:24). His own death on the cross is interpreted as a curse upon him in his capacity as the sin bearer (Gal. 3:13). And the saints of the Revelation cry out, "O sovereign Lord, holy and true, how long before thou wilt judge and avenge our blood on those who dwell upon the earth?" (Rev. 6:19). We simply cannot dismiss texts of cursing without asking about the broader picture the whole Bible gives us of the justice of God. The biblical writers and poets are crying out to God to vindicate his holy name and bring deserved judgment upon the wicked. Perhaps if we had faced a Stalin or a Hitler we would find it easier to read these texts. True, God does not delight in punishment, but desires to save sinners (Ezek. 33:11).

Nevertheless, the Bible is very plain in saying God will in the end judge them. There can be no question here of revelation progressing from false to true. Judgment is part of revelation from beginning to end and cannot be got rid of.

To take one other example, in Old Testament law the death penalty is invoked for a number of crimes, including murder, adultery, homosexuality, witchcraft, and incorrigibility. Did God really command such things, or did Israel misread his will in the matter? Please notice that we are not asking whether we should adopt this practice in modern society (that is a separate issue) but whether God expected Israel to adopt it in theirs. Does the Word of God fail us at this point, or is there some explanation?

Here we come up against a real difference between the Old Testament and modern ideas. In our society sentiment for abolishing the death penalty has been widespread (though this is changing with the crime rate out of hand), and we have considered it more just and humane to put a murderer away for twenty-five years without hope of parole (in Canada) rather than put him or her to death. In the Bible, on the other hand, God says the murderer ought to die. Have we not merely adopted humanist ideals rather than biblical ones in this case? And do we not find ourselves in a situation where the Bible's solution seems increasingly more just than our own? Whose morality is defective at this point—the Bible's, or our own?

What we have to do in these cases is consider the wisdom to be found in the ancient statutes, however peculiar they seem to us. Witches were to be executed in ancient Israel because they represented a threat to the divine plan for God's people. Homosexuals were threatened with death because their lifestyle was a gross contradiction of God's created order of sexuality and destructive of family and, ultimately, the nation. We do not know how often, if ever, such sanctions were put into effect, but they stand as a warning against theological and moral corruption in Israel.

In our permissive society, with its high rate of family breakups, it is hard for us to take seriously the Old Testament when it prescribes death for adultery. But here again, it maybe our values that need correcting. Is it not ironic and savage that the law punishes a person harshly for stealing money or goods but is very lenient toward a person who robs father or mother and ruins family and home? In terms of harm and misery, adultery is far worse than the theft of material resources. We had better be very cautious before we point out the mote in the Bible's eye, considering the beams in our own eyes.

Even in the case of the incorrigible youth who is to be put to death for stubborn rebellion, we can see the divine wisdom (Deut. 21:18–21). This becomes clear as soon as we ask what our own "superior" policy is. Do not our rebellious youth die in car crashes or spend their lives in prisons and asylums or go on destroying their own lives and the lives of others perpetually? Having this kind of sanction to back it up, the ancient Israelites had means of persuasion and hope of true reformation that we lack. Even in the hardest cases we ought not to be hasty in judging the Bible, which has a tendency to prove wiser than all its critics.

To conclude, we are not in a position superior to the Bible. God's Word comes to us in human language, it is true, and there are features in it incidental to its teaching purposes. But in "all things necessary" that the Bible wishes to teach us it is true and coherent and possesses the wisdom of God.

Human Modes of Literary and Historical Composition

At the basic level of minimum difficulty here, we have to put aside modern inhibitions and alien expectations and permit Scripture to employ whatever forms of literary composition it chooses. It is a simple question of the sovereignty of God and the freedom of the text to determine its own thrust and form. Though it is natural for readers to expect those forms familiar to them, it is essential for us to be open to surprises when the text employs literary forms now not in use. To some extent, the problem is eased by the great influence the Bible has exercised in Western culture, so that forms such as proverb, parable, and lament are familiar to us already. Nevertheless, we must remain open to fresh examples that may come out of the ongoing scholarly study of the text. It is not our right to sit in judgment on the text and measure it by our standards of appropriateness. Inspiration can make use of all forms of literature employed by human genius and make them into media of the Word of God., "We affirm that the text of Scripture is to be interpreted by grammatico-historical exegesis, taking account of its literary forms and devices, and that Scripture is to interpret Scripture."[8] The reason exegesis is important is not to satisfy academia but to enable us to understand the text better. Unless we grasp the "language game" that is being played in the text, we may not be able to comprehand what is being communicated in it. Valid interpretation requires that we pay attention to such factors as literary form.

The modern reader is able to take a large number of these literary forms in stride. We have become accustomed to Jesus using hyperbole ("hating father and mother") and picturesque speech ("the kingdom is like a mustard seed"). It was a way of communicating the truth vividly in first century Palestine, and it can still do so when people are open to it. In his use of the Old Testament, Jesus would see parallels between himself and figures and events in the sacred narrative. His own impending death was typified in Moses' raising up the serpent in the wilderness (John 3:14). He understood the Old Testament to prefigure what was going on in his own day. Occasionally, even allegory is used, as when Jesus spoke of himself as a vine, and when Paul spoke in detail of the Christian's armor. Every language also has its pithy sayings and proverbs. Because of their extreme brevity, they often express only one side of a complex truth and will be balanced out in the collection by a seemingly contradictory proverb, inviting the reader to think about the issue and decide what course to follow. Besides prophecy, there is apocalyptic, whose interpretation is made difficult by the extraordinary imagery used in representing events present and future. For the same reason, it is common for this genre to suffer misuse by those who refuse to study the original setting and the alphabet of discourse. Hebrew poetry is familiar to us because of the psalms, with their imagery and parallelism. The book of Job is a literary composition in the form of a long dramatic poem that grapples with the problem of evil in human existence. It has always been apparent that Matthew arranged his genealogy of Christ deliberately so as to create three groups of fourteen names, even though it meant dropping out some of the links given in the Old Testament. Obviously, he is following the literary conventions of Jewish historians of his day and makes good use of the possibilities they afford. Examples such as these create no real difficulty for readers of the Bible, because they do not grate upon their own literary presuppositions too harshly. We have become familiar with such things from our long use of the Bible and are happily resigned to them.

However, it is not always clear sailing. Let me list some examples, and then reflect upon the problem. Conservatives are very "touchy" about the historicity of the fall of Adam, because of its importance to their soteriology and theodicy, and, therefore, about the status of the Genesis narratives on that event (Genesis 2–3). They are reluctant to admit that the literary genre in that case is figurative rather than strictly literal—even though the hints are very strong that it is symbolic: Adam (which means "Mankind") marries Eve (which means "Life), and their son Cain (which means "Forger") becomes a wanderer in the land of

Nod (which means "Wandering")! Penteteuchal criticism is associated in our minds with evolutionary theories of Israel's religion and is deeply suspected. Nevertheless, the literary characteristics that underlie the theory are there to be accounted for: the use of divine names in certain large blocks of material, the duplication and even triplication of the same story, breaks in sequence, differences in vocabulary and syntax, and the like. These are literary facts, not liberal theories, and call for some explanation. Serious differences in the numbers in parallel accounts in Samuel/Kings and Chronicles have been noted for centuries. How many men, chariots, and horsemen were there, anyhow? It would seem not only possible but even likely that some of these discrepancies may be explained by assuming that the inspired writer took the figures as found in the official records and copied them out for his own purposes. It was enough for the chronicler, let us say, to aquaint the returning captives with their heritage to publish this material just as it was, and not necessary for the Spirit to rectify any mistakes in it. Inspiration can make use of ordinary channels of information without raising them to a standard of complete perfection. Chiefly out of a concern to defend belief in the miraculous, conservatives have been strong defenders of the historical genre of the book of Jonah. It reads like a historical account and is used by Jesus in relation to his own historical victory over death. But there are also indications that the book might be a didactic fiction, serving a prophetic function. After all, Jonah does seem to die, according to 2:2, not merely suffer extreme privation in the belly of the fish. Could it not be a storylike narrative pointing forward to Jesus Christ, as Ellul suggests? And then there is the Book of Daniel. Although it seems to be made up of some prophecies given to a man named Daniel in the sixth century B.C. there are also good indications that it is somehow tied in with events in the second century and the Maccabean revolt (Daniel 10–12). From this, many would deduce that the book stems from that later period, and that pseudonymity is the literary form used. There is at least the possibility that the book was attributed to Daniel out of godly not evil motives. In the case of Ecclesiastes, at least, it is almost universally granted that the writer was not Solomon, even though that is the impression one would get from the first verse and from allusions later on. The later writer had a good reason for putting the piece in the mouth of Solomon.

To take a few examples from the New Testament, when we read the Synoptic Gospels, it is obvious that someone is copying from someone else (what we would call plagiarism). It is also apparent that the evangelists feel somewhat free to reword the sayings of Jesus and place them in new settings. Robert Gundry has recently proposed that we understand the literary form of Matthew to be midhrashlike, and that we ought not to regard every detail in it to be historical in nature. Luke did not hear Stephen's speech, so we assume he must have reconstructed it himself from reports current. There are unusual features in the Pastoral Epistles that lead one to wonder if they might not have been written by a disciple of Paul's rather than by Paul himself. Saint Jude appears to refer to a legendary incident in the life of Moses to make a point (Jude 9).

The point I am making is this: the Scriptures have the right to choose what literary forms they will use, and we must be open to what they decide. This is not to say that we have to accept whatever speculation biblical critics advance or that we have to deny a traditional interpretation just because it is traditional. It is simply a question of our being willing to respect the liberty of the biblical writers to use the forms of literary composition they decide on, even if it shocks us and contravenes our standards of writing. Once we grant Jesus the right to use fictional stories called parables to make a point, we are on the right track. He did not use parables to deceive people about historical facts. It was not to "dehistoricize" the gospel, or anything like that. It was just a matter of him deciding that this was a good way to teach these people at this time. Therefore, we must not be too hard on or suspicious of the biblical scholars who try to inform us about these matters but give them a fair hearing, because their expertise is precisely to determine literary practices unfamiliar to us nowadays and help us to understand the Word of God better. We have our literary ideals in the Western world and must take care not to impose them upon the Bible, which has its own.

Many of our difficulties with the Bible arise from its way of writing history and from its use of precise details. We in the West are schooled to look for exact information and factual accurracy, so when we read the Bible we expect the same thing. We automatically suppose that a detail is recorded because it corresponds to factual reality and is not fictional. If it were not true in this scientific sense, we would not look kindly on it. When we read the creation story, we think immediately about evolutionary biology, not about those issues that concerned the ancient writer. We simply tend to assume without thinking about it that narrative that looks descriptive to us is necessarily what it appears. Because we impose such expectations upon the text, we create for ourselves a large number of difficult problems.[9] But we must not yield on the principle that the Bible has a right to write history the way it chooses;

it does not have to answer to us and our peculiarities. Despite history being crucial to the biblical message, we have to grant the Bible its freedom to employ the styles of historical writing it wants to. The Chicago Statement was correct in making this generous concession: "We deny that it is proper to evaluate Scripture according to standards of truth and error that are alien to its usage or purpose. We further deny that inerrancy is negated by phenomena such as a lack of modern technical precision, irregularities of grammar or spelling, observational descriptions of nature, the reporting of falsehoods, the use of hyperbole and round numbers, the topical arrangement of material, variant selection of material in parallel accounts, or the use of free citations."[10]

In essence, the problem for us is that the Bible was written long before the time when a clear line was drawn between strictly historical and storylike narrative. Whereas we are eager to distinguish the factual from the nonfactual, it cannot be said that the biblical writers always were, and we worry about the imprecision they permit in their work. We are even tempted to improve their work by making definite things they left indefinite.[11] The price we pay is a large number of biblical difficulties that subsist not so much in the text as in our own enculturated minds. A few illustrations will bring this into focus and help us think about it.

Starting with some Old Testament examples, indications of the special character of the Bible's historical writing crop up again and again. At the very beginning, we are confronted with a six-day creation and begin to wonder how the world can have been created in so short a time. When we look for other explanations, we soon notice the internal parallelism of the days (days one to three describe spheres, and four to six point to the inhabitants of those spheres) and contextual factors (the need to correct the theology of the Babylonian myths of creation). The problem seems to have been a misunderstanding of the literary genre. In the narrative of the fall of Adam, there are numerous symbolic features (God molding man from dirt, the talking snake, God molding woman from Adam's rib, symbolic trees, four major rivers from one garden, etc.), so that it is natural to ask whether this is not a meaningful narration that does not stick only to factual matters. Then there is the long life span of the antediluvian patriarchs, who lived an average of 857 years, according to Genesis 5. Are these not, perhaps, an imitation of the epic traditions of Sumer, whose kings lived many times longer still? You can tell that conservatives are bothered by the figures, since some of them posit a different meaning for the term "year" than usual (without any evidence). In Genesis 10, one can only count it strange that there are figures named Egypt and Canaan and Sidon there, supposed ancestors of those later entities. It is like reading about Mr. Canada and Miss France in an account. The Great Flood of Genesis is presented as if it engulfed the whole world in water, but we have to wonder if the purpose of that description was to have us seriously investigate the archaeological evidence for such a remarkable catastrophe. The genealogy in Exodus 6 allows for only four generations between Levi and Moses, a period of 430 years, an obvious abbreviation of the actual time span. In the chronology of the judges and Samuel, periods of twenty, forty, and eighty years are continually assigned to the various leaders of Israel. Elsewhere, it is said that Moses, Eli, Saul, David, and Solomon all reigned for forty years. It is suggested that the figure 480 years in 1 Kings 6:1 is really an aggregate number made up on the basis of twelve generations of forty years each. It is pretty clear that the Old Testament does not use numbers in the way we do today. As is well known, the numbers in the versions of the census recorded in Numbers are both confused and abnormally large. According to Numbers 1:45–6, the number of able-bodied men in the exodus wandering was 603,550, which means, if you count women and children, that the number of people must have neared three million. This number can hardly be taken literally when one considers that the Canaanites were said to be more numerous and that Israel herself was chosen even though "fewest of all peoples" (Deut. 7:1, 7). Efforts have been made to have the term *thousand* mean many fewer, but these do not work out smoothly and look like a dodge. It is probably best to admit we do not know what these numbers mean and consider them part of the epic style intended to magnify the majesty and miracle of the deliverance from Egypt. This may also be the best explanation of the chronicler's numbers. Though his are not always higher than those of the parallel accounts, he spoke of the million men who fought against Asa, and it seems that his purpose is not to give the plain facts, but to adorn the victory by exaggeration. My point is not that there are no solutions to these difficulties that bring them closer to factual truth, but simply that the overall impression is of a style of historical narration different from ours and not to be twisted against its will into conformity with ours. We may be creating many problems for ourselves because of our unwillingness to let the text be itself.

The same phenomena are found in the New Testament, though on a smaller scale. When we study the Gospels we find different wordings of the same logia of Jesus, and we find them placed in different settings. In one story Jesus will say something that someone else says in the parallel account. Many questions occur to us. How often did Jesus go up to Jerusalem? On what day was he put to death? What exactly was written on the sign above his head? How often did the cock crow? How interesting to compare the catechetical plan of Matthew's arrangement with Luke's order and his unique journey from Galilee to Jerusalem. In cases such as these, rather than force the material into an unnatural harmony, we ought simply to admit that these texts were not written to satisfy modern historians or to conform to their standards of historiography. They were written to lead people to know and love God and on historiographical principles native to the ancient world. We ought neither to charge the Bible with error nor to knock our own heads against a wall trying to eliminate what we should just accept. If we would just stop objecting to the form of the Bible for our own apologetic reasons and let the phenomena be what they are, we could be more relaxed with the Bible and do less violence to the text and to ourselves. So many of our difficulties are not in the Bible at all, but in our own heads.

The stakes are highest when we raise the question of legend in the Bible. Though perfectly natural, in the sense that legend is a universally known literary form, it is highly controversial. To admit legend is to touch two sensitive nerves at once: the factuality of biblical history and the reality of the miraculous. If we admit legend in the Bible, would we not be opening the door to a program of demythologizing that would seem to reduce the gospel to anthropology? What on the surface seems to be a simple question of literary form all of a sudden turns out to be a theological hot potato. Once you admit that Lot's wife did not turn into stone, where can you stop turning the mighty acts of God in the Bible into fables? Is the history of salvation only a way to present existential truth and not important as divine action in time and space? Surely not! Scripture does care about historical facts that prove the power of the Lord. Their existential significance arises out of their objective reality, and complements it. But to demythologize and existentially reinterpret them would be to falsify the claim that is being made.

From this it is already clear that legend is a modern problem as much as a biblical one. It is tricky, not so much in itself, but in our eyes—for modern reasons. On the one hand, we cannot rule legend out a priori. It is, after all, a perfectly valid literary form, and we have to admit that it turns up in the Bible in at least some form. We referred already to Job's reference to Leviathan and can mention also Jotham's fable (Judg. 9:7–15). There the prophet speaks of the trees going forth to anoint a king over them. Obviously, he is teaching a truth in the form of a nonhistorical tale. Jesus' parables present something of the same form. There is no good reason why we should from the outset deny the possibility of legends in the Bible, apart from our own anxieties about admitting it. It is unfortunate that Scripture is not more precise about this point. It does not label anything "legend"; nor does it rule legend out in a categorical statement. We would have appreciated either of these being done. The Bible comes from a time when it was not necessary to draw a clean line between the objectively factual and the storylike features of narrative, but today we see a need to make a sharp distinction. We are worried that once something is admitted to be legend there will be no stopping people from calling things legend that certainly are not, so we want to close the door firmly from the outset. But this we cannot do methodologically, because we are committed to facing squarely the human face of the Bible and are not free to twist the evidence to suit our own contemporary agendas. Thus we are in a bind. Legends are possible in theory—there are apparent legends in the Bible —but we fear actually naming them as such lest we seem to deny the miraculous.

It would be nice if we were able to say that for identifying legends there are a set of criteria that are purely literary and do not involve a judgment about the supernatural, but we cannot. What makes something seem to be legendary is precisely its abnormality. People do not turn to salt; they do not come out of hot furnaces unsinged; they do not live a thousand years. When we read of such things outside the Bible we do not hesitate to regard them as legend, because we prefer to think in terms of ordinary causation rather than special divine action (even though we would not rule that out in principle). Not being atheists, we know God can do anything; being reasonable, we try to discern what he does do. But "if there is nothing too difficult for God," how can we ever know that any case of the improbable is a legend? If we believe that God is active in a decisive way in the sphere of history narrated in the Bible, how could we ever come to the conclusion that something is a legend there? We cannot go beyond saying that there are legendlike features in the Bible, because the story of redemption itself is an enchanted tale (God's spell), as Tolkien reminds us, and opens up to us a realm deep in wonder and mystery. If we do not make room for the miraculous here, we may miss everything, even the whole point of the Story itself.[12]

I think it best to approach this difficult subject in the following way:

Revelation, according to the Bible, is much more than a set of eternal truths or a plain historical record. It is the disclosure of a mystery that can be understood up to a point but that goes beyond understanding. To convey this mystery, the Bible uses a wealth of literary forms. In addition to historical records, theological meditations, and poetic out-pourings, there is imagery that grips and challenges us. But aspects of the Bible's idiom offend us as modern people. We tend to think of things like myth and legend as primitive and outmoded, as practically devoid of value for reaching truth—even an impediment to the scientif-ic mind. Therefore, in our apologetics we often leave no room for such a category and try to sweep it under the carpet. We worry that if we were to allow it in Christianity we would introduce fiction and error into our religion. In this way we not only narrow down the scope of revelation but close our minds to aspects of the Bible itself.

When we look at the Bible, it is clear that it is not radically mythical. The influence of myth is there in the Old Testament. The stories of creation and fall, of flood and the tower of Babel, are there in pagan texts and are worked over in Genesis from the angle of Israel's knowl-edge of God, but the framework is no longer mythical. God is described as sovereign over history and every power and breaks down the pre-suppositions of myth. What we find of this sort are "broken myths," allusions to ancient myths but now translated into different terms. They occur now as symbols of the realm of transcendence and no longer as events and literal references.[13] But the traces are still there, and need not be denied. In Psalm 74 it is stated quite plainly that Yahweh fought with the sea-monster: "By your power you cleft the sea-monster in two, and broke the dragon's heads above the waters; you crushed the many-headed Leviathan, and threw him to the sharks for food." (74:13–14). In Psalm 29 it is plain that the writer does not deny the existence of the gods but only insists that Yahweh rules over them, whatever they are (v 1). "Yahweh is a great God, a great king above all gods" (Ps. 95:3). Not infrequently in the text we read of night hags (Isa. 34:14) and of a rock that followed Moses in the wilderness (1 Cor. 10:4). We read of a coin turning up in a fish's mouth and of the origin of the different languages of humankind. We hear about the magnificent exploits of Sampson and Elisha. We even see evidence of the duplication of miracle stories in the gospels. All of them are things that if we read them in some other book we would surely identify as legends.[14] Perhaps there is an explanation for the sun going backwards (Isa. 38:8) and the day being lengthened (Josh. 10:13), but maybe not. The category of legend would explain them all.[15] Barth has suggested that we speak of "saga" in these cases, a kind of writing that is neither myth nor exact description but a storylike expansion of God's intervention in history and not accessible to historical investigation as such.

What we really want to avoid is what has happened in New Testament criticism over the past century. Operating out of a rationalist framework, men like David Strauss argued that the entire gospel was a mythical message embodying in a primitive form the philosophical idea of God-manhood. Soon after, scholars of the history of religions school contended that the New Testament message was decisively influenced by the Hellenistic mystery religions. The mythical mystery god simply acquired a new name—Jesus of Nazareth. In our century, of course, Rudolf Bultmann has maintained that the gospel is given in mythical terms in the New Testament and needs to be demythologized and existentially reinterpreted. This mythology stands in the way of modern people believing the good news and must be eliminated. In Bultmann's positivist world every aspect of the paranormal is labeled myth and legend and discarded. Even the resurrection of Jesus must be a myth, because the dead rise not.

But being open to legend as a possible literary form does not open the door to this improbable and destructive thesis. There is no mythology to speak of in the New Testament. At most, there are fragments and suggestions of myth: for example, the strange allusion to the bodies of the saints being raised on Good Friday (Matt. 27:52) and the sick being healed through contact with pieces of cloth that had touched Paul's body (Acts 19:11–12). But these are not typical of the New Testament story. In it we find the emphasis on the bodily resurrection of Jesus as the factual occurrence that grounds the message of salvation (1 Cor. 15:14). No wonder several passages in the New Testament denounce even the category of myth, so far is the message from that hazy world of discourse (1 Tim. 1:4; 4:6; 2 Tim. 4:4; Titus 1:14). As Peter emphatically stated, "We did not follow cleverly devised myths when we made known to you the power and coming of our Lord Jesus Christ, but we were eyewitnesses of his majesty" (2 Pet. 1:16). The gospel is simply not a mythical message and should not be treated as if it were one. Only distortion can result from doing so. At the same time, we are free to inquire about any individual detail whether it is simple fact or legendary embellishment we are dealing with.

The important thing is to note carefully what the text says and implies. Matthew and Luke both present the miraculous conception of Jesus, though they differ in what they relate in almost every other respect. This makes it difficult for us to appeal to this miracle as an apologetic proof, but its location in the context of the great miracle of the incarnation that so excites the entire New Testament ought to disincline us to consider it a legend. The temptation of Jesus sounds mythical in picturing Jesus being interviewed by Satan in the desert and standing with him on a mountain from which they could see all the kingdoms of the earth. It is likely that this is the mode of presentation only, the point having to do with Jesus defining his own messianic mission in relation to dark alternatives. Satan is much more than a furtive figure one might bump into on a trip through a desert. In Capernaum Jesus was opposed by a man with an unclean spirit and overcame him. It was certainly important to Mark that the demonic was real and that it knew the true identity of Jesus (Mark 1:21–28). For ourselves, we are able to admit to the reality of the demonic too, but are usually unsure how to define and locate it. We would usually consider it part of the incomprensible mystery of evil and not be able to say much more. But there is no reason for us to deny the demonic supernatural any more than the divine. It is enough to know that Jesus has the authority to overcome the powers of darkness and to deliver us from them.

There are cases in which the possibility of legend seems quite real. I mentioned the incident of the coin in the fish's mouth (Matt. 17:24–27). The miracle is almost incidental to the pericope. It supplies the actual coin with which to pay the tax but is not necessary to the teaching here, which concerns our obligation toward taxation. The event is recorded only by Matthew and has the feel of a legendary feature. From the Book of Acts, in addition to the strange miracles I mentioned earlier, there is Paul's escape from poisoning in Malta (Acts 27:1–6). Prior to this Paul has had a number of narrow escapes from danger. God is seeing to it that his journey to Rome will be successful. It is entirely possible that God delivered Paul in precisely this manner, though one should perhaps not count on it. But it is also possible that it forms part of a hero-narrative and is not an expression of fact.[16]

On this matter we have become unnecessarily polarized. Some liberals have insisted on the nonfactual character of biblical history and its existential nature, with the result that conservatives have felt it essential to defend the factual to the last detail. But historicity and existential significance are in no kind of opposition to each other, and there is no reason to create the chasm between them that we have. History and theology are closely intertwined; little is gained from trying to pull them apart. One unfortunate result has been to make it difficult for conservatives to be relaxed in the face of the Bible where history is concerned. But our respect for the Bible must compel us to grant that the text has the sovereign right to employ the literary and historical modes of writing that it decides on.

In Conclusion

First, it must be stressed that the literary vehicle, Scripture itself, has the right to determine its own forms, not the reader. The Bible does not attempt to hide the marks of its humanity. In inspiring the Scriptures, God made full use of human intermediaries operating out of specific cultural contexts. His Word comes to us by means of a great variety of literary forms, and all of them deserve our close attention. It is inevitable that a modern reader will have difficulties with the text at numerous points, and assistance should be offered. But skirting of issues or ingenious harmonizations are not allowed, because they dishonor the Bible and discredit its supposed defenders. Simple honesty is essential. It is a crime to tamper with the text—even to save it. It is a violation of our integrity to employ the ability to understand when the results are agreeable to our presuppositions and then to abandon it when the going gets tough. It is not edifying to see liberals or conservatives tampering with the text to avoid some disagreeable detail. The distance of the text, its integrity over us, must be maintained, if it is to be our norm. And the morality of knowledge, too, is mandatory. We must be willing to face the facts whatever they are, and not cheat. I realize that honesty in religion is often in short supply. Because religion touches the deepest emotions, believers may not care much about honesty when their whole worldview seems to be threatened. They can be tempted by clever epistemological tricks that offer to ease the pain of religious doubt. But our love for the God of all truth must be great enough for us to refuse such seduction.

Second, the kind and number of difficulties in the Bible definitely vary with the expectations brought to the text by the reader. The Calvinist will want the Bible to be Reformed, the Wesleyan will want it to be Arminian. A scientific person may want it to be very accurate, whereas a literary person may glory in the symbols and the imagery. The difficulties arise where the Bible does not meet these expectations. In a sense we create them for ourselves. None of them are "in" the Bible per se. They are self-imposed burdens.

Among classical Christians, however, there is the conviction that one ought to expect the Bible to be reliable and true because it claims to be God's written Word and carries the message of salvation to the world. That is to say, the burden of expecting the Bible to prove reliable ought to be accepted as part of the revelation package of authentic Christianity. It should be gladly borne. Part I has already explained the basis for making this assumption.

But there is a debate within the ranks of conservative Christians concerning how the Bible is reliable and true and to what extent it is perfect. The debate arises from the natural desire to believe the Bible without reservation and thus prove reverent also in the sight of God, whose Word the Bible is. Conservatives feel instinctively that their faith rests upon the authoritative information and instruction the Book yields, and that it must therefore be totally trustworthy and not unreliable in any respect, down to the smallest detail. God's own reputation is often thought to be at stake in the matter. Therefore, there are a large number of evangelicals in North America appearing to defend the total inerrancy of the Bible. The language they use seems absolute and uncompromising: "The authority of Scripture is inescapably impaired if this total divine inerrancy is in any way limited or disregarded, or made relative to a view of truth contrary to the Bible's own" (Chicago Statement, preamble). It sounds as if the slightest slip or flaw would bring down the whole house of authority. It seems as though we ought to defend the errorlessness of the Bible down to the last jot and tittle in order for it to be a viable religious authority. As critics like Barr point out, attempting to bring it off, involves us in a good deal of strained reasoning.[17] Even worse, it has set brother against evangelical brother and created an atmosphere of destructive suspicion. How one answers it becomes more important than all the other great issues in theology. How can we move beyond this impasse?

Recalling what was said in Chapter 2 about the claim of the Bible to be the reliable covenant document of the church, let us place our emphasis on the focused inerrancy of the Scriptures. They claim to be able to bring us to know and to love God in Jesus Christ and to nurture us in that saving relationship. Nothing is said about vowel points in the Hebrew text of the Old Testament. Nothing is laid down about grammar or literary conventions or proper historiography. We hear nothing about original autographs and how perfect they, as distinct from our present copies, must have been. The writers do not seem embarrassed to cite the text freely or to represent its content creatively. The complexities we debate about today simply are not discussed, and we do each other wrong if and when we make too much of them. Let us not try to be more evangelical than the New Testament by drawing up a too-tight standard of orthodox belief at this point and using it to shut people out. We could not do this if 2 Timothy 3:15–17 was our guide rather than a scholastic conception deduced from it.

In saying this I have no desire to pick and choose in the Scriptures on the basis of this macropurpose we have identified. As if we could decide which of the assertions of the text we would deem worthy to stand in the privileged circle of revealed salvational truth! Such a procedure would surely put the reader in a position to gain control over the Scriptures where they were displeasing in their thrust. For example, one might not follow Paul in his teaching on homosexuality, saying it does not matter because it does not constitute salvational truth, anyhow. No, it is up to the writer and text to decide that. If the Bible asserts it, it must be part of its purpose or else it would have been omitted. The situation is rather more like this: We know well what the Bible was given to do—to be our reliable teacher for salvation and sanctification from God and to testify to God's undeserved grace for sinners. We trust it to be able to carry off its great purpose in large part because it has achieved its goal in our case. We have, in fact, come to love and serve God because of the Bible. So its reliability in the fundamental sense has been established. After all, the Bible is the medium of the gospel, and we have come to know God by reading and hearing the gospel in and through it. This is by far the most important thing.

Therefore, when we encounter difficulties in the text, we face them calmly and consider what they are and how they fit in. If we have come to know God in the Bible, they will appear to be relatively unimportant, and a little bit of the kind of help I have provided here may be of assistance. Help is at hand that can reduce the small anxiety that these difficulties sometimes cause. We are not stampeded into specious logic, but can approach them in a spirit of calmness and hope. Just as precritical Christians find it possible not to worry about perplexing features in the text, because God still speaks to them in it and the difficulties can be shelved, so postcritical believers who know more about the difficulties can also tolerate them, even when they are not solved, because they, too, know where the real authority lies and can turn a wise hand to the difficulties themselves. I suppose the real problem is the backslid Christian who is shaky in his or her assurance about the living God and loses all security if a single difficulty appears unsolved. I doubt that any number of clever solutions will be able to put that mind at rest, since what it needs is to encounter Jesus Christ afresh through the Spirit in the Bible. Once that happens, the difficulties will resume their relatively unimportant position.

Am I saying that no difficulty could successfully shake the Christian's confidence in the Bible, because it is grounded in religious experience and not in these empirical matters? Could nothing falsify one's confidence in the reliability of the Bible, then? Yes, something could falsify it, but not such things as are usually discussed in chapters like this one: whether Methuselah lived 969 years or not, whether the bowels have a psychological function or not. Phenomena on this order cannot bring the house of authority down. There is relief from (Thomas) Paine! What could truly falsify the Bible would have to be something that could falsify the gospel and Christianity as well. It would have to be a difficulty that would radically call into question the truth of Jesus and his message of good news. Discovering some point of chronology in Matthew that could not be reconciled with a parallel in Luke would certainly not be any such thing. Let us never put the church in a position where difficulties on this tiny scale loom so large as to threaten her fundamental confidence in the message the Bible exists to declare.

The Bible makes a strong claim to be true in a particular way. We have no basis for being dogmatic when we encounter perplexing features in the text. We cannot say, This is an apparent error that will be solved by our scholarly legions; nor can we confidently say, This is a flaw for which there can never be a solution. We have to take the evidence as it comes, and not rush to judgment.

CHAPTER 6

Biblical Criticism

The "more conservative" a Christian the "more negative a view he or she is likely to have toward what is called biblical criticism. The etymology of the term *criticism* itself suggests standing in judgment over a text, in this case one that ought to be standing in judgment over us. Historically, too, biblical criticism has been a principal tool in the critique of classical theology by forces of the Enlightenment. By subjecting the Bible to humanistic presuppositions and treating it as a merely human text under the control of our superior techniques, we have seen the message relativized and debunked time and again. It is not the natural term for classical Christians to use when describing the careful study of the Bible. When "criticism" comes in, very often faith goes out. This has been the experience of a large number of those who have gone into criticism seriously. It is all too easy to slide from the critical methodology to the critical theology of religious liberalism.[1]

Nevertheless, in spite of the dangers, biblical criticism has come to signify many things and many methods, not all of them hostile to the interests of faith. Under this heading a great deal of careful, reverent, scholarly study of the text goes on that builds up the church. For, just as there is a reading of the Bible for the purpose of dissecting and discrediting it, there is also a reading of it for the purpose of penetrating and grasping its message. One can also define criticism to mean analysis and discerning study of the phenomena of Scripture. As Ladd says, "Biblical criticism properly defined is not an enemy of evangelical faith, but a necessary method of studying God's Word, which has been given to us in and through history."[2] Such criticism involves asking nonprejudicial questions of the text while remaining open to its revelational function. It is the kind of criticism represented so well by F. F. Bruce and by Ladd himself, which strives to make plain the meaning of

Scripture and which has supplied the church with magnificent new tools in the form of commentaries, dictionaries, and monographs of every kind. It is a reasoned approach to the text that uncovers vast stores of historical, linguistic, and literary insight and information that in turn shed vast light upon the text. Thanks to biblical research over the past century, we grasp the biblical message more clearly and are enabled to appropriate it more adequately. The more we know about first-century Judaism, the better we can grasp what Paul was teaching on the doctrine of justification by faith; everything stands out more sharply. Such scholarly study, which today is also called biblical criticism, can assist the text to stand on its own and speak in its own way to us. True, we have to go beyond scholarship and receive the Word of God in faith. Nevertheless, scholarly analysis can help us to do so intelligently. God has communicated to us in history, and it is essential for us to attend to the historicity of the text in order to respond to it properly. This is what godly criticism can help us to do.

Biblical criticism in the modern world, then, has two faces. It can dennote positive operations in the analysis of the text of the Bible with a view to the obedience of faith. But it can be something very different. We need to have our faculties trained to distinguish good criticism from bad (Heb. 5:12).[3] Though we should not in any way minimize the real benefits that accrue from careful biblical scholarship, we must not fool ourselves into thinking that there is nothing for us to fear in biblical criticism. The time for innocence in this matter is long past. A hearty suspicion is entirely in order.

In essence, what we have to see is that criticism has been the chief means by which the Scripture principle has been overturned and, with it, the pattern of orthodox doctrine smashed. As Hodgson and King admit, "No single factor has been more important in the reconception of theology in the modern period than the collapse of authority and the emergence of the historical-critical method."[4] Why is this? Quite simply, it is because criticism is a child of the Enlightenment, as Troeltsch pointed out so plainly in 1898. It secularizes the Scriptures by treating them just like ordinary sources and, from the start, closing itself to the possibility of revelation and miracle.[5] With a single stroke, the entire assumption lying behind the creation of the Bible in the Jewish and Christian communities as God-given Scriptures was swept away and an entirely new way of reading the Bible was begun. Instead of the reader standing underneath the Scriptures to hear God's Word, the Bible was made to stand before the critics as a defendant must stand before a judge, critics who were not of a mind to consent to the Bible's central message.

The text was seen as an ordinary product of human culture to be judged by the presuppositions of modernity. Enlightenment criticism works out of a worldview that simply does not allow for the possibilities that the Bible itself announces.[6] In this framework, the Bible cannot possibly be a truth-guaranteeing vehicle of revelation. The content of the Bible is placed within the sphere of a naturalistic approach to reality that, if permitted to, must explode the system of classical theology based upon supernaturalist assumptions.[7] Such criticism is plainly incompatible with historic Christian belief and must and does lead to a new theology at odds with it. Scripture can no longer function as it once did in orthodoxy as a truth-guaranteeing vehicle, but will be made subject to human autonomy. If only more critics were as honest as Julius Wellhausen; when he saw what his work was doing to students for the ministry, he withdrew from the faculty of theology and took up a post in Semitic languages so as not to be a stumbling block to any. It is more common, unfortunately, for critics to remain in theology while holding that the Bible is only the word of some leading Christians and not the infallible Word of God.[8] Therefore, it is appropriate to sound the alarm. Gerhard Ebeling is naive, or else a dangerous theologian, when he advocates that we let everything burn that will burn in the work of criticism.[9] For if we employ criticism that is Bible-denying and really atheistic, everything will burn, including whatever vestiges of Christianity a neo-liberal like Ebeling wishes to preserve.

There is a misconception current that only conservatives have any trouble with biblical criticism. To see this, all that is needed is to ask what aspect of the text the more liberal person holds onto and then to observe that this, too, can be critically undermined. Supposing that Jesus believed in violence and the Gospel writers covered this up with a pacifist overlay. This has been argued by S. G. F. Brandon and others. Suppose that he did not consistently trust in God but lost his faith in the face of the crucifixion? Suppose that we have not understood Paul's doctrine of justification and that the apostle had something quite different in mind? All of these convictions are subject to the same critical burning. There is no part of the biblical treasure that cannot be placed in doubt by the consistent application of negative criticism. If one is a Christian at all, criticism will show its hostile face at some point. Nevertheless, it is true that criticism poses less threat to religious liberals, for the simple reason that they have already surrendered so much biblical ground to it and retreated to more minimal positions that seem less vulnerable. But the tactic of throwing meat to the wolves only puts off the time when the pack will eventually catch up and have to be faced.

Faith and Reason

In the conflict between Enlightenment criticism and Christian faith we have a prominent example of faith presuppositions colliding with supposedly rational requirements. The critics insist it is simply a question of the facts and whether Christians will be willing to face them: Bible scholars look at the text as neutral scientists and expose such errors and fallacies as there are. The method is value-free and free of presuppositions. If it does not find room for categories like revelation and incarnation, that is because the method is oriented to this-worldly causes and effects. It is just unfortunate that the approach tends to lead to a dissolution of the Scripture principle and the undermining of classical beliefs. Critics cannot be blamed for pursuing the truth in their disinterested way. They are committed to the morality of truth.

However, Christians should not accept these pretensions. This supposedly neutral way of reading the Bible is totally out of keeping with the nature and claims of the text. The Bible calls for faith in God, and to treat it as just a piece of literature is to say no to that claim. This "value-free" approach is not only an illusion but an inappropriate and unfruitful way of coming to the text. It reminds us of Jesus' denunciation of the lawyers: "You have taken away the key of knowledge; you did not enter yourselves, and you hindered those who were entering" (Luke 11:52).

To be sure, there are a number of ways one can approach an object. A flower may be approached by a bee to find nectar in it, or by a butterfly to rest on it, or by a botanist to determine its classification, or by an artist to paint it, or by a chemist to analyze it. Certainly the Bible can be studied as literature and as history as well as divine communication. But we must take into account how the Bible wishes us to approach it and for what purpose. It obviously wants us to come to know God in Jesus Christ. Therefore, we are within our epistemic rights as Christians when we insist on approaching the Bible in the spirit of faith. Further, we suspect that those who refuse to do so have really decided to reject its central claim and are really out of harmony with the essence of the text they pretend to study. The secular, academic approach to the Bible is already predisposed to reject the Bible's message. It is not neutral scientific investigation at all but has a debunking character. The whole spirit of the enterprise breathes that human autonomy that wishes to be free of God and not subject to his Word.[10]

The common critical pretension to be a value-free point of view is, of course, an illusion, in spite of the protest to the contrary. One might

say that the reason the question of God and faith is bracketed is not
because one is closed to it but because scientific methodology, even
when used by believers, brackets it as a matter of course. Scientific
method is self-consciously oriented to mundane reality and does not
bring God into problems that need solving. It is only closed methodologically, not metaphysically or theologically. Only by being closed
can it serve to get rid of the kind of superstition that plagued humanity
before the rise of a truly scientific method.

However, there is a bias here, even if some critics refuse to admit it.
It makes a very big difference whether in reading the Bible one believes
or does not believe in the God of the biblical story. If the answer is
negative, then the entire Bible becomes implausible and irrelevant in
one fell swoop. What is called methodological bracketing might as well
be a metaphysical blockade, because the result is the same. The Bible
makes it clear that in order to understand its message one must be
personally involved with the God of the gospel. The issue cannot be
effectively bracketed. Not to decide is to decide. On the ultimate question, at this point, one cannot really abstain. A "value-free" orientation
to the Bible predisposes a person to reject its message.[11]

Behind this whole discussion lurks the modern question, Why
ought one seriously to consider God when reading the Bible, or in life
generally? You cannot expect scholars to view things theistically, at
least not as scientists. It may be that on this rock the spade is turned, as
Wittgenstein said. Belief in God is a basic belief like belief in color or
causation or the existence of other minds. It is properly basic and does
not need to rest upon something more ultimate. There is no way to
verify the belief in God, which affects so profoundly the question of
how to approach the Scriptures. One simply must decide to believe or
not to believe. One is within one's epistemic rights to believe without
having to give reasons for it. For myself, this answer to the modern
question rings hollow. It gives an answer that is no answer. For the
person who asks why he or she should believe in God we ought to try
and do more than repeat the demand for faith. What can he or she
think except that bracketing God in criticism was probably the right
thing to do after all?

To my way of thinking, one ought to approach the Bible, and reality
as a whole, in the spirit of faith in God because it is the only way to
make sense of all of it. As Rahner and Pannenberg have effectively
argued, we as human beings are oriented to a horizon that encompasses and transcends us. We are driven inescapably to decide in relation to the mystery of our existence; the question of God is the question

of our own life and its meaning. The universe outside of us, too, calls for some explanation. How did it come to exist, and how did it come to exist in the intricate forms of design that it has? The story of the Bible itself, and the claim that it makes to be the historical revelation of the otherwise unnamed mystery of existence, is surely convincing too. Where else shall we encounter a person like Jesus of Nazareth, and how else shall we explain what happened to him? Most important for us individually is the experience of salvation through Jesus Christ, by which we have entered into a personal relationship with God that colors everything we see and do subsequently. Ultimately, it is a question whether to trust in God or not. But in considering how to answer, the mind is by no means passive and uninvolved. The presupposition that the Bible invites us to embrace is, I think, more deeply rational in the broad sense than the modern attempt at playing atheist. In any event, it cannot be sidestepped in the matter of biblical criticism.[12]

But even if we grant the basic point about reading the Bible sympathetically in line with its own claims, what difference does that make? How can that tell us anything specific about critical questions? In the last analysis, one still has to sift the facts and decide what they mean. Indeed, is it not important that criticism not be controlled by dogmatic presuppositions but be free to follow the truth where it leads? Surely we want to know what the Bible says and not have it filtered through dogmatic presuppositions again, as it was in the age of orthodoxy. How we analyze the composition of Genesis, for example, has little to do with presuppositions, one might argue, and a lot to do with literary characteristics that anyone can see.[13]

Granted, at the microexegetical level there is no place for corrupting exegesis by feeding traditional conclusions into the operation. As I have myself been arguing, we must face up honestly to the phenomena of the text. Fiddling with the evidence is not worthy of those who profess to love the truth.[14] Nevertheless, there is a gospel manner of approaching the Bible that inclines one to be open and positive and receptive to what it has to say. As we have shown, to read the Bible as the reliable Word of God is to read it the way the Bible itself asks us to read it. It is not an arbitrary assumption introduced into the discussion from our tradition or culture but one that arose in the first place from the text itself. And it is obviously a conviction that must affect everything in a general way. It means that we do not assume we are superior to the text and in a position to rewrite it according to our way of thinking, and it means that we shall be open and receptive to the Bible in a way critical theories often are not. How differently the Gospels will appear to the one who accepts the New Testament claim of incarnation. Is it not obvious that Gospel studies divide between those who radically suspect the text as propaganda and those who listen to it with open ears? Differences on this scale cannot easily be accounted for on the basis of empirical study but seem definitively rooted in a decision about the Bible as reliable testimony.

Now, this does not mean, in my thinking, that our confidence in the Bible cannot be shaken and that it is impervious to empirical data. Many have once held to the historic Scripture principle and then, for one reason or another, abandoned it. This can certainly happen. To use an illustration, I trust in my dentist to be a well-meaning and competent physician. This confidence is founded upon evidence of various kinds, including the experience of his or her ability. Should it happen that something changed and I could not longer trust, I would change dentists. Of course, changing gods is a little more traumatic than changing dentists, but the principle is the same. The Scripture principle could be overturned for me, as it has been for others, if it came to seem contradicted by the facts, broadly speaking. In particular, if its central message should prove to be unreliable and incredible and fail to mediate to me the presence of the absolute Savior, I would have to sadly abandon my confidence in the Bible. As Paul said, if we come to the place where we no longer believe that Christ was raised, then our faith is surely vain and empty (1 Cor. 15:14). Our approach to the Bible, then, is not unfalsifiable in principle or in fact. Nor, for that matter, is the approach of unbelief. It is perfectly possible (and this also happens, praise God!) that a nonbeliever can find the word of God to be living and powerful and find him- or herself converted to a saving relationship with the Lord who speaks to us out of the text of the Bible.

Positive "Criticism"

Since biblical criticism in the modern situation has two faces, it is necessary to sift out and discern what is positive and edifying for the church and what is negative and destructive of her life and mission. If we approach the Bible as the Scripture of the church, in a believing circularity, how shall we pursue scholarly biblical analysis? It cannot be merely a question of British reasonableness, as when Robinson suggests that we eschew a foolish cynicism that takes the Bible to be fictional and a fearful fundamentalism that is afraid to ask hard questions and go for his own committed conservatism, which somehow avoids both extremes. It is not a golden mean we wish to honor here, but the divine origin and function of the Bible as God's written Word.[15]

Positive biblical scholarship, let it be said, is a very useful thing for the church. It is a valued aspect of a sound ministry of the Word of God and serves the gospel by shedding light on the meaning of Scripture, preventing distortion of its meaning. As Hengel says, "Theological exegesis which thinks that it can interpret the New Testament without the application of the relevant historical methods, is not only deaf to the question of truth but is also in danger of distorting what the texts say and falling victim to docetic speculation."[16] Confidence in the Bible as God's Word underlines the crucial importance of getting back to the original form of the text and to the authentic meaning of it, and the scholarly efforts to do this show not censure but appreciation of the text. Because God gave his Word in a historically situated way, it is essential that we use historical methods to ascertain what the biblical statements are and what they signify. To deny the church the tools of biblical scholarship would be like denying a person a knife and fork to eat with—it would tend to impede the appropriation and assimilation of the truth. We must not bind the hands of biblical scholars, because church people need the results of their labors in order to make important judgments about the meaning and significance of the text. We Protestants who first placed the Bible in the hands of the people ought not to take it away from them now. Of course, we are well aware that historical criticism is often skeptical toward biblical claims and alienated from a faith commitment, but we must also realize that such prejudices are not intrinsic to biblical scholarship but regrettable accretions that can be cut away.[17]

A positive scholarly approach to the Bible according to the Scripture principle comes to the text not just as text but as the inspired Scriptures of the church. For these are not just human literature but authorizing and authoritative writings for believers. They have the established right of standing in judgment over us. As Luther saw, the Bible is our adversary, the merciless critic of our lives and traditions, able to pierce through our best defenses and lay us open before God. Such scholars would not be "critics" at all but criticized themselves. Their approach to Scripture would not be secular or neutral but one that identifies the text as normative inspired Scripture—trustworthy, coherent, deserving of respect. Their scholarship would be ministerial in service of the text and the community whose Scripture it is, and their goal would be to elucidate, not debunk, its claims. They read Paul on the resurrection or salvation not in order to discover where Paul got the ideas but to face up to the truth of God for us. Of course they may have to ask in the process where such an idea fits into Paul's own thought in its development, but the goal is always to attain God's Word in the text. They read each text in the canonical context as the basic horizon and concentrate on the final text, not speculatively reconstructed pretexts. This already relativizes the importance of much critical work. The speeches of Jesus in the Fourth Gospel stand there whatever critics conclude about their originality and will be heard as Jesus' words. Whether or not there ever were sources such as Q or D does not change the fact that the text lies before us to be heeded. Research into the backdrop of the text may have something to contribute to an understanding of the canonical Bible, but its results are far from assured and cannot assume greater importance than the final product of inspiration. As a preparatory study it may shed light on the text, but it cannot negate or effect a revision in it. The real work remains the exposition of the text God gave.

The attitude of positive "criticism" is one of openness and faith. It is marked by the willingness to hear the text even when it is alien and strange. It employs a hermeneutics of consent that stands open to God's work of salvation in history and to God's Word of life in the Bible. The approach is reverent in the presence of the God who speaks, humble and believing before him, ready at all times to trust and obey. This disposition to believe the Bible does not determine in advance the answer to every critical question but indicates the stance that ought to be taken. Obviously, theories will be refused that cast a shadow of doubt over the credibility of the text, but that leaves open to question a large proportion of hypotheses. And it does not lock us into traditional opinions in matters that do not have the status of the Word of God. It leaves entirely open such questions as whether J was a source used in the composition of the Penteteuch or John was the last Gospel to be written or Solomon the author of the Song of Songs. What it excludes are theories that prevent the Bible from functioning as the truth-telling Scriptures of the church. Since faith is the proper attitude in positive scholarship, it follows that the church is also the proper context for its exercise, not the secular university. The latter context is precisely one in which the claims of Scripture will be squelched and resisted. Because of the humanistic presuppositions dominant in the modern university, the Bible as Scripture cannot expect to get a hearing. Far from receiving an objective treatment, the Bible is wrenched from its natural context of the worshiping and confessing community and forced onto the procrustean bed of alien assumptions. Far from being rescued for objective study, the Bible is now examined under the control of new and alien presuppositions and effectively silenced as the Word of God.

The positive approach to the Bible as Scripture in the spirit of faith entails certain behaviors, which follow naturally from it. The goal would never be novelty for its own sake but always the hearing of God's Word. There would be a spirit that anticipates coherence in the teaching and truth in the concepts, a patient spirit that waits for the text to disclose itself and does not rush to negative judgment. Respectful of the literary wholeness of the canon, it is disinclined to cut the text up into atomistic units. It tends to be cautious in what it proposes, preferring the text itself to speculative fancies that are anything but assured. It respects the weaker brother and does not burden him with "disputes over opinions" (Rom. 14:1). It knows that critical knowledge puffs up, but love builds up (1 Cor. 8:1).

It is this attitude rather than a set of specific opinions about biblical problems that characterizes positive scholarship in the Christian context. Although it would be easier if we could just employ a checklist of approved opinions regarding Daniel or the Pastorals in order to determine whether the criticism is positive or not, doing so would only show whether it is traditional, not whether it is respectful of God's Word. How one dates John or Isaiah is not a reliable test for the spirit of faith. We look, rather, for integrity in the total operation. Such scholars may not even advertise or reflect consciously on their commitment to inspiration, but the way they carry out the work will tell decisively where they stand. Biblical studies need to be reformed on the basis of this principle and this attitude and learn again how to be active in theologically responsible ways.

In calling for a reformation of biblical scholarship, we have no basis for smugness. Often, because of our confidence in the Bible, we have not bothered to investigate it seriously, on the supposition that we had all that was necessary to hand in the final text itself. It took critics with their principle of doubt to shake the branches and see some new leaves float down out of the tree of Scripture. Has our attitude of trustful faith not sometimes led us to complacency, so that we become known for reprinting older commentaries and are not the source of powerful new readings of the Word for today?

I will now make a list of specific examples of the kind of positive work that can be done within the framework of evangelical convictions. I want it to be plain that there is considerable freedom to move within it. Positive work can be done in all the familiar fields. Results can be obtained that serve the text and the church and do not denigrate the Word of God.

Form criticism is the study of the different forms of literature in which the witness to Jesus was passed down in the oral tradition. Though often allied to skepticism regarding the historicity of the material and to a naturalistic worldview, there is value in form criticism as a literary tool that can distinguish and help to elucidate the genres of the New Testament. It is not necessary to accept the notion that the early church freely created sayings of Jesus or invented the course of his career. Bracketing such assumptions, the conservative is left with an exegetical tool for understanding the development, style, and meaning of the New Testament.

Redaction criticism is the study of the purposes and perspectives of the various Gospel writers as they put together the sources they had to form the final work as a coherent and meaningful whole. It tries to detect in the small changes made in the common material shared by the four Gospels the motives and concerns lying behind them. By studying the composition of the Gospels each in turn, one can learn more about the specific nature of the theology of the evangelist and gain a deeper understanding of his message. The uniqueness of each writer comes to the surface in this way. Often, in practice, redaction critics are skeptical about the historical basis for the redactional distinctives, but putting that aside, using redactional techniques, the evangelical can probe more deeply into why the evangelist wrote. This technique sees him as a writer with a distinctive contribution to make and emphases all his own that ought to be noticed. Instead of merging the Gospels together, redactional studies have revived our interest in comparisons between them. Of course, conservative work in this field will be distinctive: it will not push too hard on really incidental clues, or presuppose a non-historical motive as a general rule, or set the writers against each other as if their respective theologies were incompatible.

Textual criticism is concerned with recovering the original text of the Bible. Mistakes are bound to creep in when a document is copied by hand over generations, and it is the task of the text critic to spot these errors and suggest emendations. By studying various manuscripts and scribal techniques, a science of textual criticism has evolved that can aid us in attaining the original text and therefore the original meaning of its author. Conservatives often favor this field of study because it seems to be most objective and free of non-Christian presuppositions.

Literary, or source, criticism can also aid the biblical interpreter, even though it is a difficult undertaking. Several biblical writers, like Luke and the chronicler, admit to using sources, and in the case of books like Kings, which covers hundreds of years, it is apparent that sources must have come into play. There is also indication that the Synoptic Gospels consulted each other, or else made use of common sources. However, caution is always required, because unless we know sources are being combined in a passage, it is hard to be certain about it. As C. S. Lewis pointed out, if we cannot be sure of such matters in contemporary books, how can we have much confidence when scholars announce the sources used by ancient authors? Therefore, literary criticism must admit to a high degree of speculation and not claim too much for its findings—unless we happen to have a part of the source as well as the later document that makes use of it.

Even greater caution is in order in tradition criticism, which tries to penetrate behind the sources and come up with the history of the tradition before it was committed to writing. Conclusions in this area are very hard to confirm. Yet it is important in the case of the Gospels because these texts were composed after the resurrection and introduced certain alterations to the received material, as can be observed in the Synoptics' variants. Jesus is, after all, both a figure of the past and the living Lord of the churches from which the Gospels came.

Historical criticism considers the historical setting of a document, the time and place in which it was written, the nature of the events that it describes. It would ask concerning the exodus from Egypt about the nature of the literary sources and the support, archaeological and otherwise, for the event in question. Again, certainty is in short supply in these areas, and speculation abounds. Furthermore, in this case there are radical theories that allege that the Old Testament picture is quite different from what really happened, so that the people of Israel's faith that God delivered them does not rest on good historical grounds. In this and many similar cases, conservative scholars will find themselves in opposition to theories that deny the validity of the Bible. Rather than abandoning the field, they need to stay with it and help the faith of the church attain understanding.

There is value even in newer, more exotic fields like structural and rhetorical criticism. Structuralism, as the name implies, attends to the structures of language to which the particular linguistic expressions in Scripture belong and tries to explain how at this deep level the language functions. It does not probe behind the text historically, as many kinds of criticism do, but concentrates on the text itself as a literary phenomenon. It is interested in the mental structures of human thinking that express themselves in these texts and symbols. Although the structuralists tend to assume material apparently historical is actually mythical, thus denigrating the historical foundations of the Bible, it is not necessary follow them in this. There is still value in this emphasis on the text itself as a given and the attention given to the total context in which words are found. Rhetorical criticism is a supplement to form criticism that looks for those devices of speech that reveal the personal character of a writer's thought. Again, there is a concentration on the message of the text itself and the rhetorical processes by which it is propounded. It allows the text to speak and inform us of the intention of the writer and the expected impact upon readers.

In the area of the literary composition, it is certainly possible for the conservative to consider the problems with considerable liberty. There are some reasons for dating 2 Peter after the death of the Apostle Peter, for example, its appeal to Paul's letters as Scripture, its extensive use of Jude, and the kind of heresies it confronts. The conservative is not free to conclude that the letter is a forgery passed off in the name of Peter and meant to deceive the readers. But that does not shut off the possibility that a writer embodied Peter's teaching and had no intention of deceiving anyone. Posthumous publication in Peter's name does not deny its Petrine character and does not advance any deception; Peter's name can fairly be claimed for such a work. Something of the same thing arises in the case of Ephesians. Though it is likely that this epistle is the quintessence of Paul's theology and his final masterpiece, there are some features in it that suggest some shifts and further developments of Paul's thought. The tensions between Jew and Gentile seem to have been overcome, and some of the terms used are employed in slightly new senses. Were a conservative to be convinced by such factors, he or she would not be compelled to label the epistle a forgery but could see it as the work of a disciple and colleague like Luke, who faithfully represented his master's thought and adapted his teaching to a situation in such a way that it could be fairly said to be Paul's. The reason I say Luke is that a large proportion of the words unique to Ephesians among the Pauline letters occur in Luke-Acts. The same sort of question comes up in connection with the Pastoral Epistles, which use a style and language somewhat different from Paul's and treat church polity more fully than Paul did. It is also hard to fit their composition into the chronology of his life as we know it from Acts. But if we suppose that the Pastorals were written by an assistant of Paul's, all of these features would be accounted for. I am not here arguing for the truth of these proposals but simply seeking to show the freedom (and the form) that there is for positive biblical scholarship to operate within a high doctrine of the Bible. In our reaction against truly negative criticism, we must not deny ourselves fruitful avenues of research that can hold promise for a better understanding of the scriptural fact.

Now, it might be said by way of objection to my manifesto for evangelical critical liberty that the approach I have taken allows for a dressing up of most critical theories in acceptably pious clothing, enabling the scholar to remain a conservative and still do criticism like everyone else. What negative view, given a little ingenuity, cannot be framed in orthodox terminology? The simple answer is, no theory can be so framed that has the effect of denying what the text asserts. Admittedly, that question of assertion is the key one, and we have no pope to go to in order to answer it infallibly. We have to do the best exegesis in the good company of other scholars. The defenses against deceitful and unscrupulous persons are not impregnable. But we cannot surrender the liberty in interpretation we treasure and must continue to hope that those hypotheses that truly exalt the truthfulness of the Scriptures will persist and those that denigrate it will become apparent to all. Meanwhile, it is imperative that we not deny to our biblical scholars the freedom they have a right to, the freedom that, in the end, will serve the people of God through the new insights that come out of untrammeled investigation.

It might be well for classical Christians, in closing, to ask themselves whether even what they call positive criticism has not changed the Bible for them from what it was in precritical orthodoxy. Have we, too, not become accustomed to ask if this is Jesus or Luke we are reading? Was this Paul, or the work of a disciple? Ought Hebrews to be canonical? Even when we are most conservative, has not criticism lowered the certainty quotient? Can we return home to the innocence of the simple faith we have now abandoned? If the certainty referred to was really a kind of rational certainty based upon equating the words of the Bible and the words of God and not allowing for the human dimension, then there is no going home. But if our certainty rests instead where it ought to—for simple as well as for educated believers—in the effectiveness of the Bible to mediate to us salvation in Christ, then positive criticism poses no threat, but offers clarification and new light upon the Word of the Lord.

Negative Criticism

There is also a kind of biblical criticism that is inconsistently Christian at best and that operates within a naturalistic circularity. Such criticism has played a disastrous role in the lives of many believers and carried some to ruin. What kind of Bible study is negative criticism?

A negative critical approach to the Bible comes to the text as human literature, not as the Scripture of the church—thus denying its own claim and historical reality. It sees the Bible chiefly as the literary sediment of human traditions, as an expression of the religious identity of an ancient people, not as the oracles of God. It looks to the Bible to discover what people have thought, not what God is saying. It is a study of the Bible divorced from belief in its inspiration and divorced also from orthodox traditions in general. Therefore it does not expect the Bible to be true or coherent or relevant and is not bound to sit beneath the Bible's normative authority. Seeing the Bible as a library of disparate documents collected apart from any underlying divine plan, it is not inclined to treat the documents as a literary whole, and certainly not as a canonical whole. It grinds the text up into little pieces that have no meaning within a broader context. In essence, negative criticism seizes the prerogative to subject Scripture to independent rational critique just like any other book and is magisterial, not ministerial, in relation to it. It raises the serpent's question: "Yea, hath God said?" (Gen. 3:1). Instead of bringing the Bible closer to the reader, it has a distancing effect and makes the Bible appear to be a strange, antique object to be dissected rather than a Word to be heard and obeyed. In some ways, as a result of criticism the Bible is less known and respected today than before. Though it is true that the Scriptures have a historical aspect that means that they must be carefully analyzed in a historical way, it is also possible to dominate them by means of criticism and in effect bypass them as authority. Criticism itself can seize the normative position and demote the Bible to a lower status.

There is a kind of criticism based on humanist assumptions that takes mastery of the text rather than submitting to it, that does not approach it as God's Word or shrink from criticizing it. It performs as if the question whether there is a God and whether God had anything to do with the existence of the Bible were not relevant, and proceeds under the assumption he did not. Reading the Bible that way is like trying to eat soup with a fork. Worse, it is part of a concerted campaign to undermine classical beliefs in general by concentrating on their source.

The spirit of negative criticism is marked by mistrust rather than by faith and employs a hermeneutics of suspicion rather than consent. Instead of sitting under the text, it is prepared to place judgment on it. Reason is employed, not in the service of faith or in the context of the church, but in the service of a humanist world view and in the context of the academy. Very often it has functioned on the basis of positivist presuppositions that go against the special character of biblical theology and history. Supposing that reason could readily come up with true hypotheses about complex ancient texts, it has repeatedly claimed assured results of a negative kind, which for a time troubled the people of God, and delighted to come up with theories that debunk the ones that went before. Pastorally, it has had harmful effects in seeming to overturn the truth base of faith and in replacing a devotional knowledge of the Bible with an arid, academic study of it that is sterile for the purposes of worship and Christian living. We hear much about the value of biblical criticism against the danger of docetism, but not enough about the danger of the havoc criticism can wreak when its results collide with the Scriptures and destroy faith's foundations. There is room for spiritual discernment here. Much criticism goes contrary to God's Word and is issued in an appealing form that only the experts are able to evaluate. Church leaders and conservative scholars have an obligation, therefore, to watch out for the faith of Christ's little ones. "We are called to liberty; but let us not use our liberty as an occasion for the flesh" (Gal. 5:13). Critical freedom, like any other form of Christian liberty, ought to build up the community, not cause anyone to stumble. If it tears down the church and causes weak believers to lose their footing, it will come under the judgment of God.

In terms of critical specifics, I propose now to indicate the kind of negative criticism that is harmful to the Bible as Scripture and opposed to a theologically proper view of it. It consists of theories that collide with the text and its intentions and discredit the force of its assertions. To begin with, as we have already noted, negative criticism can be done in all the major fields of research. Form criticism is beset by a historically skeptical and anti supernaturalist attitude leading to minimal and unusable (by the church) conclusions. Redaction criticism often displays a condemning attitude that pronounces on the tendentiousness of one book or another and the risk of heeding what it says—for example, alleged anti-Semitism in Matthew or John. Even textual criticism can be the basis for arguing that the textual shape of the canonical Scriptures is hopeless, making slightly absurd any claim to believe in the "Bible" (what is it?). Literary and source criticism can be the sphere of endless wrangling and nit-picking about hypothetical sources, leaving the content of the text ripped apart and the text itself in tatters. Getting behind the text in tradition-history criticism is more speculative still, and often poses direct challenges to the validity of biblical teaching. In each field it is possible to develop negative theories that bring God's Word into disrepute.

Criticism of the theological content and historical substance of the Bible is where the negative approach hurts most. Consistent with the

denial of inspiration, critics now do not assume a unity in biblical teaching and often take the view that it is hopelessly confused. Disunity has
become a principle of New Testament criticism. The writers are being
understood in such a way that their several theologies cannot be sys-
tematized in dogmatic theology, and one is compelled to choose between them. The result is that the basis of orthodoxy is destroyed, and
one is free to take any direction one likes in theology and ethics. To
take a few leading examples, it is held that Jesus taught a quite different
message from the one preached by the early churches after his death.
He is supposed to have taught the coming of God's kingdom in his
day, and the early church is then supposed to have had to gloss over
this fact because of its delay. The spread of Christianity to Greek and
Hellenistic settings also required new theologies at odds with the original faith of Palestinian Jewish disciples. Jesus began to be thought of as
God, and church order began to become more catholic. One passage
will see the state as God's instrument, another will view it as Anti-
christ. The New Testament contains half a dozen different doctrines of
Christ, and these cannot and should not be harmonized. Even internal-
ly, an author may prove inconsistent in his views (Paul on the resurrection) and mistaken from our standpoint (Paul on women). The list
could go on and on—there are dozens of examples in which critical
theories are incompatible with belief in the full authority of the Bible
and must be deemed negative. One result that must flow from this
view of the Bible as a network of contradictions is that one is forced
either to select those themes one finds appealing (a theology reflecting
one's own culture and prejudices) or, more consistently, to select none
at all, since none of the viewpoints in the Bible is truer or more valid
than any other. Why should a theology critically deemed to be earlier
be more authoritative than one thought to be later? One may as well
believe that there is no possibility of establishing a normative position
now, so one might as well strike out on one's own and exercise one's
own creativity, just like these New Testament writers did long ago. We
are just going to have to find categories in our world to express what is
ultimate and beyond us. The New Testament can offer us suggestions
and stimulation, but little more. Certainly it cannot provide the basis
for any orthodoxy or any unified Christian theology that Christians
could agree on. A person or church can no longer claim to have a
unified theology and to have based it on the Bible at the same time. If
we accept the Bible as a whole, we have surrendered the possibility of
coherent theology. Everyone is free to do and think what seems right in
his or her own eyes.

What shall Bible believers say in response to this pattern of denial? We must be forthright and admit that contradiction is not something that we can consistently allow and that if contradiction exists our doctrine of Scripture is overthrown. It would have the effect of falsifying that theological assumption and would shake the foundations of our faith. But we should hasten to add that no such situation exists at present, despite these bold claims. Criticism has the distinct tendency to look for and to find differences where there are none and contradictions where there are only differences. Scholars have delighted to set James against Paul, Matthew against Mark, J against E, when it is not necessary to do so. Of course, one can see how the contrast is seen where the will to see it is present, but in every case there would follow a different result if similarities rather than differences were stressed. The believer expects to find unity, not contradiction, and in practice it is not difficult to do so. It takes effort to see why the various Christologies of the New Testament cannot participate in a unified whole model of Christ. Our task here is not to answer objections in detail but to indicate what negative criticism is according to sound evangelical principles and how it must be handled.

In historical matters, the negative critic is also not committed to upholding the truth of the biblical record. The place this hurts the most is in the career of Jesus, where the Christian message is rooted and where it assumes its most supernatural form. In a painful dilemma, one wants to investigate the life of Jesus using historical methods but finds these methods unsuited to deal with this phenomenon and producing conclusions in some cases that overturn our Christian faith. Rather than ranging widely over the field of historical denials, let us take hold of this all-important problem in historical criticism. The portrait of Christ in the Gospels is at one and the same time the presentation of a thoroughly human life and the portrayal of an episode in the life of God, hence its profound supernaturalism. God the Son dwelled among human beings in the life of Jesus of Nazareth—what can historical study make of this remarkable claim? Is it the work of mythical imagination, or did such a person actually walk the earth? It would be convenient to be able to say that in addition to believing this it is not necessary to ask if it has a firm basis in history. But it is necessary to inquire into that if it is truly a historical claim faith is making and not merely a myth. Ironically, it is our theology that gets us into this historical problem. We cannot assent to the claims of church Christology if these claims have no basis in the life and teachings of Jesus.

A good deal of the difficulty here arises from the naturalistic worldview that dominates academic and intellectual life at this stage in Western history. Though there are many signs, such as a belief in the paranormal, that may indicate we are moving out of it, at present Christians do face serious opposition to their basic truth claims. The secular mentality will not grant room for such events as miracles within scientifically intelligible reality. The pressure has caused religious liberals to redefine miracle as a religiously significant event that does not transcend the alphabet of nature's potential. Jesus cannot have walked upon the water, because such a challenge to the law of gravity (even by the creator of gravity!) cannot be permitted. It must be a mythological picture designed to express an existential truth about Jesus for believers. Unfortunately, the Christian faith rests upon such events as the bodily resurrection of Jesus, so the challenge of unbelief has to be faced rather than evaded. We have to insist that the world did not come to be through chance, and we do not know that reality is a closed system of material cause and effect. It is unfair to the Bible and to natural intelligence to declare dogmatically that miracles cannot happen before one has even looked into the evidence to see if some have occurred. Christians are not materialists and ought not to treat the Bible as if they shared naturalistic presuppositions. Of course, as Western people we have assumptions that predispose us against miracles at first, but as Christians we must deal with this cultural reality about us as we would in any other case. The Word of God stands over our prejudices and judges them. We must not suppose that our beliefs constitute absolute perspectives over all reality and that they permit us to judge negatively a central feature of the biblical message. The problem that seems so large to the secular humanist looks very small to the Brazilian Pentecostal.

The main point to make is that the historical method, although properly oriented to mundane reality, ought not to be imprisoned within a naturalistic worldview. Contingent events do not occur in such a tight causal relationship that an analogy between them can be used to deny certain events even apart from the evidence for them. Reality is not perfectly homogeneous, and though we look for similarities in history, we must be open for dissimilarities as well. There is no reason for us to accept the dogma of modernity that holds that the world is closed to God and the miraculous. If we believe that God created the world, then we believe in a miracle that dwarfs all others already. It is inconsistent to believe in creation and then draw back from the other mighty acts of the Lord. It is also inconsistent to believe in human freedom and to hold to a closed causal nexus. It is truly a mystery how Bultmann can deny miracles on the basis of a closed scientific world and then champion existential freedom as if freedom somehow escapes from scientific determinism.

But having said that, we should not react too severely to the threat of a naturalistic bias. Bultmann's outright denial of the miraculous is certainly an extreme position, but it is not necessarily typical of everyone who has a concern in this area. Our openness to the supernatural should not make us gullible and allergic to any analysis at all. After all, there were prescientific views in the air in the first century, and these may have found their way into the biblical formulations and narratives. That cannot be ruled out as impossible. To do so would be as antiempirical as ruling out miracles themselves. As Shirley Jackson Case once said, "The sky hung low in the ancient world. Traffic was heavy on the highway between heaven and earth. All nature was alive with supernatural forces." We do not need to assume that every time a paranormal event is referred to the biblical understanding of it is the only possible one. Without denying the demonic, it may be that Mark's descriptions of such possessions are not the only way to render what happened but only his way of telling it. It is no denial of miracles to ask whether the feeding of the four thousand is a variant of the more famous feeding of the five thousand and whether other cases of miracle duplication may not have occurred. The question is not whether God can affect the physical world, but when and how he has done so in each given case. Should it be true that Matthew tells the birth story in a midrashlike way, this has nothing to do with being antisupernaturalistic. One can be both metaphysically open and historically tough-minded at the same time.

The point is that what looks like a miracle at first sight may not in fact be one. Just because we are open to it does not mean that we should uncritically accept appearances. Using the ordinary rules of empirical observation, some have asked what kind of star it was shining over Bethlehem; what might have caused the series of plagues that God's judgment sent upon the land of Egypt; and how universal the Great Flood really was. It is only natural to ask these questions, and we have no right to be so hard on religious liberals who do so.[18] Being open to God's actions in history does not mean that we suppress inquiry into the facticity of them. Our problem lies in the surprise-free method of historical criticism. The limitation of the method is that it inhibits us from seeing what transcends the normal and the regular. If we heard of a man who turned into a banana, we would not credit it, because like Sarah of old, such things do not happen in our experience. Sarah laughed at God's promise of a son, not because she ruled out the possibility absolutely, but because her experience worked so much against it. She was thinking by way of analogy with the other things that had happened in her life and had trouble getting her faith around this fresh promise. Perhaps she should not have "staggered at the promise of God through unbelief" (Rom. 4:20), but her uncertainty was understandable and did not turn God away from his plan for her. Criticism is negative when it closes itself to the wonderful deeds of God, but not when it asks in a reasonable way about the specifics of the claims to which it is fundamentally sympathetic.

In Conclusion

The Bible is the Scripture of the church, which is the pillar and ground of the truth (1 Tim. 3:15). She lives on the basis of the nourishment of God's Word, while serving to defend the Word against misuse and abuse. There is great promise in the fact that there are large numbers of people expert in biblical scholarship today who can serve the Word of God and edify the church. But we would be badly mistaken if we did not recognize the perils as well as the benefits of such study. Unbelieving elements have become mixed with the procedures and methods and pose great danger to the community and its house of authority. Often denied is the reality of God, his revelatory intervention in history, and the validity of miracle and prophecy. The authority of the apostles is frequently bypassed and the historical truth of the text made light of. Such developments have to be opposed, not only as contradictory to the overall claim of Christianity based in the Bible, but also as devoid of good scholarly basis and alien to proper principles of historical method. Biblical criticism is a major unsolved problem in the church, particularly delicate because it touches faith's foundation so directly. Biblical scholars need to be sensitive to the high stakes theologians and church leaders perceive in this area and not pursue their work in blissful ignorance of them. In return for such awareness, the scholars themselves would receive less nervous attention and be more able to continue their work in the freedom they have a right to.[19]

Sound Christians who are not particularly conservative and who participate fully in critical research would also do well to listen to our warning. For they often seem to ignore the truly destructive effects that criticism has had and can have on the basis of authority in the church. They pride themselves on having graduated out of fundamentalism and having learned to appreciate the fruits of biblical scholarship, while at the same time wanting to appeal to Scripture as the definitive witness and source of truth for the church. They really must decide whether to dwell in the house of scriptural authority or not. Is the Bible the infallible norm in matters of faith and practice or not? If we believe it is, we are going to have to take a stand against the kind of criticism that denies it.

There are great areas of freedom for the Christian scholar and large possibilities for the use of skill and genius for the good of the church. But let the scholar also remember to obey the apostles and prophets and be submissive to the Scriptures that God has given us. Let the Scripture scholar maintain the dignity of God's Word and explain it so that it continues to be a source of truth and strength to pastors and people. Let the scholar pursue scholarship, not as an end in itself, but for the purpose of grasping more perfectly the sense God intended through the inspired writers, showing how it contributes to a clearer understanding of revelation and, if necessary, to the refutation of error.

But is it not inconsistent for me, on the one hand, to call for an open, inductive investigation of the biblical claims and to hold that Christian belief is a reasonable belief, and then, on the other, to maintain that we should take a stance vis-à-vis biblical criticism predisposed against conceptual mistakes and factual errors? Have I not insisted that the Bible is human and must be allowed to reveal its humanity? The answer lies in paradigm thinking. We humans not only think through to ideas, we also think with them. Atheists not only think about the reasons they do not believe in God, they also think about the world atheistically, just as theists think about reasons for faith and regard the world theistically. I am arguing that Christians believe the Bible is God's Word on good grounds that they are prepared to discuss, as I am doing, and as a result also look at it in the light of their belief. Their doctrine of inspiration provides an interpretive framework when they approach the problems of criticism. Now, if the counterevidence were to build up from an encounter with the phenomena of the text, the framework could be shattered, and this has happened to innumerable people, who have shifted away from classical faith. So the bias is not arbitrary and is not invincible.

The situation is in flux today. A few decades ago one could be sure that a conservative would reject criticism, whereas a liberal would embrace and practice it. Nowadays it is common to find conservatives deeply involved in criticism and liberals sounding a warning against doing so uncritically. This augurs well for cooperation and understanding between us in the field.[20]

Modern biblical scholarship is often oriented to a technical mastery of the text and to the secular knowledge of everything that concerns the text. Though the discoveries that are made can be very helpful to understanding it as originally given, our fundamental orientation ought to be rather different. It is friendship with God that we ought to be pursuing in the study of the Bible. Our desire is to dwell with him and be in communication with him. Like Saint Bernard, we want to taste and see that the Lord is good, and this is the direction in which our study ought to be oriented. Secularist criticism simply does not address the religious dimension that the text exists to serve and therefore fails us badly. We seek a means of approach to the text that takes it to be a text of integrity and deserving of respect. Fortunately, in some of the more recent literary approaches to the Bible we are being told to attend to the meaning of the text as a whole and being invited to engage its message personally.

We may rejoice that the debate over criticism seems to be easing. It is common now to hear liberals warning against the abuses of criticism and conservatives advocating a more scholarly study of the Bible. There is a shared perception that presuppositions have something to do with how criticism operates, and that there has been altogether too much scissors-and-paste criticism done on a test with theological and literary integrity. We seem to be closer to one another now than previously, and the days of severe polarization may be in the past.

All in all, we have to be open to the results of inspiration God was pleased to allow. Certainly the Bible is true, but we must be ready to admit how complex the category of truth is. A fact may be approximately reported, whereas a command can be neither true nor false. Jesus was in the habit of telling "true" stories called parables that were in fact fictional. Therefore, when we look for the Bible to prove true, we must open ourselves to the kind of truth it chooses to deliver and not try to limit its freedom. We have to let the phenomena of the text guide us, even when they disappoint our expectations or surprise us. It is enough for us to expect the Bible to be entirely trustworthy for the purposes God had in inspiring it. It only gets us into trouble when we impose further requirements of a deductive nature on the text. Let us rather be guided by the proverb applied to the Bible text: "If something exists, it must be possible."[21]

Part III

SWORD OF THE SPIRIT

CHAPTER 7

Word and Spirit

Introducing the Spirit into our subject may have radical implications in a number of ways. For one thing, it seems that the Spirit is missing from both sides of the liberal/conservative debate over the subject. Both sides are strongly wedded to the Enlightenment mentality that places most of the emphasis upon academic understanding and minimizes the role of the Spirit in recognizing and interpreting God's Word. Rationalistic assumptions lie behind the familiar liberal rejection of the Scripture principle, whereas the conservatives, in reaction, tend to want to prove the Bible is the Word of God by adducing arguments a liberal might be able to accept. Neither says much about the role of the Spirit in stimulating faith and understanding in us toward the Scriptures. If we were to do justice to the Spirit in relation to the Word, I suspect we might get free of some of our cul-de-sacs and find the whole hermeneutical operation loosened up and made exciting.

As was pointed out in Chapter 1, revelation is bipolar. What has been revealed must come *to* someone. Until now, we have concentrated almost entirely upon the objective side of revelation and must move to the complementary subjective aspect. Revelation has to be received and become meaningful to those whom it addresses. The external letter must become an inner Word through the work of the Spirit. We have to avoid both a false objectivity in which revelation is independent of God's present activity and a false subjectivety in which revelation is swallowed up by human experience and cannot be normative for it. We must lose neither the content of the divine disclosure nor the reality of God speaking to us today. The two aspects belong together, even though there are those who want to suppress the objective in favor of the subjective and vice versa. We need to get beyond the polarization in which the conservative downplays the subjective because revisionists make too much of it.[1]

In one sense, of course, the Bible is a past text under our examining eyes. But in another sense it is an instrument of the Spirit peering into our lives and questioning us. The Word of God is "at work" in believers and not merely something they have control over (1 Thess. 2:-13). The text can become the occasion for God speaking to us today. What was given can become fresh and new in our hearing, a fire in the bones, like honey to the taste. Though we interpret the Bible, in a sense it also interprets us if we are open to it. "The word of God is not bound" (2 Tim. 2:9). The Bible is no mere ancient text resting on the mantle like some dusty antique or museum piece. It claims that the Spirit is accustomed to rendering the text effective as the Word of God in our hearts. God himself meets us in his Word and makes the truth live.

It is not that the living Word is different from what is said in the objective biblical text but, rather, that through the Spirit what is said comes alive and becomes contemporary to us. The texts become more than they would be to the unbeliever, who only understands their historical meaning. They take on the character of personal address. The Scriptures become "living and active, sharper than any two-edged sword, piercing to the division of soul and spirit, of joints and marrow, and discerning the thoughts and intents of the heart" (Heb. 4:12). In this way the Bible leaps over the centuries and becomes present and meaningful for us today. The Spirit himself sees to it that the relevance of the ancient Word is seen and ensures that the Scriptures function as the medium of the Word of God for the church. The real authority of the Bible is not the scholarly exegesis of the text, open only to an elite, but the Word that issues forth when the Spirit takes the Word and renders it the living voice of the Lord. Therefore, it is not a text we can master through techniques but a text that wants to master us.

Not without cause, conservative Christians have been a little fearful to give much room to the subjective and the existential. They have seen what can be done when the Word is subordinated to human subjectivity. But neglecting the subjective side cannot be the answer. It can too easily result in Pharisaic legalism that handles the text in a cold, harsh way and never asks what our Lord is saying to us now through it. It can make us afraid for the fate of the Bible, so that we feel we have to defend it down to the last jot and tittle lest it prove untrue according to some rational standard. It can make us spiritless ourselves and ineffective in reaching those today who are longing for subjective immediacy in faith. Often in fundamentalism there has been a false concentration on the letter and an insensitivity to the illuminating work of the Spirit.[2] Surely, the Spirit is the key to the proper functioning of biblical authority. It is not enough for people to have their heads stuffed with biblical data if they are not at the same time appropriating the truth subjectively.

The great concern for the Bible is a wonderful thing in our day. We want to get back to apostolic foundations and recover the evangelical message. Renewal in the church is always marked by a new love for the Scriptures. But our concentration on the Bible can also be the mark of desperation, the reflection of insecurity about God. It can be a desperate attempt to recover something solid when the reality of old-time religion has faded. It can be an effort to bolster up orthodoxy rather than a result of tasting new wine. We ought to be clear that a mere doctrine of Scripture cannot guarantee soundness or life in the church unless faith in the working of God's Spirit is present also. The danger that causes Thielicke to postpone his discussion of Scripture to the end of his dogmatics, so as not to fall into this rationalistic trap, is not unreal.[3]

The Danger of Subjectivity

Although there is a danger of conservatives overreacting to the shift to the subjective pole of revelation and buying into a false objectivity without the Spirit, we must recognize that the danger of a false subjectivism is also very real. Modern theology is marked by a shift to the functional and the existential. It places tremendous stress on the subjective pole, not to complement, but to replace, the objective content of the Word of God. We want to avoid falling into either subjective irrationalism or objective rationalism. There is a very real threat in the prevalent tendency to downplay the authoritative text and pretend to go with the Spirit, who is in reality equated with the spirit of the times. In this way, the objective requirements of the Scriptures can be twisted and whittled down to suit our own specifications. The effect is to restrict the ability of the Bible to discipline the inner light of human experience and to prevent it from exercising much control over how we think. The trick is to conceive the text as *trans*formative of the believer in some vague way but not *in*formative in regard to specific doctrines and statutes. This leaves revelation without much by way of intelligible content and makes it into an existential event that happens to us. It then becomes possible for the reader to construe it in ways that suit him or her, the text having lost its true normativity. The shift is very agreeable to those who desire to be free of biblical teaching while still appearing to respect the Bible. One can still be pious while in rebellion from the doctrines of the apostles and prophets.[4]

One possible indication of this trend beginning came in the radical Reformation when Thomas Muntzer, for example, stressed the importance of the inner word, even to the point of denying the authority of the biblical text. The"spiritual" Anabaptists related the Spirit to the Word in such a way that the Bible tended to mirror religious experience rather than be normative for it. Revelation was what happens in the heart of the believer rather than objectively in history and in text.[5]

But the concentration upon the subjective began in earnest with Schleiermacher and the religious liberals. Doctrines do not have their origin in divine revelation but in the religious self-consciousness, he claimed.[6] They were humanity's way of expressing affections and emotions and not statements of objective truth. To treat them as such would be to misconceive their nature and function. To confess God as creator, for example, is not a factual claim against an evolutionist but an expression of one's sense of absolute dependence. The Bible's authority, therefore, is not to teach us infallible concepts but to shape our God-consciousness. Christianity does not consist in being ruled by an unalterable creed but in a continuity of spirit over time. The context of faith itself will vary according to the worldview of any given epoch. Religious experience is primary, not the forms in which it is expressed.[7]

The early Barth shows signs of the same sort of preference for the subjective over the objective. Although he is known for writing dogmatic theology and pays close attention to the content of the Bible, one would not guess it from what is called his "actualism." According to his theory, which stands even in the *Church Dogmatics*, Barth sees the Bible as a fallible human word that gets transformed into an existential Word by a miracle of God's.[8] In this way he hopes to preserve the freedom of God in relation even to the Bible. Revelation is seen as a contemporary event, an encounter with God, and not involving a system of truth. Fortunately, from a classical standpoint, Barth disregards his own theory when he proceeds to do theology and operates on the basis of what amounts to an orthodox doctrine of Scripture that takes the content to stand beyond criticism. This would be true also of many, like Hordern, who like the sound of Barth's theory but, like him, do not use it in practice. For if they did, no such theology as Barth's could be imagined.[9]

Rudolf Bultmann, of course, illustrates the danger we are addressing with great clarity. On the basis of a number of dubious assumptions about the New Testament as mythical and existential in nature, Bultmann proposes to interpret it as the seedbed for possibilities of authentic living in the world. We come with our existential questions to a text presupposed to be only interested in such questions, and out of the encounter with Scripture there can come an encounter with God. Bultmann respects the New Testament and takes it to be unique and irreplaceable, but for him it is not a teacher of normative truth. Its purpose is not to give general truths in theology or ethics but to issue a call for decision and to put us existentially in touch with God. It does not matter that the Bible is full of mistakes and contradictions, so long as this existential miracle occurs through it. For its authority does not lie in its content but in its proclamation of the kerygma of God's saving action for us in Christ. The New Testament never intended to give us a mythical picture of the world but aimed to issue a living word of salvation that can transform human existence.[10]

One finds this kind of teaching on every hand in modern theology. It is our knowledge of ourselves and a relationship with God that matter, says Rosemary Ruether, not revealed doctrines and miraculous events. The truth of faith is the truth found in encounter, not in objective judgments. When it gets expressed in symbols, as it must, these are relative to the historical occasion when they arose and not universally valid.[11] For Claude Geffré, revelation does not consist of truths about God but of what happened to the early Christians when they encountered God. What we want to do is to make that experience contemporary.[12] Paul Hanson does not believe that the Bible wants us to think the way it thinks but to draw us into a liberating relationship with God. This relationship must not be permitted to fossilize into a concern for facts and doctrines.[13]

Even the evangelicals, because of the pietist character of their movement, can be attracted to a version of the functional authority of the Bible. After all, is not changing lives what the Bible is about? Therefore, it is tempting to consider locating its authority in the existential realm and sidestep a lot of awkward intellectual questions. (This is, of course, exactly what attracted pietists like Schleiermacher in the first place.) One becomes very suspicious when Dooyeweerd tells us that the authority of the Bible is assigned to the "pistic" level in the scheme of thirteen modalities and when Berkouwer wants to correlate the Bible with the faith of the church, seeming to deny its objective truthfulness. People have even wondered if Rogers and McKim had anything like this in their minds when they suggested we limit infallibility to the soteric realm. In each case, it is unlikely that they had in mind anything like demythologizing. Nevertheless, the temptation is there to fall into.

What we are dealing with here is a determined effort to reconceive revelation in noninformative terms. The reason for this is an apologetic one. Modern people find it difficult to believe the Bible intellectually, but they can appreciate it in an existential way. Therefore, modern theologians oblige by dropping the demand to believe the content of the creed and withdraw to a much weaker one. By asking only for some vague relationship with the Bible, it is hoped to make the gospel less vulnerable to critical attack. The new idea is to think of the Bible not as a source of objective truths but as an instrument that can function in the transformation of persons. It is a clever move, in that changing lives is most certainly part of the Bible's purpose, but perverse in that it wholly misconceives how this comes about.[14]

It has been common since Harnack to maintain that it was a mistake to draw dogmas out of revelation. Christianity began it is claimed as a charismatic movement that hardened into the confessionalism we call orthodoxy, and this was a bad mistake. In fact, however, this is not true. The early Fathers who looked to the Bible for doctrinal information were entirely right to do so. The gospel has content, and the content can be drawn out and developed. Indeed, that is what the New Testament calls on us to do. It is obvious from Luke and Paul and John that they cared about how Christians understood the basics of the faith in history and in doctrine and instructed them to hold it fast. This idea that the New Testament does not mean to teach us objective truth is an invention of modern theologians eager not to have to believe it. It is more honest to be an atheist and turn completely away from the Bible than to profess respect for it and then refuse to submit to its actual teaching. Of course, the writers care about the existential significance of what they set forth, but not in opposition to belief in their teaching. They cared about the appropriation of them personally. It is because of these facts having happened and these truths having been given that the transformation can take place through faith. Christians are expected to build upon the foundation of the apostles and prophets and be "obedient from the heart to the standard of teaching to which [they] were committed" (Rom. 6:17). We have been given a deposit of truth by the Spirit, and we are expected to treasure and guard it (2 Tim. 1:13–14). Obviously, the New Testament cares very much about truth and fact and sees them as crucially important in a person's relating to God in a saving way. It knows nothing of Bultmann's contentless kerygma and gives no support to this modern shift away from the objective. This represents an artificial and arbitrary restriction of the meaning of the Bible to a certain set of existential questions we have decided we want it to answer. It is a plain denial of the true authority of Scripture in the guise of affirming it. Modernity, not Scripture, was the cause of this misstep.

Word and Spirit

Revelation is two-sided, divine and human, objective and subjective. There is an initiative from God, and there is a receiving by human beings. There must be a mutuality of the divine Spirit and the human spirit for revelation to become effective in our lives. As Paul says, the Spirit "bears witness with our spirit" in all these matters of salvation (Rom. 8:16). God works in a double way—he makes himself present to us and he opens our eyes to help us to receive revelation. As Calvin put it, "God sent down the same Spirit by whose power he had dispensed the Word, to complete his work by the efficacious confirmation of the Word" (Institutes I, chap. 9). First God gave us the Scriptures by inspiration, loading them with revelational potential for all generations, and second God gives us the Scriptures in order to activate and actualize this potential in our hearts and minds. The Bible is a deposit of propositions that we should receive as from God, but it is also the living Word when it functions as the sword of the Spirit. Let us consider the general relationship of the Spirit and the Word.

Because the Old Testament sees the work of the Spirit in a fairly narrow way, working among a quite restricted company of believers, it does not speak directly to this matter of the testimony of the Spirit, as Protestants call it.[15] But it does speak of it indirectly, as indeed do many texts in the New Testament as well. When it speaks of dry bones coming to life by the Word of God, and when it asks God to open our eyes so that we may behold wondrous things out of his law, then the Old Testament is talking about God doing a work in human beings to place them in vital contact with revelation personally. Jesus refers to this God-given ability to understand when he says to Peter, "Flesh and blood have not revealed this to you, but my Father" (Matt. 16:17). Not all texts that refer to this matter by any means talk about it in terms of the Spirit, but they build up the same general impression. God himself is at work to make a knowledge of himself possible. He gives an inward revelation of the truth and a certainty that cannot be obtained merely from human understanding. According to Paul and Luke, the coming of the Spirit at Pentecost was an event comparable in its importance to the incarnation itself. Having sent his Son into the world, God sent his Spirit also to make the former action historically and existentially effective (Gal. 4:4–6). The apostle refers often to the Spirit as bearing witness in our hearts (Rom.

8:16), confirming the truth of the gospel (1 Thess. 1:5), enabling people to see that his message is the Word of God (1 Thess. 2:13), giving us inward light and removing the veil and the darkness (2 Cor. 3:16–4:6). Paul speaks of the "Spirit of revelation" who operates in the believing heart to give a personal appreciation of all God has revealed and given (Eph. 1:17). How this works can be seen in the case of Lydia as she was listening to Paul's preaching: "The Lord opened her heart to give heed to what was said by Paul" (Acts 16:14). The God who caused light to shine out of darkness is able to send shafts of spiritual light into our hearts to disclose the glory of God in the face of Jesus Christ. Here is a subjectivity we must not turn away from. The saving knowledge of God depends upon it.

The Apostle John rivals Paul in the emphasis he gives to this testimonium of the Spirit. Believers, like sheep, will be able to follow Jesus because they will hear and recognize Jesus' voice (John 10:4). The Spirit when given will teach them and bring to their remembrance what Jesus said (14:16–17, 26). He will bear witness to Christ, and enable us to bear witness in the world (15:26–27). He will lead us into all truth and will take the things of Christ and declare them to us (16:13–15). Believers enjoy an anointing within them that teaches them what they need to know (1 John 2:27). Finally, John says that the Spirit is the witness to Christ, the true witness (1 John 5:7). There is a mutuality and a balance between the Word given through Jesus in history and in the Scriptures, and the contemporary witness of the Spirit enabling us to appreciate and penetrate what was given in our own lives. There is no thought of the Spirit erasing the Word of the gospel. The emphasis is on rendering it effective and relevant. The Spirit provides the link of continuity between Jesus and the later community. He points to a fine balance between faithfulness to the tradition and creativity in interpreting it. I am sure that John thought of his own Gospel as an example of how to render the original Word in a new setting and time.[16]

This truth has not fared so well in the history of the church. For a long time it was neglected, and then when people got interested in it groups like the Quakers seemed to derive from the Spirit, content against the Bible. Especially in religious liberalism, experience became the source, rather than the medium, of revelation. Theologians like Schleiermacher thought they should and could derive the content of the Christian faith from religious consciousness. This is against both Scripture and common sense. The truth of the gospel was given in history and cannot be rederived from experience. As even Tillich said, "Experience is not the source from which the contents of systematic theology are taken but the medium through which they are existentially received."[17] The Spirit was given, not to take away from the finality of Christ, but to render witness to him effective, whether in the Bible or in everyday conversation. He who gave the Bible still gives it. He helps us to receive it as the Word of God and to understand what it means for our time. He activates the information in it so that it becomes an effective communication from God. Therefore, the interpretation of the Bible cannot be left to the experts. What is needed is an encounter with God in and through the text and a discernment as to what God is saying to us now. The possibilities of meaning are not limited to the original intent of the text, although that is the anchor of interpretation, but can arise from the interaction of the Spirit and the Word. We read the text and in it seek the will of the Lord for today.

Revelation has not ceased. A phase of it has ceased, the phase that provided the gospel and its scriptural witness, but not revelation in every sense. If it had, we could not know Christ as Lord, because we would be left to our own cognitive powers. We have in us "the spirit of revelation," which causes the letter of the Bible to become charged with life and to become the living voice of God to us. The Spirit did not withdraw from the church after the canon was completed but remains in the church speaking through the Scriptures, revealing Christ to us afresh. Indeed, indications are that the Spirit continues to address us through one another, through gifts like prophecy, for example. In the church at Antioch there were teachers who communicated the faith once delivered and prophets who responded to the word of the Lord in their spirits (Acts 13:1). Paul indicates that prophecy is an important gift in the congregation, because it builds us up (1 Cor. 14:3). We ought not to despise prophecy just because we rightly fear false prophecy. The secret is to be critical of prophetic claims and discern what is authentic (1 Thess. 5:19–22). Paul even suggests safeguards, such as employing apostolic teaching as a norm and exercising communal discernment (1 Cor. 14:29, 27). The point is simply that we ought not to suppress the Spirit in his revealing work but to be docile and receptive in his presence.[18]

We have access to the message of salvation through the Scriptures that God has given to bear witness to Christ, and these words become alive and effective in us through the work of the Spirit. Thus the Bible is an instrument or tool of the Spirit to teach and shape us. As Calvin said, the Bible is like a pair of spectacles through which we can see the truth of God and his glory. Without both the Word and the Spirit we cannot do sound, nourishing theology. Scripture is a means of grace by which God's Word continues to come to us. It is not so much a static collection of timeless oracles as it is the place to stand when one wants to be in God's presence and learn of him. Through the Bible we can orient ourselves to the objective revelation that has been given and, through the Spirit, enter into it personally and dynamically. Bloesch has suggested that we think of the Bible as a sacrament, as the outward and visible sign of an inward and spiritual grace, a vehicle by which the Spirit preaches Christ to us. Without in any way denying cognitive revelation, this proposal does justice to the freedom of the Word and gets us away from thinking of the Bible in purely intellectual terms.[19] When we consider how the Bible has actually functioned in the church over the centuries as a means of grace and constant companion, it is really a wonder that it did not become incorporated in the sacramental thinking of the church. The way the early theologians like Tertullian spoke of and used the Scriptures is certainly sacramental. As Pelikan says, "The attention to the sacraments in dogmatic theology has failed to do justice to the place of the doctrine of the word of God, proclaimed but also written, within the total doctrine of the means of grace during the second and third centuries."[20] Indeed, if modern evangelicals would reflect on our essentially sacramental use of the Bible (the Quiet Time our daily office!), we might understand Catholic theology more sympathetically, too. When we read the Bible in faith, we are ushered into the presence of God. Like the bread and the wine, the words of that Book communicate the gospel and create communion with God. By the Spirit, the Scriptures do occasion fresh events of revelation, as Barth wanted to say, that are more than just the analyzing of propositions. Of course I would want to insist, against Barth, that the textual elements of this sacrament are more than merely fallible human words. But I agree with him that a miracle takes place when a person meets the Lord and hears his Word through the Bible.

Because of the Spirit, the Bible can be a channel of the grace and speech of God to us. It constitutes the privileged circle in which to stand when wanting to hear God's Word and discern God's will. And it means that there is a mystery in the way in which the Bible operates in the life of the church. The Word can be stale and dry for long periods, and then spring to life and power. The truth can lie hidden, and then come alive and break forth. Jesus and Paul met Jews who cared greatly for the biblical text but could not grasp what God was saying to them in it. The message was hidden from their eyes. In the same way, the church can languish in ignorance of the liberating message of the

Bible, and then rediscover in renewal the grace and goodness of God. This is the mystery of the Spirit and the Word.

Lovelace has concluded that the proper balance of the Spirit and the Word is the key to living orthodoxy. In order to preach Christ effectively, we must, on the one hand, depend upon a true knowledge of the incarnate Word through the written Word and, on the other hand, depend on the risen Lord and his outpoured Spirit to bring to life the information given and focus it existentially on our hearts. For spiritually energized biblical truth is the instrument through which God transforms human personalities.[21] No choice needs to be made between the content of the Bible and our appropriation of it. The Bible is like a telescope that fastens our vision upon the Lord. God may not be giving foundational Scripture anymore now that this has been done, but he is still engaged in communicating himself and filling our lives with his loving presence. He has not and never will finish illuminating the minds of believers in the truth by which they can learn to befriend and love God better.

Three Specific Operations

How does this duality and mutuality of the Word and the Spirit work out in specific ways? What difference does it really make in reading the Bible whether one has the Spirit or not? We will look at three specific ways the Spirit works in relation to the Scriptures and notice a pattern in each case of spiritual understanding being built upon the level of ordinary understanding.

Let us consider first how we come to *recognize* the Scriptures, or the gospel itself for that matter, as the Word of God. In a real sense how faith comes about is a mystery hidden in the depths of the human spirit. It is hard to be certain how it comes about even in one's own life. Nevertheless, there is a level of ordinary understanding involved in it. There are many kinds of evidences that have convinced the minds of people through the ages of the objective truth of the message of the Bible. Calvin spoke of the good and sufficient evidences that were at hand to establish the credibility of the Scriptures, having in mind such indicia as fulfilled prophecy, miracles, profundity, antiquity, coherence, and the like (*Institutes* I, chap. 8). Although he would never have claimed to be able by rational argument to bring a person all the way to saving faith, Calvin did insist that one could think intelligently about faith. We are not left in the dark in the realm of religion. The truth of the Christian faith has good credentials. It would be very peculiar and tragic if a message addressed to all people could not make good its claim in the public realm, if there were no way the believer could explain to another person in what ways faith in God made good sense.[22]

In thinking about reasons for faith in the gospel and in the Bible, we can distinguish internal and external reasons. Internal evidence would include the way in which the Bible has again and again proved itself true in human lives by supplying the understanding crucial to facing up to the questions of meaning, suffering, and forgiveness. It has a ring of truth about it and can trigger an inner response. In speaking to the deepest questions of human existence, it presents itself as a credible candidate for revelation. A text that makes deep sense, and has been able to grip the best minds of the past few millennia, obviously possesses marks of truth. The claims it makes to be a revelation from God seem to be confirmed in ordinary experience. It should be clear that when we speak of reasons for faith these need not be philosophically difficult or erudite reasons. Many of them are evidences of the kind that cohere with the grammar of ordinary life. External evidences would include those of a more objective kind, such as the evidence of God's workmanship in the universe or of God's action in the history of the world. John Locke maintained, along with a host of other Christian apologists over the centuries, that the revelation God gave was accompanied by outward signs that authenticated the revelation as such. In this way, he believed, revelation was nonarbitrary, because it possessed credentials that interested persons could examine for themselves. Although it is not possible to conclude that revelation can be infallibly established by such arguments, it can be maintained that belief in the truth of the Bible and the gospel is rationally preferred over not believing in it, because it economically explains some important data.[23]

One can, of course, go too far in this direction. There is a personal certainty only the Spirit can give us that must not be lost sight of. In our desire to prove the Bible true, we can easily locate the basis of faith in human wisdom rather than in the power of God and become more at home defending the Bible than in proclaiming its message with power. Our supposed expertise can get in the way of actually encountering the truth of the text.[24] The greater certainty aimed at by the scholars can easily damage the faith of the ordinary Christian, who probably requires less, so that the whole apologetic operation can backfire. For reasons like these, the Reformers blew hot and cold about the place of philosophy in theology. They knew that revelation had good credentials, and they referred to them, but they did not want to lose sight of the work of the Spirit in establishing evangelical certainty. Can we have it both ways?

There is nothing to prevent us from thinking in terms of there being evidence for the truth of the Bible as well as a work of God's Spirit that goes beyond it. The evidence can give us an appreciation of the Bible and incline us to crediting its claims, but it cannot give the kind of personal certitude that faith implies and that results from a decision to trust God and believe his Word. It is not that the Spirit turns poor evidence into good evidence or a bad argument into a good one but that God helps us to have the right perspective and makes us better able to attend to the evidence that is there. The resulting conviction is personal and internal, but the basis on which it was made remains public out there for people to see. Believers can explain to the inquirer what factors were prominent in their minds when they came to that conviction. These factors yielded moral certainty, if not demonstration, and were used by the Spirit in his own witness to bring the believers to rest and peace in the matter of the authority of the Bible. Such inner assurance is not the result of human reasoning alone, or the product of churchly authority, as the Reformers insisted, but an inward certainty God himself gives us when we respond to him. This personal knowledge builds upon the data of ordinary understanding, but goes beyond it. It is not irrational, but transrational. It is a confidence that commitment brings and that God gives.

The Apostle Paul often emphasized that the power of his preaching owed little or nothing to his skill at rhetoric or argument. The gospel came to the Thessalonians with power because of the Spirit's work (1 Thess. 1:5). It was not so much that Paul impressed them as that they had been gripped by God himself in what was preached. The Word was not experienced as a human message from without but as a divine energy within (2:13). Similarly, the Corinthians were not convinced by Paul's rhetorical abilities but by a "demonstration of the Spirit and power." Though this term was used in Greek to denote a compelling argument, Paul turns it right around so that it has nothing to do with argument and proofs. They were so conscious of the power of God when Paul spoke that they were not so much intellectually persuaded as spiritually converted. There is a personal certainty the Spirit gives that cannot be obtained by reasons and evidence. He enables us to hear the Word and receive it. He takes away the veil and rings the bell of truth. He enables us to live with various kinds of uncertainty, too, on the ordinary level of understanding.[25]

Second in our look at the Spirit and Scripture, let us consider the

interpretation of Scripture. Here, too, there is an ordinary level of comprehension. Anyone can investigate fruitfully the meaning of a text. It
should be possible for Christians and others to agree on the historical
meaning of the text. This is the validity in interpretation for which
Hirsch pleads.[26] One does not have to rejoice in the truth of John 3:16 to
understand basically what it is saying. We should not think of God giving
private information about the original meaning of a text to believers and
denying it to others. If he did that, the locus of revelation would shift
to subjective experience away from its connection with the Bible. Intuition would then reign supreme, and individuals could size up the meaning of the text in a flash of misunderstanding. If the meaning of the text
cannot be determined by the ordinary understanding, then it must be
free-floating and subject to all manner of distortion. Surely the plain
sense of the text must be the anchor of all true interpretation. Otherwise
the authority of the Bible will drift off into human subjectivity. Paul's
command stands good: "Study to show yourself approved unto God, a
workman who does not need to be ashamed, rightly dividing the Word
of truth" (2 Tim. 2:15).[27]

And yet there is still a crucial role for the Spirit in the interpretation
of the Bible. Who has not had the awful experience of reading a scholarly commentary on the meaning of the text, only to be so bored by
technical detail and a lack of spiritual discernment about what the Bible
is saying that there is no incentive at all to open the Bible and take it
seriously? Obviously, the truth of the text is not secured merely by
possessing historical and linguistic tools. What marked commentaries
before the rise of criticism was an orientation to want to know God
better and grow in his friendship. They did not try to master the text as
critics now do but to place themselves under its discipline and taste the
goodness of the Lord. They were, in fact, in agreement with the biblical
writers themselves as to what was important and were therefore in a
better position to grasp what these writers were saying.

First, there is the simple fact that involvement with a text like the
Bible and an open receptivity to its message puts one in a position to
understand it better. Every Bible reader knows of times when study is
dry and fruitless. But he or she also knows of times when there is a
creative breakthrough in understanding. At such a time "the penny
drops," and things fall into place. The testimony of William Lane in his
Mark commentary is worth recording:

Only gradually did I come to understand that my primary task as a commenta-
tor was to listen to the text, and to the discussion it has prompted over the
course of centuries, as a child who needed to be made wise. The responsibility

to discern truth from error has been onerous at times. When a critical or theological decision has been demanded by the text before I was prepared to commit myself, I have adopted the practice of the Puritan commentators in laying the material before the Lord and asking for his guidance. This has made the preparation of the commentary a spiritual as well as an intellectual pilgrimage through the text of the Gospel. In learning to be sensitive to all that the evangelist was pleased to share with me I have been immeasurably enriched by the discipline of responsible listening.[28]

This is by no means a call to forsake serious study of the text but, rather, a summons to link the mind and the Spirit, study and prayer, in the work of interpretation. As William Cowper put it in his hymn: "The Spirit breathes upon the Word and brings the truth to sight." There is a level of understanding that only comes through involvement with the text and a walk with the Lord. When Jesus referred to children as an example to us, he meant their attitude of openness and trust. The nonexpert in a spirit of receptivity may understand the text better than the expert with all his or her scholarly tools. This is the only way for the Bible to become a living and transforming book. Where the Spirit is active, truths become precious that once were avoided and insights stand out that once were hidden. Coming to the text with the proper faith orientation enables the reader to penetrate more deeply and pick up what the Bible really has to say. If we were to read Paul, for example, merely as a figure in the history of religions, we would be unlikely to be able to grasp the insight God gave him into the mysteries of God of which he claimed to be a steward. What is needed is the balance Paul himself urged upon Timothy when he said, "Think over what I say, and the Lord will give you understanding" (2 Tim. 2:7). Thinking about the meaning of the text and prayerfully considering the purpose of God in the text go hand in hand in interpretation.[29] Although we are often warned about the naïveté of the layperson reading the Bible, we ought to be just as cautious about the scholarly techniques used by experts that miss the meaning because they are not open and receptive to the text. As C. S. Lewis said, "The true reader reads every work seriously in the sense that he reads it whole-heartedly, makes himself as receptive as he can."[30]

Second, more is involved than just engagement with the text and a prayerful spirit. Of course, the plain meaning of a book like Romans can lie there ungrasped for years, only to be seized upon in a time of renewal and released to transform the church. But there is more to it than that. As we shall argue in Chapter 8, the meaning of a text cannot be equated with its original meaning. After all, it now stands in a collection with other books and, most importantly, in a messianically structured canon of old and new covenants. Thus, the meaning of the text is far richer than just the first sense it had. There is surplus of meaning over and above that. It is fitted to answer questions we pose at many levels. What did this text mean to Israelites then? What does it mean for Christians now? What does it mean in the light of this text over here? How does it relate spiritually to my life? How is Christ preached in it? Although we decry the multiple levels of meaning in medieval exegesis, we have ourselves fallen into a sterile condition and limited ourselves to the precise meaning of the original author. Instead of seeking a rich testimony from God in the text, we have impoverished ourselves and sold the Scriptures short. To see that, one only has to compare the International Critical Commentary with Calvin or with Matthew Henry.

If the Spirit helps the church with its interpretation, how is it that we do not agree more than we do about the meaning of the Bible? Even those who approach the Bible as the authoritative Word of God often disagree about its message. Tradition must be part of the answer. We read the text with certain beliefs already in our minds, whether cultural or theological, and these certainly affect how we evaluate what we find. Add to that the complexity of the text itself. On the various issues on which we differ, the Bible sends out mixed signals that are hard to reduce to demonstrable dogma. What does the Bible as as whole say about peace and war or about Sunday worship or about relations between male and female? Great debates revolve around such questions. Our confusion can sometimes be a reflection of a confusion already in the text. What we have to do is work hard at interpretation and be open to changing our minds. We should strive to grasp the ruling principles of Scripture in each matter and make full use of the community of the faithful. In this way perhaps we shall grow into a unity of faith in the Son of God (Eph. 4:14–15).

Third in our look at how the Spirit works in relation to the Scriptures, let us consider the *application* of the Bible. Though there is a certain amount of flexibility in interpretation, there is a great deal more when it comes to application. The Spirit has a broad area to work in, and we must be sensitive to his leading. Of course, there is the ordinary level of understanding here also. We have to take the commandments, the doctrines, the narratives, and the exhortations seriously in the form in which God gave them. We have not been appointed to revise the Scriptures, but to heed them. The Bible is the set radius for the people of God to live in. It sets up parameters to guide our paths. Very often the application is clear in the text. We ought to love one another; we ought to praise God; we ought to believe his promises; and so forth. The original meaning establishes a direction for us that ought to be heeded.

But having said that, there is also a large role for the Spirit here, in that we need God's guidance in knowing how to put the Scriptures into effect in our situation today. Over and above what the Bible says, we need the direction and discernment that the Spirit gives. The possible applications even of a text that is straightforward are multiple, and we have to make our choice and take our stand. In effect, we have to discern what the will of the Lord is for us. We need guidance in answering questions such as these: How ought we to help our neighbors in Poland or in El Salvador? How shall we understand the finality of Jesus Christ in the sphere of world religions? What is to be done in the defense of freedom? Ought women to be elders in the church? Is Sunday the day to gather for worship? How can we achieve a greater measure of economic justice? What does creation mean in relation to scientific theory? It is urgent that we give an answer to questions like these, yet the Bible does not tell us exactly what answers to give.

The Spirit was given precisely to lead us into all truth, that is, to help us to see the meaning of what Jesus said in the new contexts that would arise afterwards. The Spirit will help us to penetrate the gospel and see it in an ever-new light. What the Spirit gives does not surpass the gospel of Jesus or add to it. As Küng put it, "The Spirit cannot give a new revelation, but through the preaching of his witnesses he will cause everything that Jesus said and did to be revealed in a new light. The Spirit is not needful because Jesus' teaching was quantitatively not complete, but because Jesus' teaching must qualitatively become a new revelation through the church's preaching."[31] In this way revelation can constantly present a new challenge in fresh situations.

We see this happening in the New Testament itself. We see it in the different ways in which the gospel is presented to various audiences in the Acts and by the great New Testament theologians. We see it in the four different Gospels. We see it in the way the writers employ the Old Testament texts so that they speak directly to the Body of Christ. They read it in the light of what had happened to Jesus Christ, a greater David and Solomon and Jonah. They did not simply read ancient texts for what they had to say but read them in a spirit of openness to what God might be now saying through them. It seems clear that Paul combined the text and his spiritual charisma to come up with fresh insights —in Romans 11:25–27 and Galatians 3:8, for example. Or consider the way in which Stephen reinterpreted the Old Testament in the light of what Jesus had said about the destruction of the temple (Acts 6:14;

7:2–53). Or consider the decision that was reached at the Council of Jerusalem concerning how the Old Testament laws regarding foods were to be applied to the Gentile converts (Acts 15:6–29).[32] These Christians did not limit themselves to the original sense of the passage, but sought the will of the Lord in the reading of the texts such that it became a Word of God to them. Do we not have the same experience ourselves when we find meaning in texts for our own lives that really extends the meaning in a new direction? How vividly I recall Edith Schaeffer applying to L'Abri an Old Testament prophecy about the nations flowing to the mountain of God (Isa. 2:2–3). I do not believe she was wrong to do this. Texts can function as the Word of the Lord with a sense different from that originally intended. This is simply to recognize the reality of the Spirit at work in the church. He is able to apply the Scriptures to us very directly.

Thus, the task of theology today is to find the applications of the Word that are in the will of God. How can we bring the text over the hermeneutical gap of the centuries and have it address our situation? In part, it must be through careful reflection about what the dynamic equivalent of the text would be, and in part it must involve the believing community listening for God's Word in its prayer and worship. The obvious danger of this liberty is that it may be used to sanctify our own causes, even though even a legalistic use of the text can do the same thing. It is easy to claim to have a translation of the text in modern terms that is really a transformation of it: for example, to claim that Heidegger is saying just what Paul meant, or that Hartshorne captures exactly the dynamic biblical model of the divine action, or that Marx supplies the theory that the Bible's teachings on justice requires us to use. Despite the dangers of distortion, the liberty to pursue the contemporary significance of the Bible is precious and not to be suppressed. Liberty can always be used "as an opportunity for the flesh," but it does not have to be misused in that way (Gal. 5:13). As a check against such abuse, we should distinguish the objective authority of the text in its original meaning, which is canonical and universal, and the subjective authority of our own insights into current significance, which are local and corrigible. What the text originally meant provides the fixed point of reference for everything else. What we discern in the text for our situation, which may go beyond its scope into a fresh insight for today, has the character of a discernment into the will of the Lord for us. As such, even though it was received in connection with the reading of the Bible, it should not be equated with the text as canonical. Rather, it should be held forth as a contemporary conviction of ours into the way God seems to be leading us. Such convictions are, of course, to be evaluated in the light of reason, tradition, and the instincts of the people of God around us.

We are used to thinking about the guidance of the Spirit in the realm of our life decisions, but clearly we ought to be seeking it also in the work of exegesis and application. Guidance is something we know we can expect God to give us, yet we are aware how easy it is to sanctify our own whims as God's leading. Therefore, we must be in an attitude of prayer when we are listening for God's voice (cf. Acts 13:2–4) and have a hearty respect for the wisdom of our fellow Christians who are prayerfully open in the same way. One is a fool who is not open to the opinions of other saints. As James said, "The wisdom from above is first pure, then peaceable, gentle and open to reason" (James 3:17). The same belief in the Spirit's guidance applies to other Christians, too, and ought to make us open and receptive to the applications they see to be approved of God.

In conclusion, we need to keep in mind both the objective and the subjective poles of revelation and of Scripture. The objective pole gives us an anchor of stability and an authority for all seasons. It prevents us from wandering into free-floating subjectivism. The subjective pole, on the other hand, gives us vitality and flexibility and rules out legalistic and insensitive pseudo-orthodoxy, which is so often merely an absolutism of the hermeneutics of one or two centuries ago.[33]

But if it is true that the presence of the Spirit is essential for the work of interpretation to be effective, then it follows that the practitioners must be believers filled with the Spirit. They must be people who are personally in touch with the reality of God in our midst pointed out so vividly by Saint Luke. They must be those on whom the power has fallen (Luke 24:49), who operate out of radical faith and in the gifts of the Spirit that bear directly upon discerning the will of the Lord. Yet is it not true that biblical interpreters today often seem to lack the ability or willingness to speak confidently of their personal walk with God and in joyful praise of him? Are they not often specialists about religion, engaged with one another in arcane debates about details—members of the academy, oftentimes dour, preoccupied, and introspective, and not the kind of spiritually liberated persons the New Testament says Christians ought to be? Do we not often find ourselves ressembling those Ephesians who had not heard that there was a Holy Spirit and those Samaritans on whom the Spirit was not yet poured out? (Acts 19:2; 8:16). If so, then we need, in addition to our rational training, a liberation of our spirits by the Spirit of God, so that we might be the kind of interpreters of Scripture that it deserves.[34] Both religious liberals and conservative evangelicals have conspired to leave the Spirit out of hermeneutics, and this must come to an end. The liberals have done so because they are afraid to make it too obvious that they believe in God, whereas the conservatives have done it because they are worried about the uncertainty that could be created if we let any amount of experience into the interpretive equation. The New Testament rebukes both of them and summons us to trust in God for the light that has yet to break forth out of his holy Word.

> Come, Holy Ghost, for moved by Thee,
> Thy prophets wrote and spoke;
> Unlock the truth, Thyself the key,
> Unseal the sacred book.[35]

CHAPTER 8

Unfolding Revelation

There is a sense in which, on account of the Spirit himself, any text he used would be rendered dynamic, even if it were itself undynamic. But this is far from the case. There are a number of ways in which the Bible is well suited to his dynamic ministry. By their own form and structure the Scriptures lend themselves to the Spirit and a dynamic interpretation. I make reference to the internal dynamic in which the biblical traditions develop and change over time, and also to the depth of meaning that belongs to a literary document of this sort. The Bible is more like a wind tunnel than a pile of bricks, and more like an orchestra than a solo instrument. Though an objective given, the Bible is also an inexhaustible resource for the church because of the development of its themes and the fecundity of possible interpretations. In this way, the Bible makes itself available to the Spirit for fresh and subtle uses (and to human obtuseness for fresh and subtle misuses). It gives room to the Spirit to bring the text up-to-date and apply it in the new situations that never cease to arise. It is with good reason, then, that we read the Bible expectantly, in hope of finding treasures new and old.

The Development of the Biblical Traditions

The Bible does not present a revelation given all at once. The truth it offers was communicated over a very long time and by a very dynamic process. The text seems to breathe, to expand and contract, to grow and build toward the full actualization of salvation, the coming of God's kingdom. The truth is given dialectically in a process of conversation and refinement, which makes for a dynamic experience of interpretation. The Bible does not take the form of a systematic theology, but that of a great narrative that presents the grace of God in action for the redemption of the nations. Therefore, the truth it yields is not cut-and-dried but balanced and nuanced. The truth is given and applied, and then reinterpreted and reapplied. Older material is appealed to again and again and put to new uses. Fresh insights appear out of this process of refinement.[1]

Liberal scholarship is likely to dwell upon the freedom to adapt traditions that we see in the text, because it fits in with the desire to be free to adapt the gospel to changing circumstances. Nevertheless, conservatives should note that respect for what was given obviously did not prevent biblical writers themselves from interpreting the text in new ways for new circumstances. They were concerned both for the meaning of what was given and for the fresh significance it might have for them. It is vital for the work of interpretation today to take note of this. Evangelicals need to give greater recognition to the fact that Scripture itself does not often cite earlier revelation for its own sake, but for the sake of what God is saying through it now. Biblical writers were not slaves to the earlier traditions but felt free to use them in new and different ways. They did not see God locked in the past but free to update his program of salvation and ring out new meaning from what had been given before.[2]

As I brought out in Chapter 1, God's grace and offer of salvation has been operative from the beginning of history. "He has never left himself without witness." We should not limit our conception of salvation history to the relatively recent biblical stories from Abraham to Jesus, but see it as something that encompasses the whole history of the world. Because God is one who desires all to be saved, we can be sure that he reveals himself in one way or another to everyone, and invites them to make a decision for or against him. Around every soul there swirl the winds of sin and grace. But our concern here is for the way in which the conversation develops within the Bible, where we encounter the definitive word of salvation and the struggle to understand it. In Jesus Christ and the biblical tradition, the saving presence of God makes itself most tangible and accessible and issues the proclamation of the soon-to-be victorious saving plan of God.

Starting with the Old Testament itself, we find a text that is oriented to the future of God's salvation. There is the awareness that God has promised to crush the head of the serpent and bless all the nations through Abraham and his offspring. But there is also the sense that God is going to do more and reveal more concerning his purpose and plan. We need to learn to look, not only at the finsihed products of revelation up to now, but also at the ways in which the biblical traditions dynamically developed. The Old Testament is, in fact, an ongoing hermeneutic of the fulfillment of the promise of God.[3]

One can read the Old Testament in such a way as to bring out the concepts that arise from reading the text as a whole, or one can read it more chronologically, observing the successive epochs in the history of revelation and tradition and noting the transitions and changes that were introduced. The content and the unfolding of the content are both important to a full understanding of the Bible. What Stephen does in retelling the Old Testament story of salvation and judgment is going on throughout the Bible all the time.[4] One marvelous way to bring this out is to refer to God's promise and observe how this promise is unfolded and actualized over time in the Bible.[5] It was given in a nutshell to Adam and Eve, then opened up in the specific, though still general, promise to Abraham, and then formalized in the covenant of the Mosaic period. Following this, it went through stages of judges, monarchy, exile, and return, in all of which the direction and meaning of the promise was progressively clarified and pointed. What was originally given was expanded and focused in changing circumstances, resulting in an overall picture of rich proportions. Progressive may be too simple a term to describe what happened. We cannot exactly say that Haggai was an advance over Isaiah, or Ecclesiastes an improvement of Proverbs. But there is nevertheless an unfolding and a deepening even in dialectic tension of the picture God wants us to have of his character and purposes.

Let us look at two illustrations that pertain to the promise to Abraham. In Genesis 12, God promises to bless Abraham and his seed and to make them a blessing in the earth. Much later, Isaiah picks up this promise and elicits a word of comfort for Israel. God will make her wilderness like Eden and her desert like the garden of God (51:1–3). But Ezekiel, when he meditates upon this promise, takes it in a quite different way. He tells the people that they cannot depend on God blessing them if they persist in disobeying him and prophesies judgment upon them (33:23–29). People like that cannot expect to claim promises that implied quite different behavior. In Genesis 15:7, God declares himself as the one who brought Abraham out of Ur, and in Exodus 20:2, he is the one who brought Israel out of Egypt. When Jeremiah reflects upon the theme, he says the phrase will be replaced with one that speaks of God bringing the people out of the north country (16:14–15). Clearly, the promise given can be grasped in fresh ways as the Lord leads in new situations.

There are abundant examples of the interpretation and reinterpretation of earlier material in the Prophets, because they were spiritually gifted and conscious of the call to update and apply the Word of God. They had the ability and charisma to discern what God was now saying through what had been given. The false prophet Hananiah knew the text about the promise of God to Israel but did not properly discern how to apply it to Israel facing exile. Jeremiah had to call his interpretation into question and point out the greater severity of the situation (Jeremiah 28). In the same way, Amos knew that God had chosen Israel and Judah as his people and vehicle of salvation, but he was convinced that the promise could not be appealed to without reference to the people's conduct in relation to the convenantal stipulations. The promise does not make Israel and Judah immune from the judgment of God —in fact, their privileged position puts greater responsibility on their shoulders (3:2). In an outburst, Amos tells them God hates their worship and cares as much for Philistines as for them! In this he was clarifying issues about the original promise as well as recalling it. Isaiah also warned them to look twice at the covenant and what it means and not believe the scoffers of Jerusalem who deny God's alien work of judgment could ever apply to them (18:14–22). Hosea, too, recalls God's tender love in the wilderness, but warns of God's freedom to turn fierce like a lion if the people continue to be indifferent to him. Jeremiah speaks of a coming day when the old covenant and the ark of the Lord would be replaced by God's throne and a new covenant (3:16; 31:31). Or consider the different reactions to the exile: To some it was an unmitigated disaster. Some hung up their harps. Some blamed God, or their ancestors, or their enemies. It was a crisis of faith for Israel and presents us with the same pattern of richly varying responses.[6]

Just because it was written over such a long period, the Old Testament is full of good examples of dynamic in interpretation. We only have to look at the various books to see the dynamic shaping of earlier traditions. The history of the chronicler is a theological reworking of the same events that are recorded in Samuel and Kings. Legal and cultic material have been brought together in Exodus and Leviticus from various places and times. Books like Job and Ecclesiastes seem to have been written to introduce correctives into the way in which the covenant might be misread. Psalm 139 uses the metaphor of space to illustrate God's continual presence, whereas Amos turns it to warn of inescapable judgment (9:2–3). The text shows us how an earlier text or image can be used again in a variety of valid ways. Out of this treasure the scribe can indeed bring things old and new (Matt. 13:52). This is exactly what God intended. The text is a stable factor, but it is a dynamic factor as well. New insight can be brought into contact with the original text and the Word of the Lord grasped afresh. It is important for us to notice not only the continuity but also the discontinuity and revisions wrought in the tradition that leads to Jesus the Christ. We ourselves are the result of a merging of traditions that determine the character of our homes and ourselves. The biblical revelation that lies before us, too, is a complex text, analogous to our own experience and able to become the vehicle of revelation for us and for generations to come.[7] It is not necessary to exaggerate the twists and turns of the developing tradition in order to pick up the richness of the Word God is giving us.

New Covenant and Old

Even more obvious is the way in which the New Testament appears to be a reinterpretation of Old Testament tradition. A new and unprecedented act of God took place in Jesus Christ in fulfillment of Old Testament hopes. All the earlier material is looked at afresh in the light of this event. Promises are seen to have been made good, and correspondences are noted everywhere. The Old Testament makes it possible to understand the New Testament, but the New Testament also penetrates more deeply into what the Old Testament was aiming at. The transition from Old to New Testament was the single most dramatic illustration of dynamic updating in the canon of Scripture. A whole new perspective now influences the field of vision, and everything appears in sharper detail, oriented to the meaning of the incarnation. Updating and reinterpretation were going on within the Old Testament, but nothing on quite this scale. A covenant of consummation has been struck that fulfills all the covenants that went before.[8] The text is not read as if it were an inflexible code, but as a pre-messianic trajectory, an occasion for the Spirit to testify to Christ, and it is by no means limited to what the Old Testament may originally have intended.

One would have to admit here that the church, when it took over the Old Testament from the synagogue, did not adopt the Judaic Scripture principle per se. Even if it sounds as if it did when one reads some conservative and traditional authors, in fact, Christians use the text not as binding law but as flexible, messianic promise. Not everything in it is now relevant to Christians: Do we eat pork? Do we wear tassels? Do we observe Sabbath? Are we monogamous? The Old Testament is the written Word of God, but, because of Jesus, it is not binding on us in the way it is binding on the Jewish faithful. There can be no question of abandoning it (contra Marcion) or violating its meaning. It is, rather, a question of reading it as a subordinate standard in light of what the New Testament says, not as an independent authority.

This becomes obvious when we consider how the New Testament uses the Old Testament. The latter was considered to have been written for Christians and was applied to them. "Whatever was written aforetime was written for our instruction" (Rom. 15:4). It was written "for our instruction, upon whom the end of the ages has come" (1 Cor. 10:11). The Old Testament became a book full of lessons for Christians and full of intimations of the coming Messiah, who was identified as Jesus of Nazareth. Somewhat in the way in which the Qumran community around the same time read the text in the light of their contemporary situation, so the early Christians saw everything in a new and revelant way.[9] The difference would be that the Christian "pesher" of the text was Christological as well as eschatological, and that made all the difference. But in each case, the past text is modernized and placed in the contemporary setting, even if adapting and modifying is required.

Jesus himself is presented in Old Testament terms. He is the stone that the builders rejected, the one betrayed by his friends, the shepherd of a scattered flock, the one numbered among the transgressors. His birth gave deeper clarity to the promise given to King Ahaz, and he is always being compared to Adam, and Moses, and David, and Solomon, and Jonah. The text is alive with references to the Old Testament, both direct quotations and allusions. The Old Testament foreshadowed the life and redemptive ministry of Jesus, and the ever-unfolding delight of this realization is constantly on the minds of the New Testament writers.[10] The Lord himself repeatedly placed new constructions upon old, familiar texts. In the Sermon on the Mount he pressed Old Testament ethical insights to even greater consistency and rigor. He boldly stated that the essence of the whole law could be summed up in the love for God and one's neighbor. He could drop part of a text out, setting himself up as an authority even higher than that of the Old Testament (Luke 4:18–19). When it came to the laws about ritual purity, he could undermine the whole distinction between clean and unclean foods by speaking about the sins that really defile (Mark 7:15). He felt able to dismiss Moses' permission of divorce because of the higher principle he saw in the creation ordinance (Matt. 19:3–9). As for Sabbath, he displayed such freedom of action on that day as to suggest that even this commandment was due for some adjustment.

Paul's letters afford ample opportunity for us to see the same phenomenon of the adaptation of the Old Testament to the messianic situation. In 2 Corinthians 3, he develops a parallel between Moses' ministry before Christ and his own apostolic calling. Paul saw himself as minister of a new covenant with much more splendor. In Galatians 4, he presents an Old Testament story in an allegorical fashion to bring out its meaning for Christians. In 1 Corinthians 9, he finds a lesson pertaining to the financial support of Christian leaders in an obscure Penteteuchal regulation. In Romans 10, he refers almost casually to Deuteronomy 30 to put into words what he wants to say. In Galatians 3:16, he finds great meaning in the grammatical singular "seed" and refers it to Christ as the true seed of Abraham. In Ephesians 4, he cites a variant form of the text in Psalm 68:18 to express what he has in mind. As an apostle of Jesus Christ, Paul felt he had been given special insight into the mystery of God, and one implication of this consciousness was a certain liberty in adapting the Old Testament to the new era. Nowhere was this more dramatically plain than in Galatians where Paul contends that the law does not possess the validity it did before Christ came, and that circumcision in particular was not to be required of the Gentiles who had become sons of Abraham by faith.[11]

Even within the New Testament, one finds interesting differences in the way the text can be adapted. Paul and James quote the same verse from Genesis 15:6 and relate it to the same doctrine, justification, but do it in very different ways. It is reminiscent of the different ways Isaiah and Ezekiel hark back to the same Abrahamic covenant. Whereas Matthew tends to quote the Old Testament to stress fulfillment, John refers to it to bring out more of a contrast. Whereas Paul sees the Old Testament as a witness to the righteousness of God apart from law, the Book of Hebrews declares the old covenant obsolete now that the new has come.

What we see happening here is the earlier text being reinterpreted in the light of the higher stage of revelation that has dawned. The New Testament is not trying to give us an interpretation of the Old Testament just in terms of what it originally meant. Rather, it is proclaiming the gospel, making use of premessianic Scripture, to render the new substance of the gospel. The operation is much more creative than what we today would call exegesis. Though we would object to a person setting up a canon within the canon on his or her own authority, the New Testament is, in fact, such a canon in the Bible as a whole. We reinterpret what was given before in the light of it, because revelation in the Old Testament is progressive and finds its fulfillment in Christ.[12] The economy of preparation is interpreted in the light of the economy of fulfillment, as Carnell put it.[13]

This means that Christians read the New Testament into the Old.

Genesis 3:15, about the serpent having its head crushed, means a great deal more to us now than it did originally, because of the coming of the Savior to destroy the works of the Devil. What was only hinted at then has become a full-blown understanding. Light has been cast on the protogospel by the gospel itself. Peter linked what Joel said to what happened on the day of Pentecost; James linked what Amos prophesied to the Gentile mission that was getting under way. God's installation of his king in Zion becomes a witness to the enthronement of Christ at God's right hand. The text of Psalm 2:6 has dramatically opened up and become significant to the whole world. What God is saying to us in the gospel sheds light upon what he said to Israel in former days. The New Testament does not care simply about the meaning intended by the original author. It seeks to understand the Old Testament in the light of the climactic revelation in Jesus Christ. Out of the encounter of text and gospel came the Word of God for the church. It is important to remember this in some of the hermeneutical problems we face, too. How Christians ought to act politically is closely tied in with how the Old Testament relates to the New. How we come down on the issue of a just war may be reflected in the weight we give to Old versus New Testament texts. How we think of the Sabbath will depend on how much novelty we think the New Testament introduces into the question of holy days. How tolerant we are toward polygamy will hinge upon how we construe the ongoing validity of the Old Testament. The Bible we respect is not flat, and how we measure its contours and changes will affect a number of questions we wrestle with.[14]

Dynamic Within the New Testament

In the case of the New Testament, the time span is really too small to prove development of theology. All the documents were written in the first century, and the exact dating of them is not certain. But there is enough diversity to show, on a smaller scale, the same kind of hermeneutic dynamic that is visible in the Old Testament. The New Testament, too, is a complex composition and collection, manifesting surprise and suspense, variety and balance.[15]

One prominent example of hermeneutical diversity is the fourfold Gospel itself. In each of these books, a portrait is presented of Jesus in which certain features are made to stand out. They are not repeats of one another, but individualized remembrances that by being placed together in the canon yield great depth of perception. We are led to believe that the truth about Jesus transcends any one presentation and that several biographies are required to give an adequate sense of his importance and significance. In each Gospel the material is shaped and interpreted by the writer to bring out certain points and insights. Alongside a historical purpose to tell the story of Jesus, there is a theological and pastoral purpose to present the truth from the angle required by the situation into which the evangelist is writing. The result is four portraits or redactions of the life and significance of Christ. The four Gospels are not "snapshots" that give us the plain facts, and they are not pieces of "abstract art" that relate only remotely to their subject. They are "portraits" that present the Jesus of history from a particular angle relevant to the community that first received the work. The material is not taken as sacrosanct and fixed, but as something to be thought through afresh and applied to ever changing situations.[16]

This is easy to illustrate. Matthew shows an unusual interest in Jesus as one who fulfills Old Testament prophecies. Therefore, there are many quotations designed to call attention to this fact. He is also concerned to show how the Christian faith, once confined to Judaism, became a universal message due to the ministry of Christ. Unlike Mark, Matthew balances the emphasis on eschatology with an emphasis on ecclesiology as well. He is the only evangelist to use the word *church* at all and wants to show that Jesus originated it and provided for it. Mark, on the other hand, is a Gospel of action. It has the style of a drama quickly moving toward the cross. Much less teaching is included, and some of the Jewish texture in Matthew is missing. Mark seems to be writing for Gentiles. He presents Jesus as the divine Son of God with tremendous power over nature and demons, and stresses the suffering that will be the lot of those who follow him. Luke is especially interested in the universal scope of the gospel. His Gospel and Acts together show his understanding of the momentum of salvation history as it moves inexorably toward the conversion of all nations. He shows a special interest in Jesus' attitude to the disadvantaged, such as women, children, and the poor. He likes to write about Jesus' prayer life, the power of the Spirit, and the joy experienced in salvation. John's Gospel is even more distinctive than the Synoptics are from each other and stresses themes such as light, love, truth, and life. He alone plainly states a Christology in terms of the full deity and personal pre-existence of Christ. The very term *incarnation* was coined from his remarks (1:14). There is a great deal of teaching, but it is different in content from the blocks of teaching we find in Matthew. All this is simply to say that the work of interpretation is already in full stride in the New Testament itself. We are confronted with a text that forces us to go deeper as soon as we appreciate the diversity.[17]

Another prominent example of interpretive dynamic would be the several theological styles of presenting the Christian faith in the New Testament. Paul, and Hebrews, and Peter, and Luke each have their own way of saying what is important and essential. Each employs its own terminology, and there is, in effect, a dialogue between them right in the New Testament. If one is going to expound the Testament according to major themes, it proves necessary to distinguish what the different writers have to say about them in order not to reduce their witness to a banal lowest common denominator.[18] A study of the Spirit would require noticing the unique nuances brought out by the various authors in their work.[19] A certain amount of diversity is canonized in the New Testament in this way, suggesting, perhaps, that varieties of perspective in the church today are not such a bad thing after all.[20]

A good deal of the diversity is due to the circumstantial nature of New Testament teaching. Longenecker calls attention to the "faith of Abraham" theme that occurs in three New Testament writers—Paul, James, and Hebrews. It is used differently in each case owing to the varying requirements of audience and situation. Paul appeals to Abraham in Romans and Galatians to bring out the patriarch's trust in God as the key to his acceptance with Him. It was not obedience to law, but faith, that led to his being justified. James, on the other hand, saw the need to emphasize the good works that ought to issue from a right relationship with God. He has seen how Paul's emphasis can lead to ethical indifference and an abuse of the grace of God. Therefore, he stresses that faith must be much more than bare assent to truth. It must be a vital decision and relationship that transforms the believer's life. Otherwise, it is worth nothing and leads to nothing. Paul and James are speaking into different situations, and this can account for their decidedly different presentations. Hebrews, for its part, brings out the forward-looking character of Abraham's faith. He obeyed God when he was called, and ventured out on a pilgrimage where nothing was certain except the goal of the city of God. This is what the audience needed to hear, since it was apparently being tempted to go back into Judaism. They needed to see that the significance of Abraham was his going forward without looking back. This would help them to get their own priorities straight. This is a good illustration of the way in which early Christian teachers, like the rabbis themselves, would take the truth handed down and relate it creatively to different circumstances.[21]

Theoretically, it is possible to see differences and developments with an author's own work. Some have suggested that Paul the Apostle changed his mind on a number of topics. But it is very hard to be sure, since the epistles cannot be dated with certainty, and the evidence is fairly fragmentary. All we can confidently say is that his focus might have shifted around the time of the writing of Ephesians, for example, and that the different situations he faced would have led him to change his emphasis and approach from time to time. I think it is rash to suggest that Paul changed his mind on any important subject during his career.[22]

In summation, the Bible is obviously a wonderfully complex library. It is like a reader in theology, in which various viewpoints are presented. In it we hear an orchestra of sound, not merely a single, solo instrument. It gives us many more than one approach to the important themes it treats. This makes the Bible rich and inexhaustible. The text unfolds before our eyes and flowers like a rose in the morning sun. It draws us into the hermeneutic of the Word of God that was going on long before the canon was fixed. Now that it is closed, the same process of reflection goes on in the community in the form of exegesis, as Christians continue to weigh the significance of what they read. In this process, there is a subtle dialectic to be observed. On the one hand, we must not despise the original sense of the text, which has validity in that God gave it. We have no right just to treat it as something to trigger some ideas in our minds that then become the real authority for us. On the other hand, it would be very wrong to ignore the dynamic potential the text has to call attention to fresh applications in our situation. It can and ought to be reinterpreted again and again. There ought to be a continual dialogue between the text and the reader's situation. We cannot confine its possible significance to what has already been noted.

On one side, then, we want to avoid diminishing the dynamic of the text. The phenomena of Scripture that we have surveyed here are the enemy of a flat reading of the Bible. It is not legitimate to pull texts out of their context in the canon and harmonize their meaning all on the same level. Though we may sympathize with the desire to have texts speak beyond their immediate circumstances, we do not have the right to wrench them out of context and flatten them out so as to make every text say more or less the same thing. Luke has the right to make a point about the Spirit without having to make it in Paul's manner. Just because Paul speaks of the Spirit coming at the point of faith into a person's life, Luke should not be prevented from envisaging an infusion of power later on as well. Though it is certainly legitimate for systematic theologians to seek a coherent picture of the whole of biblical teaching on a given topic, they have to be careful not to treat texts as pieces of a flat puzzle and try to force them together, in case there is something to be learned precisely from their *not* fitting neatly. Our desire for rational, propositional truth must be placed beneath the necessity to let the text say what it wants to. Just because the text has been brought into a canon of Scripture, it does not follow that its historical orientation can be suppressed and put aside. It does not follow that the truth is equally distributed in all parts of the Bible. Leveling the text dehistorizes it and is disobedient to the text as given by God. It is wrong to snatch a text from Scripture and pay no attention to the place where it was found or to other texts that bear on the same matter. The flat-book approach to reading the Bible leads to unbalanced thinking characteristic of fundamentalism. If we just pick up on the future hope, we may leave out the truth about the possession of eternal life here and now. If we focus on justification only in the forensic sense, we may be deficient in our theology of sanctification and community. Each of the circumstantial perspectives of Scripture has a role to play in deepening our own understanding into the full-orbed fullness of the truth. The very diversity helps us to avoid becoming lopsided and unbalanced. It also teaches us to be tolerant toward other people's views, once we recognize God's Word to be many-sided and inexhaustible.

On the other side, we need to avoid exaggerating the diversity and dynamic of the Bible. For there is a strong tendency in liberal theology to stress the contradictions of the Bible and to relocate the meaning of the text in our situation. In some of the liberation theologians, for example, there is the tendency to see the situation as the authority and the text as a resource quite under our control. The Bible itself does not support the notion that it moves from false to true, from discredited earlier insights to later progressive teachings. Nor does it encourage us to look exclusively at the twists and turns in tradition history and not to notice the continuity of teaching that is being interpreted. The picture is that of a canon in which the truth unfolds gradually and dialectically and pulls us into the process of grasping the divine self-communication. In the canonical context of the final text, we find both the truth and its ongoing reinterpretation, and we are invited to pay attention to them both. The text is normative over us, but the significance of the text for us needs to be searched out. The canon lays out the area for us to reflect on, while stimulating us to seek the will of the Lord. It constitutes a normative and foundational witness to guide us in our own reflection. Without predetermining all the results of our study, it does provide an anchor and baseline for the church. Like a road map, it lays out the ground and the different ways of moving around in it. There is freedom, but not unlimited freedom. The text makes a great deal possible, indeed, more than we have yet realized. But there are limits, too. It does not make just anything possible. Despite all its variety and dynamic, the text is still sufficiently directed and focused to ensure that we not stray too far in this way or that.

The Surplus of Meaning

How can we explain the fecundity of the text as a source of instruction apart from the freedom of the Spirit? What is it about the literary nature of texts, and the Bible in particular, that lends it to this dynamic use? What are the sources of this richness?

Several features of literary texts permit this to happen. They are not like compact stones but are open and available to almost endless reflection and interpretation. First, we ought to point to the effect of placing all these biblical texts in a single canonical collection. Books like Luke, Jonah, Ecclesiastes, and Ruth, as well as countless smaller literary units, were originally penned in a situationally oriented and independent way. But they have been placed in the company of many other compositions, which now impinge upon their subject matter, and vice versa. Whereas earlier they would be read on their own, now they are read in association with other books, whose teaching is bound to be linked up to theirs. Without thinking about it, the Bible reader places what Isaiah and Jeremiah say alongside one another in his or her mind, creating a fuller effect than could have existed before. A book like Jonah is now read in relation to the total setting of the Old Testament and, even more important, in relation to Jesus and what he said about the sign of Jonah and his own resurrection. It is now impossible to read Jonah, as once one could, in isolation from the sacred collection. It has been grafted onto the canonical vine. Mark and John, Romans and Hebrews, Galatians and James come together now in this collection, and the result is a fuller picture than before. All the originally separate units are part of a combined text, and the possibilities for fresh insight flowing from them are greatly increased. This placing of diverse texts alongside one another affects all of them. Not only does it give them an audience the writers could not have imagined, it gives them a new setting that transcends the original situation. In effect, the text can now say more than it did before. A new world of meaning was opened up by this decision, and the collection was able to speak to countless different persons.

Paul Ricoeur has written about the world of the text that is created when an author commits his or her thoughts to writing. When thoughts become text, they become a world a little separate from the writer, less under the writer's control than before. Factors like gesture, intonation, and context fall away, and the text takes on some independence. We cannot always be certain what the author meant, and it is too late to ask him or her to clarify. All we can do is to operate in the world of the text and face its demands. In a sense, the text stands between author and reader. It is free, in that the writer has loosed it and let it go, and the reader has no real choice but to accept it as it comes, and not force an agenda upon it. There is a certain elusiveness in interpretation such that the reader may not presume to be in full control of the text and its meaning. Inescapably, there is a degree of uncertainty and tacitness involved with a written text. We cannot be absolutely sure what was meant and are never in a position to conclude we have drawn all the meaning out. Certainly, the text sets up certain parameters for us, but it does not make interpretation a cut-and-dried procedure. Various interpretive options always exist, forcing the reader to engage in a dialogue with the text and with God.[23]

Imagine meeting a person running down the street shouting, "Hurry! The train leaves at two!" The command and the statement are both clear, but many questions are left unanswered. Why should I hurry? What train am I supposed to be catching? What are you talking about? Interpretation has to overcome ambiguity built into speech and text events. I am not saying that we cannot be sure what the Bible teaches, for many things are quite plain and often repeated in several places. But I am saying that there is a tacit dimension to texts and that there is a freedom in interpretation that cannot be eliminated and should not be denied. This forces the reader to be prayerful and discerning in seeking out the Word of God in the Bible.

Implied in the biblical texts being situated in a canonical collection is the expectation that they will be read as a whole. Each text has internal relations with every other. The meaning is not found in the Old or New Testament alone but in them both together. Using the analogy of Scripture, we read passages alongside others and try to grasp the meaning of the whole, the Word of God in the total text. We do this in response to the biblical writers themselves finding Christ in Exodus and making connections between the different parts. The canonical context was bound to influence how each text was read. What Ezekiel said is no longer limited to what the prophet intended (something we cannot entirely recover, in any case). It can now be viewed in numerous new combinations and assume new proportions of meaning. By being placed here, it has not only a past but also a future.

The decision to incorporate texts in a single collection was itself an act of authorship. It meant that originally independent texts would be read together and take on meaning arising from the association with the other texts. The Bible as a whole constitutes the universe of discourse in which God's Word is now sought. We are compelled to look at the Bible as a whole, with all of its tensions and rich conversation. It is important, for example, that Job should exist in the collection with Deuteronomy and Proverbs, because it sounds a critical note that orthodoxy always needs to hear. It calls into question a shallow reading of God's covenant promises and forces one to go deeper. Job's friends had done a superficial reading of the covenant, and Job forces them to reconsider their interpretation. Just because it contains such a rich selection, the Bible is always forcing us to go deeper. It presents us with a rich conversation of various voices designed to challenge us and make us grow. by choosing four Gospels and not only one, the church committed us all to hermeneutical variety. It is not our business to isolate one line of interpretation or one insight among many and make it our private canon within the canon. The task of interpretation is to deal with the whole world of the text in its totality. Only this will prove fruitful for our own world and all its needs.

The Bible is rich in symbolic and metaphorical language, and this creates a second source of fecundity of meaning for us to examine. There has been a tendency for conservatives to think of Scripture as containing only one kind of language, chiefly offering bits of information and propositional truths. Of course, we know better, but this has not prevented us from a narrow orientation dictated by the polemical atmosphere. But the language of the Bible is rich in exhortations and commands, in figures of speech and typology, in poetry and parables, and in symbolism. We are required to do justice to this variety of expression in our interpretation. When Jesus says, "I am the door," and when he claims that God's kingdom is like leaven, he is making assertions that transcend the strictly literal and point us in the direction of profound understanding. There is a splendid versatility to such a mode of expression that sets up a range of possible meanings that can scarcely be exhausted. Although the general point is usually plain enough, other possibilities will always exist. What Jesus meant when he said, "The kingdom of God is in your midst [or within you]" will never be reduced to a definitive explanation that will allow us to dispense with the text. All language, but especially metaphor and symbol, contains a great deal of tacit and implied meaning, and the greatest challenge of interpretation is to try and bring it out into the open.

The Bible is full of great symbols that bear testimony to mysterious reality that cannot be completely reduced to propositions. It speaks of the Fall, the Cross, the Resurrection, the Kingdom, the Light, and so forth. To an extent, we can understand what they mean, and to a degree, the Bible itself explains them to us. But they go beyond such explanations and have the power to transform our lives at many levels. It is hard for a classical Christian to speak of biblical symbol, because of what has been done in the name of it by liberals like Paul Tillich. He had a way of deliteralizing the content of the Bible and using the evacuated concepts to hang his own Hegelian philosophy on.[24] In this way, a bad name has been given to symbol. But we cannot allow the term to be stolen from us, because the Bible is deeply symbolic. It is full of rich pictures: of exodus, of exile, of a descending dove, of a slain lamb, of a thundering mountain, of a wedding feast. The same goes for the great themes of the Bible, like kingdom, new birth, creation, heaven, bread of life. This kind of speech is uniquely able to draw us into itself and to have a transforming effect upon us. And it opens up to us realms of awareness not easily made accessible by discursive speech. Its meaning cannot easily be nailed down, and its value is more one of putting us in touch with truth that cannot be captured easily and of giving rise to thought and reflection. In this way symbols contribute to revelation in the Bible by working on us in a dynamic way. Like the Lord's Supper, they are able to point in so many directions and touch such depths of the personality that they are simply inexhaustible.

Conservatives are certainly right to insist that the core content of the symbols that the Bible provides be kept as the parameters for their possible use. The truth and content of revelation must not be imperiled. In the name of symbol, one can easily float off into realms of feeling and speculation and lose the truth God is communicating to us. The cross, for example, is a symbol whose meaning cannot be exhausted, but it is also the subject of much plain biblical teaching that informs the use of it as symbol. This teaching does not close off deeper participation in the symbol but anchors it in the system of truth given in the gospel. The propositions cannot substitute for the symbol, but neither can the symbol float free of the content given in the Scriptures. Dulles is on target when he says: "Christian doctrine sets necessary limits to the kinds of significance that can be found in the Christian symbols. Without doctrines we could hardly find in the cross of Christ the manifestation of divine grace and redemption."[25] Thus, the symbols not only give rise to thought in us, they also give guidelines that ought to shape the thoughts we have in response to them. Speaking of symbols in the Bible, then, does not rob the images of their clarity of content. Rather, it opens up to us the holistic realm of truth that transcends the merely propositional.

In the same manner, speaking of the symbol of exodus does not mean to deny the factual nature of the deliverance of Israel from Egypt. If this did not happen, we have no right to use the symbol, at least according to biblical thinking. The wider meaning of exodus, such as the new exodus of the gospel, or the release of modern peoples from slavery, rests upon the proven fact of God's ability to deliver. These mighty acts of God are both facts and symbols—they made a difference to an actual historical experience, and they continue to have impact upon our lives in pointing to ongoing divine activity of delivering. We must utterly reject the notion that symbolic events cannot have both factual and theological significance. It is very clear that Luke, for instance, thought he was writing both history and theology at the same time.[26] As Paul said, had the resurrection not happened, it could not serve us as a symbol for faith to grasp (1 Cor 15:14, 17).

A third instance of this depth of truth we can point to is the fullness of meaning that a text can have as a piece of literature. Like a musical score or a painting, the biblical text is available for fresh interpretation without end. As a text, it occupies a position between writer and reader and has a life of its own. That is not to say the text is autonomous and can mean anything at all, subject to the whims of the readers. For it is still anchored in the original situation and still bears the content intended by the writer. To know what a text means, we have to consult the text, not merely the feelings or thoughts it evokes in us.[27] The meaning resides in the words of the text, not in our imagination. Nevertheless, granting these solid parameters of meaning the text lays down, it is still true that, like a symphony or a sketch, the text cannot be exhausted and can always be seen in new and challenging ways as the angle of vision alters and the Spirit speaks. Christians find more in Genesis 12:3 than Jews do, because they relate the promise to Jesus Christ and its opening up to the Gentiles according to Paul. A text can be seen to possess more significance later than was noticed or even intended at first. As God's purpose becomes clearer, we can go back and see more clearly what God was getting at back in the earlier situation. Raymond Brown defines this fuller sense as "that additional, deeper meaning, intended by God but not clearly intended by the human author, which is seen to exist in the words of a biblical text when they are studied in the light of further revelation or development in the understanding of revelation."[28] In a seed lies the potential of a tree that will develop out of it. At first we cannot see the potential, but after the tree has grown we understand the seed better. In the light of the redemption that is in Christ Jesus, we can see in Genesis 2–3 a foreshadowing of the whole history of salvation. From the seed of the woman has come a Savior to destroy the Satanic serpent. But this is much clearer to us now than it was to the author of the passage in Genesis. Indeed, much of the Old Testament is opened to us by the fulfillment of it in Christ. The text can take on deeper meaning when we become more informed of the purpose of God in the world.[29] Language possesses a dynamic fullness that permits an excess of meaning to emerge over time. Like works of art, literary texts open up a field of interpretive possibilities and allow for ongoing reflection and discovery. Authors are responsible for the words they record, but they cannot exclude, even if they wanted to, the fullness of which I speak. After it is written, the text is not the writer's to control altogether. There is always much more for the reader to find and enjoy than the author might have thought of.[30] As Tracy points out, the Bible is the church's religious classic and has unlimited power to impinge the Word of God upon us.[31]

Strange as it may seem precritical exegesis was far more likely to grasp the rich fullness of the Bible's message than is the technology of modern scholarship. For centuries Jewish and Christian communities have poured over these texts and listened to them in all sorts of ways not approved of by the academic guild today, and as a result, they experienced the truth of the Bible in ways closed to the secular reader. The "archaeology" of the text that modern scholarship attempts to do with some success is only the beginning of the work of grasping the sense of the Bible. Until we see it as a literary whole, as willed by one Author, we are not likely to get very far or very deep. Our modern exegesis is so "scientific" that it is impoverished. It discourages readers from putting themselves in the text and therefore misses at least half the point. If it has gained something in focusing more precisely on the original meaning, it has also lost a good deal in closing off other approaches to the text that are also fruitful.

David Steinmetz has shown that precritical exegesis, though it cared about the original meaning a text had in its own situation, also granted the legitimacy of implied meanings that became visible when different questions were posed to it.[32] As Origen noted long ago, a biblical story may have both a historical sense and some spiritual meaning. Do we not all recognize in the wilderness wanderings of Israel both of these dimensions? Do we not see in the sacrifices of Leviticus both the offerings themselves and the vision of Calvary? Are there not patterns in the history of the Old Testament that foreshadow the ministry of Jesus and the experience of the church? Can we not see in the indignation of the psalmist about Babylon a way to apply his words to the atrocities of communism? It is not a question of giving free rein to the imagination and breaking the link of the text with history. The literal sense does control what can be done with the text. But it does not close off the real possibility of spiritual and theological meanings that go beyond what the writer originally intended. Thus, the songs of David can be my Christian songs as well.

The point is this: The texts of the Bible have a definite meaning in the historical situation in which they were written, and that meaning is the touchstone and anchor of all the interpretations that may legitimately be made of it. But their total meaning is not restricted to what can be discovered in a scholarly way about the original thrust. Texts can carry implied meanings also, and these may be picked up by later readers in different settings. A text cannot just mean anything we want it to, but it does open up a field of possible meanings, not only one. The idea that a text has only one meaning is a modern "scientific" prejudice that does not correspond either to the Bible's own view of itself or to Christian experience of using Scripture. For an interpretation to be valid, it must fall within the range of possible meanings that the text itself creates, whether or not they were all the intention of the writer. Having said that, the meanings of the text are obviously multiple and not single.

We ought to hold to a middle way. A text consists of both letter and spirit. Because we respect the text, we grant it the right to lay down the parameters of its own meaning. And because we are open to such other meaning as may be implied in it and intended by God, we listen for the rich and fuller meaning it can open up for us. The text sets forth a field of possible meanings, and we are free to seek the Word of the Lord within this abundant set of options.

Some Conclusions

Quite evidently, there is a lot of room for the Spirit to use the text of Scripture in dynamic ways in the church and in the Christian life. It is not a collection of timeless oracles given all at one time, like the Koran, but a developing and dialectical text on which endless reflection can be made. One thing we may conclude from this is the dynamic character of the divine pedagogy. Why did God give us his truth in such a manner? After all, a flat text is easier to grasp, and the Bible turns out to be open to misinterpretation on account of its complex character. What advantages does this mode of disclosure afford?

The only conclusion we can draw is that God must want to force us to think as mature people. Socrates presented the truth in dialogue and probing questions to help his disciples to think more profoundly themselves. He wanted to convey, not only information, but the skills of learning that would be usable throughout their lives to grow into mature understanding.[33] The Bible in the form it comes to us is the kind of teacher that draws us into the process of learning and helps us learn to think theologically and ethically ourselves in new situations. God seems to have made a decision to instruct us in this way in order to bring us to greater maturity. As Paul said to the Galatians, God did not want them to remain immature children and slaves ordered around by law. Rather, God's will was that they operate in Christian freedom and learn to respond to the Spirit (chaps. 4–5). True, there is a risk in giving us so much liberty, and disasters occur, partly because of it. Sin itself came into the world because human beings were created with finite freedom. But the same risk in freedom can be productive of the kind of maturity God has as a goal for our lives. Hence, the Bible has the shape it does.[34]

It is not my position that the diversity and the dialectic arose merely from the experience of the people of God over time. If that is all it is, then the Bible would deserve very little respect as our teacher. I see this dynamic process as divinely willed, not fortuitous. I see it as the divine pedagogy, giving us both form and freedom, liberty and law. I see the Bible as God's tether, which keeps us connected to the center and gives us abundant room to explore and roam. God gave his truth to humanity gradually and dynamically in order to lead us to maturity, from the stage of drinking milk to eating meat. The rich diet is suited both to nourishing babes in Christ and to satisfying the maturer appetite.

A second conclusion that should be drawn relates to our interpretation of the Bible. Because it is a complex and developmental text, we have to take this dynamic into account and cannot just interpret the text as if it were flat. We have to take into account the kind of text it is and pay attention to diversity and dialogue in it. But this is what orthodoxy tends not to want to do. Because we believe the text is inspired by God, we tend to suppose it must be flat and immutable that each text stands on the same level as every other text and speaks with the same absolute authority of God. However sound this deduction may seem to be, it is not the view the Bible itself invites us to take, as we have seen. It may be characteristic of the Judaic Scripture principle, but it is not true of the Christian principle. The Pharisees may have seen Scripture as a set of timeless oracles, but Jesus certainly did not.

What is called for is a dynamic reading of the Bible that takes account of the features we have noted and incorporates them into our interpretation of the Bible. It will mean that the interpretive task will be more like climbing a large mountain than exploring a vast plain. The mountain has valleys and cliffs, meadows and rocky slides, and can always be climbed from a different side and angle. It always stands there inviting us to climb it, and never ceases to challenge. It is not right to read the Bible in a flat, static way; it will only lead to false dogmatism and unsound conclusions. Because of the inner dynamics in the text, it follows that we must have regard for the canonical wholeness and balance of the Bible and be in agreement with the inner harmony and movement of the total witness. God's Word is most likely to be heard when we take the historical context of texts seriously and when we heed the inner canonical dialogue. We are likely to miss it when we pick out isolated texts without regard for their setting and look at them all as of equal significance, to be harmonized into some rational system of our own making.

Some of our disagreements over interpretation arise from a flat-book approach to the Bible that ignores historical contexts and regards every verse as equally binding upon Christians. Although it is sometimes called literal interpretation, it is a way of twisting the Bible God actually gave us and making it do our pleasure.

A third conclusion also relates to interpretation. In this case, it is to rule out a pseudoscientific approach to the text, whether liberal or conservative. The evidence of dynamic features in the Bible means that the sense of Scripture is richer and broader than what can be proven by means of scholarly techniques. There is a place for Spirit-led interpretation that makes use of the inexhaustible possibilities of the text. On account of symbol, dialectic, and the fullness of language, there is always more to discover in the Bible than has yet been found. The writer may have had a single objective meaning, but the text often leaves open more than one, and when it comes to applying the text in its significance for us today, the range is rich indeed. And the truth for us today may well be better seen, as Jesus said, by children than by the wise of this world.

Finally, the textual dynamic ought to humble us hermeneutically. It is not so easy to grasp precisely what the Bible is getting at on every occasion. We cannot so readily dismiss other opinions than our own, as we sometimes do. It is hard to be certain one has got the perspective just right, so as to be able to say confidently this other reading is false and perhaps even badly intended. We will have to listen to the Lutherans, the Catholics, the Arminians, and the Pentecostals with more of an open mind than is customary. We will have to grant that the Bible gives license to a fair degree of hermeneutical pluralism. People do believe and act differently on the basis of the same Book. Not that we shall have to become theological relativists. A position will still have to be shown to be scriptural in the public arena and not just in front of friends and admirers. But we will have to admit that interpretations are not as clear as we used to think and that an open mind is appropriate when it comes to considering the merits of hermeneutical proposals.

Is God not teaching us through this that it is more important to be fully convinced in one's own mind and to love one another, and that he is not concerned that we all talk and look alike? The Bible as our authority also gives us much liberty to think and decide about things. This calls for toleration and biblical pluralism, as we seek to grow into the unity of faith and the stature of Christ.

CHAPTER 9

The Act of Interpretation

At long last we come to the goal of the matter. How can readers engage the text so that they can have God speak to them through it? An answer needs to be given to the one who asked: "How can I understand unless someone guides me?" (Acts 8:31). How can we become "workmen needing not to be ashamed, rightly dividing the Word of truth?" (2 Tim. 2:15). There are few questions more crucial to the life, mission, and theology of the church than this one. We need to know God's promises if we are going to be able to intelligently trust him. We need to learn God's commandments if we are to rightly obey him. We need to become acquainted with God's nature if we are to acceptably worship and praise him. It cannot be assumed that just because people revere the Bible they will know how to use the Bible effectively. It may be the reverence of nostalgia, which has no practical effect upon them. Somehow we must gain the skills that will open the way for Scripture to influence our lives profoundly. The goal is "to bring about an active and meaningful engagement between the interpreter and the text, in such a way that the interpreter's own horizon is reshaped and enlarged."[1] It is crucial, too, on the broadest scale, since almost all our theological and ethical differences stem from hermeneutical decisions ultimately and will need to resolved finally with reference to the Bible text.

The basic key to the art of interpretation is at hand in what I have presented in the book up to now. There are two sides to hermeneutics. First, we listen to the text as God's Word in human language given to us, and second, we open ourselves to God's Spirit to reveal the particular significance the text has for the present situation. Interpretation involves a bipolar ellipse, and moves back and forth between the historical meaning of the Bible and our standing before God. It therefore involves fidelity to the text and creativity in the context. The first provides the objective content and control, and the second opens us up to God's leading and direction. Thus, the interpreter is not autonomous but subject to the text, and avoids frozen legalism by being open to God's Spirit. In this way errors of the left and the right can be avoided.

My hermeneutical proposal is that we hear the Word of God in the interaction between the Word and the Spirit, not through Scripture alone and not by means of meditation alone. This makes interpretation an art rather than a science or technique. It is a skill that has to be acquired by a combination of study and prayer. It cannot be reduced to a set of rules.[2]

Points of Clarification

First, can it be so simple? After all, books about hermeneutics, like books about epistemology, are among the most difficult to understand! But yes, I believe it is quite simple in essence. How else could God's Word make wise the simple? How could ordinary believers search the Scriptures to see if things are so, if the art of interpretation were not within their grasp? Of course, I would grant that, although the basic operation is simple, issues can come up that are not as easy. For example, in particular cases a person may be struggling to understand a given text or concept that is giving difficulty, so that help may be required. Or, because of our culture and traditions, aspects of the message may pose serious problems for us and need special attention. Or, scholars like Gadamer may get into analyzing the condition of interpretation, just as they get into analyzing the act of knowing, and unquestionably this thinking about thinking is the hardest thinking to understand. But still the heart of the matter is not complicated. We interpret the Bible effectively when we attend to the text in a spirit of openness to God.

Second, what I am presenting can for the purposes of exposition be discussed in the form of a two-step operation. But in reality it is a single act that has two dimensions rather than two separate steps. Two things go on at the same time in interpretation. We do the reading, and God gives the understanding. We attend to God's Word, and the Spirit gives us discernment as to its significance. It is not as if the Spirit only comes into play on the second step.

Third, scholars, in writing about interpretation, often refer to the two horizons, that of text and reader. This is an important observation; however, it can tend to be secular in orientation, as if there were no difference whether it is the Bible or Plato under discussion. Well, there is a difference. We are speaking about an inspired text and a Spirit-filled reader, not about just any old text and reader. Because we believe in both inspiration and illumination, in contrast to Heidegger and probably Gadamer as well, we are in a mood to expect the living God to honor his Word and cause it to live in our experience. I have no reason to expect the Bible to come alive and prove intelligible where the reader has not been converted and received the Spirit (1 Cor. 2:14).

Fourth, there is an urgency in my proposal. Great damage can result from neglecting either of the two sides of the interpretive act. Valid interpretation in the Christian sense must come as a result of fidelity to the text and openness to the Spirit. Were we to neglect fidelity to the Word and choose the Spirit over the letter, subjectivity would go wild, and all manner of heresies would follow. Were we to neglect openness to the Spirit and choose the text over the Spirit, legalism would confront us, and the truth of God would come under human control. Knowing God's Word would become a mental exercise and nothing more. The text would be locked in the vaults of the past and hindered from breaking loose and addressing our situation.

Fifth, we might ask which error would be the more serious: the liberal rebellion against submitting to the dictates of the text, owing to the liberal's own undeniable modernity, or orthodox legalism, in which the mint and the cumin are tithed and the real meaning of the text is passed over? Both errors are strongly denounced in Holy Scripture. Those who twist the text and transform the gospel into a form that suits their own liking are condemned (2 Tim. 4:3–4; 2 Pet. 3:16). But there are no stronger denunciations than those Jesus hurled against the legalists he ran into (Matt. 23:1–36). The wise course must be for us to attend to the error we ourselves may be guilty of and correct that, hoping others will do the same. For it is not right to point out the beam in our brother's eye when there is a speck in our own.

The key to hermeneutics is to recognize that God has given us the Bible, his written Word, and enables it to function by giving the Spirit, who brings a comprehension of its truth and a certainty of its divine origin. As Erickson puts it, "The objective Word, the written Scripture, together with the subjective word, the inner illumination and conviction of the Holy Spirit, constitutes authority for the Christian."[3] Not the text by itself, as in Fundamentalism, or the Spirit alone, as in charismatic excesses, but in the fruitful combination of the two. The written Word, correctly interpreted, and the illuminating work of the Spirit—these are the objective and the subjective base in the pattern of Christian authority.

The purpose of revelation is encounter and communication involving two parties. A divine giving and a human receiving are both involved. Even God cannot complete his revelation of the gospel: there must be a human response to his initiative. But because of human estrangement, revelation must include a liberation of our cognitive abilities so that we will perceive God's majesty and grasp his will. The "Word" stands for the giving of revelation, and the "Spirit" represents the possibility of hearing the Word. The Spirit opens our hearts and minds to receive the things freely given to us by God. Objectivistic and subjectivistic approaches are both wrong. The duality of Word and Spirit must be preserved.

But we do not have two sources of information here, the Word and the Spirit. It is not as if we can explore the truth of the Spirit apart from and beyond the content of the Word—or take the Spirit for granted, as if he were always present in the text. There is a bi-unity or perfect complementarity in the working of the two. The Word supplies the message of God, while the Spirit inclines us to attend to its truth, so that the Word can become effective and relevant in ourselves.[4]

True, it has not been easy to make this point clear. There has been a tendency either to take the Spirit for granted and think of the Word as working automatically, or else to separate the Spirit from the Word and see it as an independent medium of the Word. The secret is to interpret the Spirit's work as primarily referential, as witnessing to Jesus Christ and opening our hearts to the gospel. It is an inner work in us that brings about the personal recognition and appropriation of the truth for ourselves in our situation.

New Testament Hermeneutics

Abundant confirmation of this two-sided model for interpretation is provided by the New Testament itself. On the one hand, it cares very much about the text God gave, and on the other hand, it is able to locate fresh significance in it. Now I grant that we cannot imitate New Testament exegetical methods in every respect. First, these writers stood upon a revelational plateau and could take liberties with the Old Testament because of their privileged position. We would do well to be much more cautious. Second, the New Testament employs rabbinic styles of exegesis that we need not copy. For example, the Jews would comment upon texts in a midrashic manner, embroidering and elaborating upon what was written. But even taking these two points into account, it is important not to miss the conviction that underlies New

Testament interpretation. There was a vital sense of the Spirit using the text in dynamic ways to guide and instruct us. These writers believed fervently that the Word of God could speak to people in whatever contexts they found themselves in. The Word and the Spirit, the text and the situation, exist in a dialectical relationship, which means that God can speak to us in every new situation.

We can see this both in the New Testament's use of the Old Testament and in the New Testament's use of its own traditions. In regard to the use of the Old Testament, it is obvious that the text gets adapted to the New Testament message and interpreted in a Christian way. Paul can detect in the fading glory of Moses' face an analogy to the relation between the old and the new covenants (2 Corinthians 3). The rock that Moses struck in the wilderness is a type of Jesus Christ (1 Corinthians 10). The "seed" of Abraham in the ancient promise is none other than Christ (Gal. 3:16). The New Testament does not go to the text just to learn premessianic foundations but to discuss Christian themes in relation to the text. God had done something wonderful and new in Christ, and the Old Testament can now be read in the light of it. A subtler example of this adaptation would be the use of different text-types and translations to bring out the very point required by Christian teaching. In Romans 1:17, Paul is not very concerned with what Habakkuk may have meant but is very interested in the meaning the words now can have because of the gospel. The same would be true in his use of Psalm 68 in Ephesians 4 and Deuteronomy 31 in Romans 10. And what can we say about Matthew 2:23, which quotes a text that does not seem to exist? We have to face the fact that the text often is not cited because of its original meaning, but because in one form or another it may express what the New Testament writer wishes to say.[5]

Extraordinarily, conservative writers like Warfield tend to pass by the evidence of adaptation and refuse to see its relevance to the doctrine of Scripture. As a result, they give us a rather legalistic view of authority, not unlike the one Jesus encountered in his Jewish opponents. There is a tendency to generalize on divine inspiration and neglect the other side of the coin, the divine illumination. The belief that the Spirit is active alongside the text, helping us to see its significance for us even though it was not originally written to us, is an important part of the New Testament doctrine of Scripture. The text was seen to be a dynamic text capable of saying fresh things to Spirit-filled readers. When Luke repeatedly referred to the text as something the Spirit was saying, he did not have in mind only an inspiration of the past but also a continuing breath that enables the text to speak prophetically to the

Christian community (Acts 1:16; 4:25; 28:25).[6] The text was not viewed as a frozen document that could theoretically be exhausted, but as a flexible utterance that could meet the needs of every changing circumstance. I see no other way to comprehend the neglect of this factor in conservative theology except in reference to the polemical situation. We worry that if we were to recognize it we might be vulnerable to Scripture twisting in the name of dynamic interpretation. This is a real danger, but it cannot be grounds for denying part of the evidence of what the Bible claims.

In regard to the New Testament's use of its own traditions, we find the same conviction that the truth is dynamic and able to be adapted to changing circumstances. It is of particular importance in that it is not a question of different levels of revelation, as in the relationship of Old to New Testament. The flexibility cannot be entirely due to a dispensational change, but must be principial. The dynamic we noted within the Old Testament can be found within the New Testament as well, and it tells us something important about how revelation through texts works.

All one has to do to grasp this is consider the way Jesus' deeds and words are used by the different Gospel writers—how they are ordered and reordered, phrased and rephrased, how they are expressed so as to bring out the needed emphasis in the evangelist's community. A text like the one on divorce, for example, can be made to function differently in Mark than in Matthew. In Matthew, the famous "except" clause is added in order to interpret Jesus' meaning to a Jewish Christian audience (19:9). And the words about clean and unclean foods that come out so strongly in Mark 7:14–23 are toned down considerably by Matthew (15:10–20). The Markan parenthesis ("Thus he declared all foods clean" [7:19]) is dropped out entirely. The Gospel writers could not have been legalists about the logia of Jesus when they made adaptations like these. We are forced to ask whether it is right and proper to appeal to these texts legalistically now, if indeed the Spirit is wanting to help us determine their significance in our situation. It would seem as if we ought to be very sensitive to the original contexts of the verses and then ask prayerfully what the Lord might be saying to us now. It would be difficult to be hard-nosed on such questions as divorce and remarriage today if we did so.

In the same way, Saint Paul was no legalist. His stated policy was to be all things to all men (1 Cor. 9:19–23). The truth of the gospel could be adapted to all manner of persons and was not an inflexible mass. He could take the truth and work it into different contexts. It was not a case of opportunism, but of a proper flexibility of approach and elasticity of attitude, that made this strategy possible.[7] The truth is not so inflexible that it cannot be resituated again and again. I think this is how we ought to view the difference between Paul and James on the doctrine of justification. It is not a matter of one being right and the other wrong. It is a case of the truth of justification having to be put one way in one context and another way in another. The different formulations were required precisely to maintain the truth. The same word had to be put differently if it was to have the proper impact on the different audiences. Legalistic concern for the letter can be a way to suppress, not maintain, the burning relevance of the truth.

We are required to be liberal and conservative at the same time—liberal in the sense that we are eager to discern the ever-fresh application the Bible may have in the ever-changing situations of life, but conservative in the sense that we respect the text of Scripture as God's written Word. We must be the sort of liberal who respects the infallibility of the Bible, and the sort of conservative who seeks the direction of the Spirit and is not a legalist. The place this would make quite a difference would be in the behavioral area, no doubt. What would it mean today to heed Peter's word about jewelry and Paul's word about the veil? Surely the particulars in these directions are culture-relative and invite faithful flexibility in considering what they mean for today. It might even help us with a text like 1 Timothy 2:12, where Paul seems to forbid a teaching role for female believers. Susan Foh has noted that, apart from this single verse, the opposition to female elders and teachers cannot be biblically proven.[8] So if we weigh the situational factors that may have influenced Paul's negative tone in this passage, view it in the light of his own (and Jesus') practice of working along with women in the Christian ministry, and remember what he said about their standing in Christ and their being gifted along with men by the Spirit, this text really is unable to silence the concern in our day to give recognition to female ministries and to base it in the New Testament itself. It would seem that we have become hung up on this issue because of a tendency to handle the text legalistically, not dynamically as Scripture itself would encourage. How many other issues might be eased were we to stop resisting biblical, as distinct from merely traditional, hermeneutics?

Submission to the Text

Let us step back now and take a closer look at the two sides of biblical hermeneutics. The requirement emphasized by conservative theologians is the obligation to submit ourselves to the demands of the text. If theology has an obligation to be faithful and creative, then this is the fidelity side.

The basis for our submission to the text is the doctrine of Scripture I have already expounded. God gave the text to us as his written Word, and we care about what God says in and through it. This is the most important piece of preunderstanding with which to approach the text. We come to the Bible believing it to be God's Word in human language and are disposed to submit ourselves to its ministries of teaching, exhorting, and shaping us. If it were only a fallible human document, we would feel free to twist, discard, demythologize, decry, or reject part or all of it. But our belief in the inspiration of Scripture leads us to submit our prejudices to its authority rather than subject Scripture to our biases. God gave the text in all its objectivity and distance, and we care deeply about what it says. If this is what God said to those ancient people, we want to understand what it was. We want to determine, if we can, what the writers were saying in the Bible. The primary task must be to understand what is being said there. What did the writer intend the readers to understand? What was God's Word to them? This question needs to be answered before we inquire about its significance for us. To believe in biblical inspiration means to care about what God said to his people in past historical situations so that we might consider what his Word to us is. In our interest in knowing the contemporary significance, the past meaning must not be covered up and confused. We must now allow a "fusion of horizons" to distort what the Bible is saying and turn it into an instrument of manipulation.[9] Let the text be heard in the exact shade of its sense and meaning as it was first given and not be overwhelmed by the centuries of later interpretation. Let the text be understood faithfully before it is applied creatively. How else can it stand over the church as its norm and judge? Seek ye first the original meaning, and all these relevant applications will be added unto you!

In saying this, we declare ourselves in opposition to trends in interpretation that would subjectify the operation and make the text practically autonomous. This would have the effect of rendering its meaning indeterminate and of nullifying the truth claims made in the text. There would be no way left to decide between competing interpretations, leaving the reader in control again. Scripture would be subject to the reader's whims and desires. We must hold to the primacy of the intended sense of the biblical texts. Writers have been stimulated by the Spirit to communicate with us through literature, making it possible for us to receive communication from them. They have encoded a message in the text, and we read it in order to receive the word. We read the Bible to construe the text, with a view to grasping its intended sense. Because of the variable claims Scripture makes for its teaching, we are on a ceaseless quest for the meaning of the message of the text.

Similarly, we oppose arbitrary presuppositions that would slot the intended meaning of the text into limited channels such as symbolic or existential significance. Granted, there is much in the Bible that addresses the life of the subject and raises issues of ultimate concern for him or her. But there is also much that relates to the way things are in the world and in the kingdom of God that we ought to heed. As Packer has noted, before the nineteenth century there was no significant Christian thinker who questioned the right of the Bible to instruct us in historical and doctrinal matters or who declared a moratorium on the truth content of the text in any significant way. It was taken for granted that Scripture was given to teach us in matters of faith and practice, that the categories and arguments employed to tell us about Christ and salvation were God-given and of abiding validity. But in recent times, a basic shift has occurred in which, instead of seeking the divine message in the Bible, people read it as if it were a merely human religious document, opening up for us the dynamics of experience but not delivering to us the message and truth of God. In this way we open ourselves to the personalities of ancient writers but not to the beliefs they set forth. This leaves us in complete control of the content of the gospel and its applications in the world. The only proper way to read the Bible is to seek to learn its truth and to incorporate it into our lives. We have no right to ignore or twist or deny its contents.[10]

If indeed it is crucial to ferret out the meaning of the biblical text, something should be said about the great challenge this presents. We will need to heed Paul's word to Timothy: "Study to show yourself approved unto God, a workman who does not need to be ashamed, rightly dividing the Word of truth" (2 Tim. 2:15). It will take everything we have by way of scholarly ability to arrive at the knowledge of what is given in the text.

In ordinary life, the work of understanding goes on all the time, without a great deal of consternation and confusion. When a person addresses us, we usually do not need to think about how we understand him or her or to consult a set of hermeneutical rules. Our understanding is spontaneous, and comes from belonging to a shared culture and language. But when it comes to the Bible, an ancient book from another culture, complications set in. There are blocks to our understanding thrown up by the Bible's strangeness. Even when we feel comfortable in our interpretation, we can be quite mistaken about it. So we are forced to think about how understanding occurs. There are obstacles that have to be overcome. We do not find ourselves in the same historical situation as the biblical writers. We view what is written from our perspective. The languages of the Bible are foreign to us both in vocabulary and expression. There are differences in worldviews that pose difficulties. It is because of such things that hermeneutics, the science of understanding, becomes important.

In a general sense, we have never been in a better position to recover what the Bible means than we are today. Though they pose some difficulties (as noted in Chapter 6), the biblical critics also provide tools and techniques that are exceedingly helpful in helping us to root out the original sense. We have at our disposal an imposing array of interpretative resources designed to help us overcome the obstacles to understanding. No set of exegetes has ever possessed as fine a set of tools as we possess in terms of textual studies, lexicography, linguistics, and social, cultural, and literary history. Even though we are more aware than before of the problem of historical consciousness, we are also heirs to the means of overcoming such difficulties. They can help us hear the Bible speak on its own terms and exercise its authority over us. Readers with their biases come and go, but the text stands from generation to generation. Serious interpretation must let the text speak and call the reader into the service of God. Our goal is that the Bible be able to challenge the ideologies brought to it and bring about true conversion.

Marshall calls attention to 1 Corinthians 16:22 as an example. "If any man love not the Lord, let him be anathema. Maran atha." The text had to be partially translated in the first place for the English reader. The word *anathema* is familiar to us because it is a Greek word used in English to mean "accursed." As for the Aramaic phrase *"maran atha,"* we have to learn that it means "our Lord is coming" or something close to that. We have to ask if it is a declaration of his coming or a hope expressed for it to happen soon. In seeking to understand the meaning of this text, we are involved in some scholarly reflections that can assist us to get inside the text. We are forced by the text into linguistic and historical considerations.[11] What this helps to ensure is that the text will be respected in its historical distance from us, and be protected from having our ideas read back into it. This is why our study of the Bible must include a careful investigation of its nature and contexts in the ancient world. Divine revelation is historical in nature, and that means that we must take account of all the factors that bear upon understanding it.

We have to learn to listen from within the text in such a way that *it* generates the meaning and *we* do the listening. This will mean attending to text carefully and becoming aware of the literary forms being used and the images being employed. And we will need to go behind the text, too, and consider the context that cradled the message. We will be concerned to discover the function of a text in the broader canon as well as within its own setting, and to become informed about the specific historical setting in which the text was written. It will be important to learn of any religious, cultural, economic, and political factors that might have played a significant role in the creation of the text.[12]

Granted, we do not want to deliver the church into a papacy of biblical scholars. Certainly the ordinary reader is capable of grasping the things necessary to salvation without the help of a professional. At the same time, however, biblical scholarship is one of the gifts of God to the church to help us all grow in grace and in the knowledge of God. The scholars have a useful role to play in helping the rest of us overcome the difficulties of interpretation and in making us better stewards of the Word of God. Without them, we cannot know the exact meaning of the text as it comes out in the Hebrew or the Greek. They can assist us to catch the exact shade of meaning intended by the biblical writers. At stake here is whether we communicate our own ideas cloaked in biblical phraseology, or really deliver what Scripture says.[13]

Interpretive Biases

But how can one get back to the original thrust of the text when contemporary beliefs and presuppositions seem to block the way and distort all our interpretations? How can the text assume such a determining role over us, given our own place in history? How practical is it to maintain that the Bible ought to exercise decisive influence over us, when distorting assumptions are impossible to remove?

One thing is certain: naive realism is out of the question. We cannot fail to pay some attention to the fact that Bible readers, including ourselves, encounter the text burdened by all manner of presuppositions. We come to the Bible with a twentieth-century orientation, with convictions about politics, philosophy, theology, and history. What we hear from the text, and what we decide to do about its message, is heavily influenced by the baggage we carry with us. We cannot claim that our interpretation will be purely objective and without any presuppositions at all. The reader as a neutral observer of biblical data is a myth. There is no such person. Modern consciousness is deeply convinced that we understand everything in relation to what we already know and believe. It is obvious, at least in the case of other people, that interpretation is strongly affected by the historical context. How else could so many German Christians have consented to what Hitler did to the Jews? The temptation is always there to want to use the Scriptures for our own purposes rather than to let it be a norm for our own beliefs and behavior. If we are honest, we will have to admit that this is also the case with our own interpretation. Our own historical horizon colors what we see in the Bible. We do not live in a vacuum—we cannot jump out of our own skins.

Should we give up trying to be fair, then? Shall we stop even trying to recover the meaning the Bible originally had? Of course not. What is needed is critical, instead of naive, realism. We have to take account of the bias factor when we go about hermeneutics. This does not make us skeptics, thinking that we are trapped in the present and unable to know what the text is saying. It simply requires that we be very careful and self-critical in our work of interpretation. Getting at the original meaning is harder than we used to think, and it calls for greater effort. We have to work at transcending our historical situation and struggle to hear the Word of God in the text. No one is saying it is useless to understand what Paul was teaching, for example, only that it is harder than we used to suppose and requires a lot more effort. But the goal is the same. We want to know what the Bible is saying and to subject ourselves to it. If we were satisfied with the contemporary context, we would not need to consult the Bible in the first place. The key to success in this endeavor is to see the work of interpretation as a spiral motion. We do not reach the goal of the original sense all at once in a single move, but through repeated approaches and by spiraling in on the target.

The whole point of the doctrine of inspiration is that the text of the Bible rule over, rather than be ruled by, the assumptions of the reader. It is our rule and norm, not the reverse. The text was given precisely to prevent us from following the devices and desires of our own minds and to put us in touch with the mind of God in matters of faith and practice. Therefore, we must handle this problem of assumption and bias with care and respect. It must not be allowed to be a screen for Scripture twisting and denial.

It should be noted at the outset that not all assumptions are negative and prevent good exegesis. Some of them can help us identify with what the text is saying and sensitize us to it. As Tillich pointed out, the situation contributes to theology by setting a useful correlation between the Word of God and the hearers of the Word. The encounter of the church with revelation takes place in a particular historical situation, and God's Word becomes effective in yet new ways. Of course the biblical message sets the norm, but the historical situation is the medium in which it is interpreted and is seen to be relevant. True, the message judges the fallen, distorted character of that medium, but it is only in this medium that the norm becomes effective.[14] Thus, for example, the awful fact of the Holocaust caused Christians to examine afresh the place of Israel in the economy of God according to the New Testament. Modern science has forced us to consider much more carefully what we believe in relation to creation as it touches upon beginnings. Social developments in the West are requiring a closer consideration of what the Bible says about gender roles. Calvin's belief that social structures could be changed helped him to be able to see the "Christ, transformer of culture," theme in the Bible in a new way. The Pentecostals have helped us to see what Luke was getting at, whereas the Catholics help us understand passages oriented to the church as institution. The more international the church becomes in the coming years, the more we will have to read the Bible with new questions in mind and the more we will discover there to instruct us. Modern assumptions send us back to the text with all sorts of questions and put us in a position to grow in our understanding.

A problem arises when these assumptions find themselves opposed by Scripture, when there is a collision between the authority of the text and the authority of contemporary opinion. When that happens, according to the doctrine of Scripture being developed here, Scripture must rule and the assumption be deemed negative.

Some of these negative assumptions are innocent and unwitting. They are not deliberately held. There is no intention to deny Scripture. They are part of the theological and cultural baggage we bring to the text. But it is not our intention to suppress the text by means of them. We may hold strong political views and resist some of things the Bible says, or we may hold strong denominational commitments that make us uneasy with certain biblical passages. A Latin American pastor may be surprised and shocked by what he finds a Russian pastor believes on the basis of the Bible. The church has not yet come to the unity of faith in the Son of God and has a lot of growing together to do. But ordinarily these disagreements do not arise from any intention to deny Scripture. They are honestly held differences of opinion and occur in a context of utter respect for God and his Word. They are benign spiritually and morally and are corrigible in principle. Some, perhaps all of them, can be removed under conditions of mutual study and prayer.

The really serious problems we face today are from the negative assumptions deliberately held, self-consciously in opposition to Scripture. Since the rise of religious liberalism, it has been quite common to find people holding to certain presuppositions that they will not permit Scripture to correct and with which, in fact, they critique even the Bible. They maintain that certain modern beliefs of theirs are so authoritative that they warrant even the criticism of definite biblical teachings. In this case we face a spirit of rebellion, a moral defect, a deliberate twisting of Scripture, a malignancy in theology that really constitutes a crisis.

This is undoubtedly an area in which it is necessary to walk very cautiously. Jesus said we were not to judge other people. He seems to have been warning against the harsh and negative kinds of judgments we humans so often engage in, not to be ruling out discernment per se (Matt. 7:1–6). But it requires us to be awfully careful not to confuse an honest difference of opinion in interpretation with a deliberate decision to deny Scripture. Nevertheless, rebellion is what we are often facing today, and it would be cowardly not to name it. For it not only constitutes a threat to the church, which lives out of the truth of the Bible, but hastens that loss of clarity and impact that is currently undermining Christian civilization and world evangelization.

With the rise of religious liberalism, theology passed over a critical threshold. Before that time Christians had taken for granted that one should consider what the Bible taught and then try to put it into effect. But now, for many people, the modern experience constitutes a second source of authority that entitles them to critique the biblical source where it is not "relevant." Our modern standpoint has become "an intrinsic and determinative element for understanding God's revelation," as Schillebeeckx puts it.[15] Unless we find the Bible helpful and supportive in relation to what we already believe to be true, it need not be taken very seriously. We face today a critical theology that does not submit itself to the Scripture principle. This means in practice that the text is brought under the judgment of modern people and edited according to their will.[16]

William Hordern has made the distinction among theologians between the transformers and the translators. The translators keep the content of the Bible but try to explain it in the most intelligible way they can. Transformers, on the other hand, make major changes in the content of Scripture in order to bring it into line with modern beliefs. We are talking here about transformers who hold that people in the modern world cannot believe what the Bible teaches unless it is deliteralized or demythologized. The only option we really have is to modernize

Christian belief, according to their opinion.[17] By construing Scripture as the precipitate of faith experience, Schleiermacher was trying to make it unnecessary to critique or suppress the biases of modernity. By putting the emphasis upon the existential "kick value" of the New Testament, Bultmann could boldly announce that modern Christians do not have to believe those doctrinal and factual claims in the text that offend their up-to-date opinions. By stressing symbol, Tillich could ease away from the literal content of the Bible and promote his own ontology under the guise of biblical terms. The liberal transformers, old and new, are in rebellion against the content of the Bible and are determined to adapt it to the "itching ears" of the present time. A clear case of this was the "death-of-God" or secular theology of the 1960s, but we should not suppose it was a fanatical and untypical phenomenon. As we know, people like Robinson and Altizer proposed that belief in God be dropped, at least in the traditional and biblical sense, simply because modern people would find it difficult to believe. Humanity was said to have "come of age," and it would be necessary for theology to tailor the message to modern requirements. Modern thought is taken to be the standard of truth, and nothing that is not reasonable under its standards should be retained in Christian theology.

According to this mentality, it is obvious that a belief in a miracle of the magnitude of the incarnation, for example, cannot stand in a truly modern theology. Therefore, something has to be done. A strategy must be found. There are three options currently being tried out. First, there is the frank denial preferred by the modernists. It is the easiest to deal with from a conservative point of view. The modernists simply declare that they cannot live with the traditional and biblical belief and draw up a new Christology they can accept. It is not crucial that it be biblically defended, though if this can be done to some extent so much the better. Second, there is biblical reconstruction. No doubt the New Testament as it stands witnesses to a Christ both truly human and mysteriously divine. But what if we could show the historical Jesus and the original kerygma as not so clear-cut and definite? What if we could uncover a Jesus who called for existential decision and little else; could he not be the real canon within the New Testament, enabling us to avoid the orthodox conclusions that otherwise seem justified? Third, there is hermeneutical ventriloquism, which is difficult but has great promise for appealing to Christians at large, who have an instinct for wanting to believe the Bible rather than the critic. Maybe we could show by fresh exegesis that belief in the incarnation is limited to a small sector of the New Testament, or maybe not even present at all.

Granted, this is not easy to do, but J. A. T. Robinson, at least, was busy trying to do it.[18] In this way one could simultaneously deny the incarnation in the traditional sense and seem to defend the real meaning of the Bible. This is, of course, historically the preferred way for theological aberrations. A heresy will have the most effect upon the church if it is presented in the guise of an overlooked scriptural truth. It may even be the false teacher's personal opinion that this is exactly what it is. In all such cases, therefore, the church ought to practice a sympathetic investigation of the debated point before concluding, as it might be forced to do, that theological deception is being practiced.

The problem of opposition to Scripture is widespread and has begun to affect how people approach the Bible. It has become commonplace to hear human opinion and sentiment boldly exalted over God's Word. Let me list a number of familiar examples. How can we call God "father" in the age of women's rights? How can we believe Jesus is the absolute Savior in a pluralistic world? How can we consider the Jews in need of Christ after Auschwitz? How can we consent to the notion of divine judgment when we reject retribution? How can one say gay lifestyles are wrong when some psychologists now tell us they are normal? How can we believe in an age of secular economics, that countries may be rich or poor according to their response to the law of God? The fall of Adam is out of the question as far as history is concerned. Atonement through a vicarious sacrifice is meaningless, or worse. God can exist but only in terms of a process metaphysic. The New Testament is true, but only in an existential way. Satan is a good symbol of deep-seated evil, but we cannot be expected to believe he is a created angel. The Bible is socially relevant so long as it is interpreted along socialist lines. Women can affirm Scripture in the feminist parts but reject the texts that suggest patriarchalism. The list could go on and on. Everywhere, the Bible is being questioned; we need a Martin Luther to rise up again and make his stand.

No one is free from the temptation to substitute what he or she believes for what Scripture says. At point after point conservatives, too, pass over what they do not want to hear. We may not want those troublesome charismatic gifts. We may not want to face the Bible's call for involvement in issues of peace and justice. But at least our biases are corrigible in principle. We acknowledge the written Word of God as binding on us and might just come to repentance. The challenge today is to know what to do about self-conscious rebellion against Scripture, when people are deliberately allowing nonbiblical assumptions to corrupt the Word of God. In response we must insist on the binding authority of the Bible and upon its right to set limits on the epistemological and ethical rights of human beings. The Bible, not modernity, is normative, and our thoughts are to be shaped by its teaching, not the reverse. Only by acknowledging this can we prevent revelation from being buried under the debris of human culture and opinion and from disappearing as a liberating Word from outside the human situation. A stance of determined faithfulness to Scripture is what our day calls for.

Openness to God

Having looked at the need to be docile in the presence of an authoritative text, let us go on to consider the second requirement, the importance of being open to the Spirit in hearing the Bible as a Word to us today. This is a valid concern that religious liberals are much burdened with and that conservatives need to pay closer attention to. It points to the fact that theology can be creative as well as faithful.

Underlying our hermeneutics is a belief in the reality of the Spirit of God, who helps us to recognize God's Word for what it is, aids us in grasping the point, and assists us in applying it to our circumstances so that it speaks as a living Bible within our horizon. It ought to be part of our daily experience to feed upon God's Word in God's presence and have God speak to us personally. Such is the sacramental nature and potential of Scripture in the Christian life. We pray with Samuel, "Speak, Lord, for thy servant heareth."

Donald Bloesch has written: "Evangelical theology holds that what Christ says today does not contradict what his witnesses say in Scripture but may go beyond it, as the Spirit of Christ clarifies and makes explicit what may be only implicit in the text. Against an orthodoxy that is content to live in the past and does not seek a fresh word from God in Scripture, evangelical theology shares the confidence of the Puritan divine John Robinson that 'The Lord has more light and truth yet to break forth out of his holy Word.' "[19]

Five hundred years ago Martin Luther found truth in Romans and Galatians with which to reform the church's theology of salvation by grace through faith. But he did not just read Paul in a detached and objective way. He adapted the text to conditions in the sixteenth-century church and drove the point home. One would not read Luther in order to find the best commentary on what Paul originally meant but to see how God's Word can, by the power of God, come to life in the encounter of text and situation. If we approve of this Reformation, surely we must approve also of reading the Bible with a view of discerning its true significance for our day. The Spirit gives the text a dynamic pointedness so that the text can be resituated and become fresh revelation for us. Beginning with the inscripturated Word out of the past, the Spirit leads us to the Word for us in the present. Making use of the sources of flexibility we noted in Chapter 8, the Spirit goes on to apply the Word to our needs, so that it becomes sharp and powerful within our situation.

On this point we may note a discrepancy between evangelical theory and practice. In practice we know very well that God's Word is heard in an interaction between the text and our walk with God. We listen to God speaking to us from the pages of the Bible. We place ourselves in front of the text and try to be open to God's creative Word, which can free us up to live the new life. We put ourselves in the biblical contexts and gaze upon our image as in a mirror. We strive to respond to what the text is calling on us to do. We meditate upon the Word and expect God to address us in our situation. Bible study is not only a scholarly science, it is a spiritual discipline of prayerful expectancy. We refuse to trust the interpreters who do not pray. God leads us through verses not originally addressed to us at all. Did we not know at L'Abri that the people were coming to "the mountain of the Lord"? Do we not constantly take the promises and warnings of the Bible as directed to ourselves? Is not God saying these very things to us today? These are not simple, pious thoughts that the educated Christian should get away from. They are the highest wisdom and the key to the Bible as a living authority.

But our theory is often quite different. It sounds as though there were no Holy spirit, as if all one had to do were recover the original meaning and nothing more, as though the interpretive operation were best performed by a trained technician. I fear that this imbalance is due to the polemical atmosphere. Faced with the kind of blatant Bible denial I just reviewed, classical Christians are frightened of anything that might seem to deviate from an essentially legalistic authority. Seeing some stray from the text causes others to stick very closely to it, and even to minimize the work of the Spirit for fear that it would introduce unpredictability into hermeneutics. But this is just overreaction. First we tended to deny tradition for fear that Catholics would use it to obscure the message of the Bible, and now we are minimizing the Spirit for fear that in the name of the Spirit people will wander far from the text. In neither case are these fears unjustified. But fears must not be allowed to shape our theology so much. They must not lure us into an orientation toward Scripture that sees it in an academic way as a frozen text very much as do the liberals we fear. Upholding the authority of the Bible is going too far if it minimizes the spiritual dimension of interpretation or disregards completely the relevance of the history of interpretation.

Far from being something we should be afraid of, the dynamic character of the Scriptures through the Spirit is the glory of our doctrine. We can actually count on the activity of the Spirit to help us bring the text into the twentieth century. The Bible is up-to-date, not so much because of our wise efforts at theological translation, but because the Spirit takes these time-transcending themes and makes them live. There are those who maintain about how out of date the text is and the gigantic hurdles that stand in the way of effective communication today. It is an impossible task, we are told, to make the Bible relevant for modern people. Ultimately, the reason we are not discouraged by these Cassandras is not that we are impressed with our own apologetics, which bring out the undoubted relevance of the Bible, but that we have seen how the Spirit is able to make contemporary the Word of God, time after time, in culture after culture. What seems impossible from an intellectual standpoint is made gloriously and effectively possible by the Spirit of God. Aside from our possible negligence in thinking through hard issues of hermeneutics for our time, evangelicals are less anxious than liberals generally are about the problems of communication because evangelicals tend to retain greater confidence in the Spirit's ability to bridge the gap of the centuries.

Validity in Interpretation?

There is an obvious danger in all of this. What constitutes a valid interpretation if we loosen up the link between text and meaning? How is the Scripture our authority if its meaning for us is different from what the text actually says? What is to prevent this kind of two-sided hermeneutics from becoming a cloak for Scripture twisting and subversion? Have we not landed ourselves in the liberal camp by a circuitous route? Is it not fatal to give up total continuity between what the text says and what it means for us? Is not the door wide open to private revelations in interpretative guise?

In response to these questions, we would have to admit that looking to the Spirit does introduce a certain elusiveness and mystery into the hermeneutical operation. It is not such a cut-and-dried activity as it is in legalistic usage. God can indeed surprise us when we listen for his Word in the Bible. There is no set of tests that can absolutely determine validity in interpretation. Openness to the Spirit makes inflexible legalism impossible for us, even though it is as attractive to us today as it was in New Testament times. But attractive or not, we have no right to quench God's Spirit, whose ministry alongside the Word is undeniable. We have to live with the fact that we will have to be more open when we evaluate claims about the meaning of the Bible from readers different from ourselves. It will not be as easy as it once was to distinguish a faithful from an unfaithful rendering. If spiritual involvement with the text is important, we will have to be less quick on the draw when it comes to shooting down false doctrines.

But we are not left with chaos. There are some highly effective safeguards and controls that fend off radical subjectivity. The most important of these is just the text itself. Any claim to interpretation has to appear credible in the light of the text itself. It has to be a legitimate and possible use of it. One can claim that process theism or Calvinist soteriology or revolutionary politics are what the Bible signifies for us today. But one must be able to go on and prove such hypotheses. Does the text fairly interpreted support any or all of these proposals? "To the Word and the Testimony." The Bible is not a defenseless waxen nose that can be twisted at will. It has a backbone. It has a way of resisting over time false claims made about its meaning. The text sets up often well-defined parameters that discipline its interpreters—or else destroy them. We must not exaggerate the novelty that is possible when one opens oneself to the Spirit. There are definite limits to its range. A large part of what is involved is simply the Spirit causing the content of the text to live for us and become experientially vital. He can help us to apply the text creatively to our lives and circumstances. After all, the text leaves open what directions should be followed within our contemporary horizon in order to apply the Word faithfullly to it. What should we be doing as individuals and as congregations to obey the Lord? It is here primarily that the Spirit is active in using the Bible as an instrument of guidance and direction.

There is also the safeguard of past hermeneutical wisdom—what we call tradition. We are not the first Christians to read the Bible. The Spirit has been active in people's lives for centuries already. Seeking the insight that was achieved in tradition is an act of respect for all our fathers and mothers in the faith. We should not so emphasize the authority of the Bible that we fail to see the positive significance of tradition. Indeed, Scripture itself came out of the life of the early community and has been proclaimed and preserved by it ever since. Slogans aside, the Bible is not "sola" among the factors that influence us. No one can leap over twenty centuries and grasp the text uninfluenced by the understanding of previous generations. Radical biblicism is a delusion. Very often it is the cloak for absolutizing the theology of the last century.

The positive role played by tradition is the guidance it gives us embodied in the distilled wisdom of the ages. In particular, it guards us against Scripture twisting. Is it not a common joke that any pious fraud can cite Scripture to support his or her case, however, weird? Tradition is a defense in the church against individualism in interpretation. It is needed in order to protect God's people from private misinterpretations of the Bible. The church would be foolish to turn its back upon tradition. As Macquarrie puts it, "To deny fundamental doctrines, like that of the Trinity; to reject the creeds; to set aside the beliefs of the early councils of the still undivided church—these may be actions to which individuals are impelled by their own thinking on these matters, but they cannot take place in Christian theology, for they amount to a rejection of the history and therefore of the continuing identity of the community within which Christian theologizing takes place."[20] Tradition plays a stabilizing role in hermeneutics. It places a "fence around the Torah," as it were, to protect the text from heretical pillaging. It makes us raise our eyebrows when we encounter a novel proposal and requires such a proposal to be very well supported. There is little chance that a theory that John does not teach incarnation or that Paul really supports gay lifestyles will ever be widely accepted. Common sense, which is in good measure sense informed by tradition, will help us differentiate plausible interpretations from merely possible ones. Tradition cannot and should not prevent new insight from edifying the church, but it can and should have a voice in evaluating its reliability.

The authority of tradition is one of counsel, not of command. It is fallible, not infallible. There can be uncritical and excessive regard for what it teaches. It can become merely dead tradition that impedes the legitimate development of interpretive insight. We may well need to ask if the ban on female ministry or the bias in favor of infant baptism or even the pattern of Sunday observance—all of which are strong in the tradition but unclear in the Bible—are truly in keeping with Scripture. But that does not change the fact that tradition in general represents a life-giving complement to Scripture and cannot be set aside without harming the identity of the community.

Another safeguard is the living community of believers who collectively hear the Word and assess the interpretation. It is illustrated at

Corinth when Paul says that when prophets speak, "Let the others weigh what is said" (1 Cor. 14:29). Even as authoritative an utterance as an inspired prophecy should not go unchecked by the spiritual instinct resident in the community as a whole. Similarly, the Bible is the book of the church, not of individuals only. Therefore, the community has the right and the responsibility to evaluate the interpretation it hears. God has given gifts to the Body that should be adequate to assess the quality of interpretation. Proposals have to be tested, not only or primarily in front of academic colleagues, but before believing people. And in our denominational pluralism, this means sharing the insights of one community with others in order to test for cross-community validation. Needless to say, this presupposes a congregation both Spirit-alive and well informed. It may be necessary to seek out a live, joyful, prayerful church to experience this.

Hermeneutics as Translation?

Earlier, we condemned the practice of theological transformers, who force the Bible to fit modern beliefs, and by implication commended the work of translators, who genuinely try to convey the message of the Bible in a fresh and intelligible way to the modern audience. If it is necessary to render the Greek of the New Testament into modern tongues, surely it is right also to render the categories in new forms that would bring out the same meaning for the twentieth century. Surely theological translation is what we ought to be doing to help people grasp the message of the Bible. As the theologian Gabriel Fackre says, "The crucial task of translation is to find ways in each generation and location to bring the basic convictions of the Christian faith into the thought world of its hearers."[21] Other terms will be brought into service to convey the meaning of the Christian story. In Fackre's case, the image of liberation is one that can make the biblical message live for people today.

On the surface of it, this suggestion sounds fine. It takes the content of the Bible seriously and tries to express it faithfully in modern times. No classical Christian could object to translation, if that is what really happens in it. However, we would be quite naive if we did not notice that something very different usually goes on. Transformation of the biblical message is often done in the name of translation. Both Tillich and Bultmann think of their work as translation. They claim to be taking the biblical categories and expressing them in modern terms, but they are doing no such thing. They are substituting for biblical content twentieth-century philosophical ideas. As Kelsey observes, what these theologians offer as translation bears very little resemblance to what the New Testament had in mind. They are simply stretching the term *translation* to make it coincide with transformation. They may have reasons for the substitution, but they have no right to pretend they are translating.[22] Translation implies true conceptual continuity between what the Bible teaches and what our theology says. It can only be used by those who believe that the task of theology is to explicate the content of the Bible by translating it into contemporary idiom; it cannot be used by those who have no such intention.

Translation of the content of the Bible into contemporary idiom is what we ought to be doing. In this operation exegesis is properly basic. Normativity is located in the expressed mind of the biblical writers as far as we can determine it through assiduous study. Explanation of the text precedes and underlies any translation of its meaning. Application of the text to the contemporary setting builds upon the exegeted content and does not supply its own. In application we ask the question, if God said thus and so in those circumstances, what can we suppose he is saying to us now? We take the Scriptures to be providing us with trajectories of perennial significance and paradigms always relevant to discerning how God deals with his creatures. In the Bible our human minds come into contact with the revealed mind of God shedding light upon our path. Scripture gives us divine instruction, and our duty is to apply it faithfully and creatively.

The key words are *dynamic equivalence.* We are certainly free to go beyond merely explaining the content of the Bible to trying to render it meaningfully in images native to our culture. But the result must be truly equivalent and not a crude substitution. Experience in cross-cultural communication is what interpreters need, because their work involves taking a text that was intelligible in one (ancient) culture and situating it in another, remaining sensitive to the perceptual factors that help or hinder good understanding. We start with the original communication and determine what was being said; then we attempt to encode that message in the modern hearer's frame of reference such that both the communication and the response are dynamically equivalent to those of the original situation. And because translation will always be culture-specific, we must be open to unfamiliar ways of doing it in contexts other than our own.[23]

Translating the Bible involves both distancing and fusion. On the one hand, we have to distance ourselves and allow the text to say what it means to regardless, and on the other hand, we want to bring the text into our own situation and have it address us. First we want to understand what Paul meant, and then we want to be grasped by it—as Luther was—and made new. Allowing distance ensures that the text is truly heard in its own right, and seeking fusion help us to become engaged with the text. In reading a parable like the Good Samaritan, we will need to listen to the original story in terms of what was really going on between these four individuals in the ancient context, and then consider how the same kind of impact could be achieved within the modern world. There needs to be faithfulness to the Word as first given and creativity in placing it in the contemporary context.

What did *shepherd* mean to the Hebrews? What associations surrounded the figure of Satan for them? How can we render the truth of an atoning sacrifice? What would the Jews have taken a resurrection to mean? How does the nearness of the return of the Lord function in biblical language? First of all, we want to understand the teaching of the Bible itself as accurately as possible, so that we will not be guilty of reading our own prejudices into it, and then we want to consider how to express that in modern terms. What did Paul mean by his instruction to slaves, and what does this mean now in our Western world where there are no longer slaves?

The goal is that our translation be both dynamic and equivalent. Heretical proposals are usually dynamic but not equivalent, and ineffective exegesis is often equivalent but unrelated to life today. We are called to be faithful and creative both. Our creative imagination should be placed in the service of the Word of God. We have no right to invent new doctrine, but we do have the responsibility to render the meaning of the text in an understandable way. Amos listened to the story of bondage in Egypt and noticed that some people in his day were treating the poor much as the pharaoh had treated the Israelite slaves long ago. The meaning of the text was not entirely welcome, but it was right on target. Similarly, when we read Jesus' harsh words about certain Pharisees, we should consider where this kind of perversion of religion is occurring today and not simply take it as the indictment of a past group.

Conclusion

Good interpretation is a skill, like swimming and horseback riding. It cannot be achieved merely by applying a set of rules. It requires both scholarly diligence and a readiness to hear and obey the Lord. Paul gave Timothy good advice when he said, "Think over what I say, and the Lord will give you understanding" (2 Tim. 2:7). He was to ponder carefully what Paul actually said and think it over himself in openness to God. In one sense we are not alone in this. We can benefit from generations of interpreters before us as well as from the Body of Christ now living. The interpreter is not a solo virtuoso but the member of a interpreting team and fellowship that collectively seeks to know the mind of God for the whole of life.

Our two-sided proposal indicates how we ought to proceed. It will help us avoid the disobedience of religious liberalism with regard to the givenness of the text as well as the inflexible legalism of the conservative camp that overreacts to the liberals' misuse of Christian freedom. It may be able to help us get back on track and heal some of our divisions and misunderstandings. But it is not more than a general guideline. It describes the playing field on which the game of hermeneutics ought to be played. The game itself is what matters now. And as we get into specific cases in our study of the Bible, there is no way to predict what joyful discoveries, as well as painful struggles, we will experience. This is also the way of our whole life with God.

Conclusion

I have argued that the Scripture principle belongs to the essence of Christianity and constitutes a crucial component in its pattern of authority and revelation. My aim has been to present a systematic treatment of the concept in the context of a crisis of the Scripture principle and a struggle to maintain it in the light of some difficult questions. God gave the Bible to the church to bear an authoritative witness to Jesus Christ and the gospel. It is something to be treasured and defended. Salvation, of course, rests upon sincere faith in God the redeemer, but the well-being of the church and her mission to the world depends upon keeping this conviction clear and strong. One thing evangelicals are surely called to do in contemporary theology and church life is to add their voice to the weight of tradition on behalf of this doctrine and to offer a sturdy defense and an intelligent exposition of it. This I have sought to do both here and in my earlier book *Biblical Revelation* (1971).

Wittgenstein has emphasized the importance of having a good model when one tries to make sense of reality. Confusion results from having a false or inadequate paradigm. My aim and approach has been to supply a general orientation to the Scripture principle that would open up our understanding in fruitful ways and lead us away from traps and pitfalls. I feel it to be important to call attention to the three really crucial dimensions of the subject and to work them through. If we do not embrace the divine inspiration of Scripture, we will run the risk of losing our apostolic norm and truth standard. If we neglect the human character of the Bible, we will not be able to grasp what it is saying and will give it misplaced respect. If we forget about the Spirit, we run the risk of falling into legalism and losing the freshness of scriptural piety. I think it would be wise policy to orient ourselves to these three guiding lights. In Scripture, too, we can say with Saint Paul that we have a divine treasure in human vessels empowered by God (2 Cor. 4:7).

In the course of working this out, I have interacted with other Christian thinkers. On one side, I found it necessary to oppose, quite strongly at times, the denial of biblical authority that I see in religious liberalism to this day. A great deal is at stake here, it seems to me, and strong emotions are to be expected. For this reason, it has not been easy to be fair and charitable and to place the best interpretation upon that work. I recall with regret how difficult it was for Luther and Rome to understand one another and how their discussion broke down into bitter polemics and schism. I see how important it is to heed the words of Saint Ignatius of Loyola:

In order that the one who gives these exercises and he who makes them may be of more assistance and profit to each other, they should begin with the presupposition that every good Christian ought to be more willing to give a good interpretation to the statement of another than to condemn it as false. If he cannot give a good interpretation to this statement, he should ask the other how he understands it, and if he is in error, he should correct him with charity. If this is not sufficient, he should seek every suitable means of correcting his understanding so that he may be saved from error.[1]

It gives me no pleasure to say that I think some are wandering from the truth in the matter of the Scripture principle. Yet a great divide does seem to dominate the scene, not, this time, between Catholics and Protestants, but between classical Christians of every kind and liberals who seem bent on shifting the church from her scriptural foundations. If this is not so, I will be the first to rejoice. But if it is, we are in for another long, hard struggle.

On the other side, I did some jousting with my fellow conservatives. In relation to them, I have two things chiefly to say. I see a danger of our being too much affected by the polemical atmosphere caused by our reaction to religious liberalism, which pushes us in directions we ought not to go. Obviously, it makes us defensive and uptight, even nervous, with respect to the Bible. We can become afraid to see what is there and feel we have to force the text to meet requirements we establish out of our concern to preserve a high doctrine of inspiration. Clearly this is not right, and goes against our own view of the Bible's self-determining authority. But worst of all, it throws our focus off. Deep in our hearts we know that the central purpose of Scripture is to bring people to know and love God, and that it achieves its purpose even though the existing Bible has unresolved problems in it.

Its truth and power are not nullified by this fact. Even though it is not perfect at the present time, it is wonderfully able to make us wise unto salvation and to teach us all things needful. Even though the Bible is not inerrant at this present moment, it can accomplish exactly what is claimed for it. The difficulties there are do not obscure the good news and do not prevent the Spirit from using the text in human lives. Can we not stand back from the battle and see this? In its present condition the Bible is proving reliable, nourishing, and precious.

Part of the problem is that we have been tricked into defending the Bible in the wrong way. The liberals, fresh from the modern Enlightenment, look at the Bible from a human and academic point of view. They raise difficult academic questions, and we try to answer them. But in the process, we are maneuvered into an alien defense formation. We agree, in effect, to discuss the issue on the basis of scholarly considerations divorced from the life context of proving the Bible true. This, in turn, requires us to tighten up the intellectual side and nearly bracket the spiritual side of this question. All of a sudden it becomes essential to argue with all sorts of scholarly apparatus for a Bible more perfect than the one that exists and it becomes an embarrassment to admit that Christians have always found the existing Bible, with its difficulties, quite sufficient in authority and truth. It has even caused some evangelicals to turn on others, questioning whether this procedure is really wise and helpful.

My suggestion for avoiding this unpleasant and ill-conceived dispute among us is to recover the Christ-centered and nontechnical approach that the Bible itself seems to take. There is something terribly wrong when we argue about the Bible more and enjoy it less. God gave us his Word to make us wise, to instruct our minds, to revive our spirits, to guide our feet in his ways. We stand together with all those who are of this disposition. This is what the Bible itself claims, and this is what really matters.[2]

I wish also to state my conviction that it would be wise for us to continue to speak of biblical inerrancy. Though the term is not ideal by any means, it does possess the strength of conviction concerning the truthfulness of the Bible that we need to maintain at the present time, while offering a good deal of flexibility to honest biblical study. I recognize that the Bible does not make a technical inerrancy claim or go into the kind of detail associated with the term in the contemporary discussion. But I also see a solid basis for trusting the Scriptures in a more general sense in all that they teach and affirm, and I see real danger in giving the impression that the Bible errs in a significant way. Inerrancy is a metaphor for the determination to trust God's Word completely. True, it is used by some to say much more than that and is applied to the Bible in such a way as to require text twisting. But careful and responsible definitions of the term do not do that. I refer to the Chicago Statement and to many commentaries from within that circle.[3] The burden of the term *inerrancy* is to preserve the principle of the Reformation that Scripture can be trusted in what it teaches and relied upon as the infallible norm of the church. All classical Christians should support this concern and not overreact to the language being used at present to represent it.[4]

For historical reasons, inerrancy has come to symbolize in our day that full confidence that Christians have always had in the Scriptures. The wisest course to take would be to get on with defining inerrancy in relation to the purpose of the Bible and the phenomena it displays. When we do that, we will be surprised how open and permissive a term it is. Inerrancy has to take into account the literary genre and language being played in any given passage. Truth has to be evaluated in context. But this is true not only with the Bible but with Plato and Shakespeare as well. There is nothing artificial or unreasonable about asking what is really being affirmed in a text, as opposed to what is there in a supporting role. Of course, one can make fun of it and say that inerrancy is dying the death of a thousand qualifications. But that would not be true. Inerrancy is relative to the intent of the Scriptures, and this has to be hermeneutically determined. It will certainly be necessary to explain how many curious features of the text do not actually overthrow the truthfulness of the Bible, but surely this is not too high a price to pay in order to be able to maintain a trustful stance.[5]

The point to grasp is that *inerrancy* is a term with strength and flexibility. We need it because it highlights the conviction that the Bible tells the truth when it speaks. If we could not believe and affirm that, the whole biblical faith would be in peril and jeopardy. I know what it is to struggle with this issue. At times I have felt like rejecting biblical inerrancy because of the narrowness of definition and the crudity of polemics that have accompanied the term. But in the end, I have had to bow to the wisdom that says we need to be unmistakably clear in our convictions about biblical authority, and in the North American context, at least, that means to employ strong language. If inerrancy means that the Bible can be trusted to teach the truth in all it affirms, then inerrancy is what we must hold to.[6]

In closing, let us offer as a prayer the collect for the second Sunday in Advent:

Blessed Lord, who hast caused all holy Scripture to be written for our learning, grant that we may in such wise hear them, read, mark, learn, and inwardly digest them, that by patience, and comfort of thy holy Word, we may embrace, and ever hold fast the blessed hope of everlasting life, which thou hast given us in our Savior Jesus Christ. Amen.

Notes

Preface

1. James Orr, *Revelation and Inspiration*, p. 1.

Introduction: Maintaining the Scripture Principle Today

1. Edward Farley, *Ecclesial Reflection: An Anatomy of Theological Method.**
2. Along with other confessional statements of its kind, the New Hampshire Baptist Confession can be found in Philip Schaff, ed. *The Creeds of Christendom*, vol. III, p. 742.
3. Bruce Vawter, *Biblical Inspiration*, pp. 20–43; and Geoffrey Bromiley, in his chapter "The Church Fathers and Holy Scripture," in *Scripture and Truth*, ed. D. A. Carson and John Woodbridge, pp. 199–220.
4. Though a polemical book directed at refuting another by Rogers and McKim, *Biblical Authority*, by John Woodbridge, is an excellent source of information about the classical belief in full biblical infallibility.
5. Occasionally Barr seems to be aware of how ancient belief in biblical inerrancy is, but for the most part he just batters away on the heads of conservative believers, from whose company he himself moved away awhile back. See his venomous book *Fundamentalism*.
6. Donald Bloesch is one of my favorite observers of theological trends, and I would recommend to the reader his latest title, *The Future of Evangelical Christianity*.
7. Bromiley, "The Church Fathers and Holy Scripture," p. 217.
8. G. C. Berkouwer, *Holy Scripture*, pp. 9–38.
9. Karl Barth, *Church Dogmatics*, vol. I, part 2, pp. 517–19.
10. Virtually all evangelicals, including myself, have done this in times past, so eager are we to enlist such great worthies as Augustine on our side in the great battle with liberalism. Edward Farley calls our bluff on this practice very effectively *Ecclesial Reflection*, pp. 83–105.
11. The subtitle of Woodbridge's book cited in note 4 is *A Critique of the Rogers/McKim Proposal*, and effectively refutes the view that classical theologians limited the inerrancy of the Bible to matters of faith and practice. The book referred to is by Jack B. Rogers and Donald K. McKim, *The Authority and Interpretation of the Bible*.
12. Wolfhart Pannenberg, "The Crisis of the Scripture Principle" in *Basic Questions in Theology*, vol. 1, pp. 1–14. I appreciated the candid humor of Maurice Wiles near the

---

* For complete bibliographic information, see the following Bibliography of Works Cited.

end of his book *The Remaking of Christian Doctrine*, when he asked himself, in view of the radical nature of the changes he was proposing, whether the title of the book ought not to be "the unmaking of Christian Doctrine." His instincts are on target, of course.

13. Peter C. Hodgson and Robert H. King, ed. *Christian Theology: An Introduction to Its Traditions and Tasks*, p. 35.

14. For direct denials, in addition to the work of Farley and Pannenberg already referred to (notes 1 and 12), consult C. F. Evans, *Is "Holy Scripture" Christian?*; James Barr, *The Bible in the Modern World*; and *Holy Scripture: Canon, Authority, Criticism*; Gordon D. Kaufman, *Theological Imagination: Constructing the Concept of God*.

15. For indirect denials, note the shift of the "functional" authority of the Bible in a whole range of modern writers who take the Bible to be authoritative, not in its teachings or history but in its power to occasion new experiences of revelation in us. See David H. Kelsey, *The Uses of Scripture in Recent Theology*. For Langdon Gilkey, the Bible is a fallible human witness reflecting all the biases and fears of its age and is subject to our correcting its errors. What he holds to be true is the symbolic structure and its power to illuminate our existence. See Gilkey, *Message and Existence: An Introduction to Christian Theology*, p. 52 f. Many prominent theologians make the shift to the functional while continuing to pretend they are operating within the classical picture. Hodgson and King name Bultmann, Tillich, and Barth in this category: *Christian Theology*, p. 53.

16. Farley, *Ecclesial Reflection*, pp. 153–65.

17. Farley, *Ecclesial Reflection*, pp. 135–40.

18. Auguste Sabatier, *Religions of Authority and Religions of the Spirit*.

19. This is a favorite theme of liberal Christianity. See Edgar J. Goodspeed, in *The Interpreter's Bible*, ed. George A. Buttrick et al., vol. 1, p. 63.

20. Edward Farley, *Ecclesial Reflection*, pp. 272–81.

21. Compare Richard J. Coleman, *Issues of Theological Conflict: Evangelicals and Liberals*.

22. James Barr, *Holy Scripture*, p. 19.

23. Benjamin B. Warfield, *The Inspiration and Authority of the Bible*, pp. 210–14.

24. See J. I. Packer, "The Necessity of the Revealed Word," in *The Bible: The Living Word of Revelation*, ed. Merrill C. Tenney, pp. 31–49.

25. John W. Montgomery enters an eloquent plea along these lines in "The Relevence of Scripture Today," in Tenney *The Bible*, pp. 201–18. This is also the great motivating factor behind Carl F. H. G. Henry's magnum opus, *God, Revelation, and Authority*.

26. No conservative book I know of responds to anything like the full range of hard critical questions, though most of them are treated helpfully by someone somewhere. I hope this book will fill this important gap satisfactorily.

27. People are just beginning to take account of the amazing diversity in evangelical theology and to classify the various genres by approach. The best taxonomy I have seen is, sadly, as yet unpublished—Robert M. Price, "The Crisis of Biblical Authority: The Setting and Range of the Current Evangelical Crisis."

28. Barth and Berkouwer see themselves in line with the historic doctrine of biblical authority and address themselves to the contemporary discussion, but neither one, partly because of the European context, and partly because of their emphasis upon event rather than content, really speaks for or to the evangelicals in the English-speaking world. Carl Henry is the only one thus far to fulfill my prescription *(God, Revelation and Authority)* unless my own *Biblical Revelation* be mentioned as a poor second. There are signs that better work will come forth from the diverse circle that groups itself around the Chicago Statement on Biblical Inerrancy. The appearance of Millard J. Erickson, *Christian Theology*, vol. I, which will grow to three large volumes, is the best treatment of the subject so far in a full-scale systematic theology.

29. Paul's text is discussed helpfully in Edward W. Goodrick, "Let's Put 2 Timothy 3:16 Back in the Bible," *Journal of the Evangelical Theological Society* 25 (1982), pp. 479–87; and Howard J. Loewen, *Karl Barth and the Church Doctrine of Inspiration*, chap. 2.

30. While still wary of fideism, I understand better what scholars like Daane, Berkouwer, Rogers, Bloesch, Barth, Wink, and Grounds have been trying to tell conservatives like me who have an overly rationalist bent.

Chapter 1: Pattern of Revelation

1. F. Gerald Downing, *Has Christianity a Revelation?* A more convincing account can be found in Avery Dulles, *Revelation Theology: A History*; and Gordon D. Kaufman, *Systematic Theology: A Historicist Perspective* chaps. 2–3.
2. Avery Dulles, *Revelation and the Quest for Unity*, p. 48.
3. Bernard Ramm, *The Pattern of Authority*.
4. Avery Dulles, *Models of Revelation*.
5. William Temple seems to keep a balance between these two kinds of revelation. See his *Nature, Man, and God*.
6. See Karl Rahner's challenging treatment in *Foundation of Christian Faith: An Introduction to the Idea of Christianity*, chaps. 1–4.
7. The best treatment of this whole subject is Bruce A. Demarest, *General Revelation*.
8. Kenneth Hamilton writes trenchantly against earthbound theology in *Revolt Against Heaven*.
9. James Barr rightly speaks of the time before there was any canonical Scripture as such, although he depreciates somewhat the fact that Scripture was present even then and was in the making—*Holy Scripture: Canon, Authority, Criticism* (Philadelphia: Westminster Press, 1983), chap. 1.
10. Walter C. Kaiser portrays the entire Old Testament as the developing story of the unfolding promise of God given first to Eve and then to Abraham, Moses, Isaiah, and the others, leading up to the coming of Jesus, the messianic seed of Abraham and of Eve—*Toward an Old Testament Theology*.
11. On the revelational modality of the historical event, see Bernard Ram, *Special revelation and the Word of God*, chap. 4.
12. John Goldingay, *Approaches to Old Testament Interpretation, pp. 74–77*.
13. Christopher B. Kaiser devotes a fine chapter to God's revelation of himself in the Old Testament period—*The Doctrine of God: An Historical Survey*, chap. 1.
14. Avery Dulles provides a nice summary of the pattern of revelation in the Old and New Testaments in *Revelation Theology: A History*, chap. 1.
15. As a cultural anthropologist, Charles Kraft has unusual insight into cross-cultural communication and into the incarnation as "a case study in receptor-oriented revelation"—*Christianity in Culture*, chap. 9.
16. Lapide engaged in a dialogue with Hans Küng, see Küng, *Signposts for the Future*, p. 85.
17. Royce G. Gruenler sees Jesus as the source of the high Christology that characterizes both the New Testament and the orthodox faith of the church—*New Approaches to Jesus and the Gospels*.
18. Wolfhart Pannenberg, *Jesus—God and Man* (Philadelphia: Westminster Press, 1968), chap. 3; and Gary R. Habermas, *The Resurrection of Jesus: An Apologetic*.
19. John 1:1–18; 20:28, but also Phil. 2:6; 2 Cor. 8:9; Heb. 10:5; Col. 2:9; Titus 2:13.
20. Stephen T. Davis, *Logic and the Nature of God*, chap. 8.
21. Karl Barth, *Church Dogmatics*, vol. 4, part 2, p. 85.
22. Joachim Jeremias, *New Testament Theology: The Proclamation of Jesus*, pp. 76–96.
23. George T. Montague, *The Holy Spirit; Growth of a Biblical Tradition*; and James D. G. Dunn, *Jesus and the Spirit*.
24. Sallie McFague seems to be pointing in this direction, in *Christian Theology: An Introduction*, ed. Hodgson and King, pp. 334–35.
25. Dunn, *Jesus and the Spirit*, p. 356.
26. Carl Henry and Ronald Nash hammer this point home. They may overdo it, but something had to be said—Carl F. H. Henry, *God, Revelation, and Authority, vol. III*, thesis 10; and Ronald H. Nash, *The Word of God and the Mind of Man*.
27. Warfield, *The Inspiration and Authority of the Bible*, p. 210.
28. Edward Farley, *Ecclesial Reflection*, pp. 140–52.
29. James Barr, *Holy Scripture*, p. 13.
30. John W. Wenham supplies the abundant data on which this judgment rests in *Christ and the Bible*.

31. On Scripture as product of special revelation, see Bernard Ramm, *Special Revelation and the Word of God*, pp. 161–187.

32. Geoffrey Wainwright, *Doxology: The Praise of God in Worship, Doctrine, and Life*, p. 180.

33. Brevard S. Childs has a good feeling for how this works—*Biblical Theology in Crisis*, chap. 7.

34. Klaas Runia critiques and corrects Barth's tendency to exclude the scriptural text from the revelation it attests in *Karl Barth's Doctrine of Holy Scripture*, pp. 18–56.

35. Rahner develops the idea of Scripture as charter and constitution in *Foundations of Christian Faith*, pp. 369–78.

36. David Tracy celebrates the Bible as the Christian classic, but I judge him not to mean more than that it is a human document lacking in reliable truth in all its parts— *The Analogical Imagination: Christian Theology and the Culture of Pluralism*, chap. 3–5.

37. Carl F. H. Henry develops fifteen magnificent theses on revelation in vol. 2–4 of *God, Revelation, and Authority*.

38. John Baillie, *The Idea of Revelation in Recent Thought*, chap. 1.

39. Richard J. Coleman compares and contrasts the approaches made to revelation by liberals and conservatives in *Issues of Theological Conflict*, chap. 3.

40. Avery Dulles sketches in the history of the doctrine of revelation in the nineteenth century in *Revelation Theology, A History*, chap. 3.

41. Rudolf Bultmann, *Existence and Faith*, p. 85.

42. Schubert M. Ogden registers the same criticism in *Christ Without Myth*.

43. See Avery Dulles, *Models of Revelation*, chap. 7.

44. Rudolf Bultmann, *Kerygma and Myth: A Theological Debate*, chap. 1.

45. Farley, *Ecclesial Reflection*, chap. 7.

46. See the critique by Royce G. Gruenler, *The Inexhaustible God: Biblical Faith and the Challenge of Process Theism*.

47. Norman K. Gottwald, *The Tribes of Yahweh: A Sociology of the Religion of Liberated Israel*.

48. Paul D. Hanson, *Dynamic Transcendence: The Correlation of Confessional Heritage and Contemporary Experience in a Biblical Model of Divine Activity*.

49. James D. Smart considers it the crisis beneath all other crises the church faces—*The Strange Silence of the Bible in the Church*, p. 10.

50. I. Howard Marshall, *Biblical Inspiration*, p. 15.

Chapter 2: The Biblical Witness

1. Norman L. Geisler gives us a nice example of how not to sift the evidence in this case. He solicits a list of proof texts scattered here and there in the Bible and leaves the impression that one can determine the "Bible's view of the Bible" from reading them. Geisler knows the goal he has to reach and cites a few texts that give the impression he reached it inductively. The appearance is inductive; the reality is deductive—*Decide for Yourself: How History Views the Bible*, chap. 1.

2. James D. G. Dunn maintains that "in order to clarify what the doctrinal passages mean, we must observe how Jesus and the NT authors used the OT." See his stimulating article "The Authority of Scripture according to Scripture," *The Churchman* 96 (1982), p. 222, n. 62.

3. Brevard Childs has established this point with force and conviction in *Introduction to the Old Testament as Scripture*.

4. Meredith G. Kline, *Treaty of the Great King*.

5. A moderate, sensible theory is offered by William S. LaSor, David A. Hubbard, and Frederic W. Bush, in *Old Testament Survey: The Message, Form, and Background of the Old Testament*, chap. 6.

6. Meredith G. Kline speaks about the updating of treaty documents in *The Structure of Biblical Authority*.

7. Bruce Vawter discusses anonymity in the context of a social concept of inspiration in *Biblical Inspiration*, pp. 104–13.

8. Joachim Jeremias, *New Testament Theology*, pp. 27, 82–85.
9. John A. T. Robinson, "Did Jesus Have a Distinctive Use of Scripture?" in *Christological Perspectives*, ed. Robert F. Berkey and Sarah A. Edwards, pp. 49–57; R. T. France, *Jesus and the Old Testament: His Application of Old Testament Passages to Himself and His Mission*.
10. James Barr registers an effective protest against this practice. *Fundamentalism*, pp. 72–85.
11. Richard Longenecker, *Biblical Exegesis in the Apostolic Period*.
12. Richard Longenecker, "Can We Reproduce the Exegesis of the New Testament?" *Tyndale Bulletin* 21 (1970), pp. 3–38.
13. Moises Silva, "The New Testament Use of the Old Testament: Text Form and Authority," in *Scripture and Truth*, by D. A. Carson and John D. Woodbridge, pp. 147–65.
14. Schubert Ogden is quite adamant that we relocate the canon from the New Testament text as such to the earliest stratum of apostolic testimony we can uncover by critical means in *The Point of Christology*, p. 103–4.
15. Earle E. Ellis, *Eschatology in Luke*, p. 19.
16. John W. Wenham, *Christ and the Bible*, p. 113.
17. Edward Farley refers to "the myth of apostolicity," but it is a reality well founded in the historical documentation: *Ecclesial Reflection*, p. 119, and Hans Küng, *The Church*, pp. 344–59.
18. Rosemary R. Ruether, *The Church Against Itself*, pp. 96–121.
19. Peter Richardson, " 'I say, Not the Lord': Personal Opinion, Apostolic Authority and the Development of Early Christian Halakah" *Tyndale Bulletin* 31 (1980) pp. 65–86.
20. B. F. Westcott, *The Gospel According to St. John*, pp. v–xxviii.
21. Robert H. Gundry, *Matthew: A Commentary on His Literary and Theological Art*, pp. 609–22.
22. J. A. T. Robinson, *Redating the New Testament*, pp. 259–311.
23. Wenham, *Christ and the Bible*, p. 122.
24. Theo Donner, "Some Thoughts on the History of the NT Canon" *Themelios* 7 (1982), pp. 23–27, and F. F. Bruce, "Tradition and the Canon of Scripture," in *Tradition: Old and New*, pp. 129–150.
25. The canon seems to have revealed itself to the church as she used the available writings in the context of her life and worship: Geoffrey Wainwright, *Doxology*, p. 168, and Carl F. H. Henry, *God, Revelation and Authority*, IV, chap. 18.
26. Jaroslav Pelikan, *The Christian Tradition: A History of the Development of Doctrine* I, pp. 59, 119, 120.
27. Herman Ribberbos, *Studies in Scripture and Its Authority*, pp. 20–22.
28. As in Edward Farley, C. F. Evans, and James Barr, and in such older liberal authors as Harry E. Fosdick, *A Guide to Understanding the Bible?* and Harold DeWolf, *The Case for Theology in Liberal Perspective*, chap. 1–2.
29. Like Karl Rahner, I wish to see Scripture as an intrinsic part of God's formation of the church and his rule over her. The inspiration of Scripture is an element in the definitive establishment of the church and a way to guide her in faith and life: Rahner, *Inspiration in the Bible*.
30. The measure of suspicion in this area can be noted when those who place their emphasis on Paul's own point about profitability in 2 Tim. 3:15–17 are immediately asked, Does the Bible err, then, outside this practical circle? No such deduction is intended.
31. Chapter 9 will be given over to a model of dynamic but biblically faithful hermeneutics.
32. I used to think that it did—*Biblical Revelation*, chap. 2. Numerous conservative evangelical scholars still believe that it does. See John W. Wenham, *Christ and the Bible*, chap. 1. They can do so only, I believe, by reading the data selectively.
33. Evangelical philosopher Stephen Davis applies his logic to this and other topics in this whole area in *The Debate about the Bible*, pp. 61–65.
34. E. F. Harrison, in C. F. H. Henry, ed. *Revelation and the Bible*, p. 238.

35. Richard C. Lovelace offers some rare historical wisdom on this question and how to proceed with it in *Inerrancy and Common Sense* Roger R. Nicole and J. Ramsey Michaels, eds. chap. 1.
36. I. Howard Marshall, *Biblical Inspiration*, p. 30.

Chapter 3: Inspiration and Authority

1. Edward Farley, *Ecclesial Reflection*, pp. 153–65.
2. James I. Packer gives us a superb discussion of the kind of hermeneutics that operates out of a biblically defined doctrine of inspiration in *Scripture and Truth*, ed. D. A. Carson and John D. Woodbridge, pp. 325–56.
3. David H. Kelsey would have us suppose that the proper function of the Bible in the church is the function a person decides to grant it—*The Uses of Scripture in Recent Theology*.
4. Ernst Käsemann, *New Testament Questions of Today*, pp. 272–73.
5. Paul D. Hanson is afraid of this happening—*Dynamic Transcendence*.
6. Don S. Browning, *The Moral Context of Pastoral Care*, p. 93.
7. William J. Abraham is quite concerned that conservatives so often sound as if they mean to conceive of inspiration in mechanical and docetic terms—*The Divine Inspiration of Holy Scripture*, chap. 1.
8. Paul J. Achtemeier has called attention to the inadequacy of the prophetic model for representing the biblical category of inspiration in its fullness—*The Inspiration of Scripture: Problems and Proposals*.
9. Bruce Vawter, *Biblical Inspiration*, pp. 162–66.
10. Barth writes: "Apostolic means in the discipleship, in the school, under the normative authority, instruction and direction of the apostles, in agreement with them, because listening to them and accepting their message": *Church Dogmatics* Vol. 4, part 1, p. 714.
11. Schubert M. Ogden, *The Point of Christology*, pp. 97–105.
12. James Barr, *Holy Scripture*, pp. 130–71.
13. Hendrikus Berkhof, *Christian Faith: An Introduction to the Study of the Faith*, p. 88.
14. Paul K. Jewett, *Man as Male and Female* (Grand Rapids: Eerdmans, 1974).
15. Willard M. Swartley has a better idea—*Slavery, Sabbath, War and Women, Case Issues in Biblical Interpretation*, chap. 4.
16. As Brevard Childs reminds us—*Biblical Theology in Crisis*, chap. 8.
17. Mortimer Adler defends the existence of angels as a rational belief in *The Angels and Us*.
18. Clark H. Pinnock, *Biblical Revelation*, chap. 3.
19. John W. Montgomery discusses theological theorizing in "The Theologian's Craft," in *The Suicide of Christian Theology*, pp. 267–313.
20. Anthony Thiselton points out just how complex a category like truth can be in the article "truth" in *The New International Dictionary of New Testament Theology*.
21. See James I. Packer, "Upholding the Unity of Scripture Today," *Journal of the Evangelical Theological Society* 25 (1982), pp. 409–14.
22. Walter Bauer, *Orthodoxy and Heresy in Earliest Christianity*.
23. James D. G. Dunn, *Unity and Diversity in the New Testament*.
24. Bernard M. G. Reardon, *Religious Thought in the Reformation*, p. xi–xii.
25. Van A. Harvey, *The Historian and the Believer*, p. 24.
26. Donald Guthrie, *New Testament Theology*, p. 59.
27. H. E. W. Turner, *The Pattern of Christian Truth*.
28. D. A. Carson critiques Dunn in *Scripture and Truth*, pp. 71–77.
29. Walter Kaiser sees promise as the key to the developing theology of the Bible—*Toward an Old Testament Theology*.
30. James D. G. Dunn points to the diversity in New Testament Christology in his exaggerated way—*Christology in the Making*.

31. D. A. Carson, *Divine Sovereignty and Human Responsibility: Biblical Perspectives in Tension.*

32. G. C. Berkouwer loves to work with pairs of truths and resists rationalizing harmonizations. See J. C. DeMoor, *Towards a Biblically Theo-Logical Method.*

33. See the chapter on dialectic in Bernard Lonergan, *Method in Theology.*

34. Brice L. Martin, "Some Reflections on the Unity of the New Testament," *Studies in Religion* 8 (1979), pp. 143–52.

35. Karl Rahner, *Foundations of Christian Faith,* pp. 335–42.

36. Bultmann says, without proof: "The doctrine of Christ's pre-existence a given by St. Paul and St. John is difficult to reconcile with the legend of the virgin birth in St. Matthew and St. Luke." *Kerygma and Myth, A Theological Debate,* p. 34.

37. James D. G. Dunn, *Unity and Diversity in the New Testament,* p. 251.

38. Harold Lindsell stoked the fires of controversy that threatens to radically divide evangelicalism—*Battle for the Bible.*

39. Donald Bloesch, *The Future of Evangelical Christianity,* foreword.

40. Millard J. Erickson, *Christian Theology* I, p. 233–34.

41. Edward Farley is clear and informative on this matter; *Ecclesial Reflection,* chap. 4.

42. Hans Küng goes into this in *Infallible? An Inquiry,* pp. 144–50.

43. Hans Küng, *The Church,* Section D, Part III 1–2.

44. Oscar Cullmann, "The Tradition," in *The Early Church,* pp. 59–99.

Chapter 4: Incarnation and Accommodation

1. G. C. Berkouwer is particularly concerned about the possibility that the conservative doctrine of Scripture will take a docetic attitude to the Bible. He feels that it is motivated by too great a preoccupation with apologetic reasoning—*Holy Scripture,* chap. 1.

2. Tony Thiselton brings this point out forcefully in an article, "Understanding God's Word Today," in *Obeying Christ in a Changing World,* ed. J. R. W. Stott, chap. 4.

3. David Tracy articulates the principle that the Christian classic, the Bible, must be interpreted historically in *Blessed Rage for Order,* pp. 49–52.

4. Edward Farley calls attention to this tendency in *Ecclesial Reflection,* pp. 42–46.

5. Willard Swartley shows a keen sense of the positive role of criticism in reverent biblical interpretation—*Slavery, Sabbath, War and Women,* pp. 92–95, 243–45.

6. George E. Ladd, *The New Testament and Criticism,* p. 33.

7. Paul Achtemeier notices how conservatives try to save the Bible from its own phenomena—*The Inspiration of Scripture,* pp. 95–99.

8. John Goldingay, *Approaches to Old Testament Interpretation,* pp. 125–45.

9. Helmut Thielicke, *The Evangelical Faith,* vol. 3, p. 103.

10. Langdon Gilkey, *Message and Existence: An Introduction to Christian Theology,* pp. 52–53.

11. See, for example, Donald E. Miller, *The Case for Liberal Christianity,* pp. 36–37.

12. Edward Farley, *Ecclesial Reflection,* pp. 135–40.

13. David Tracy, *Blessed Rage for Order,* p. 62, note 58.

14. Karl Barth, *Church Dogmatics,* Vol. 1, part 2, pp. 506–14.

15. Grant Wacker, "The Demise of Biblical Civilisation," in *The Bible in America: Essays in Cultural History,* ed. Nathan O. Hatch and Mark A. Noll, pp. 121–38.

16. Robert M. Price puts his finger on this painful feature of unreflective conservative thinking in *The Crisis of Biblical Authority,* chap. 6.

17. See Michael Novak, *Confessions of a Catholic,* pp. 35–41, 49–58.

18. Two fine critiques of Bultmann's theological method are Robert C. Roberts, *Rudolf Bultmann's Theology: A Critical Interpretation;* and Barry Smith, *Rudolf Bultmann's Hermeneutical Theory.*

19. J. I. Packer takes on D. E. Nineham and his contention that the differences between the way the Bible thinks and the way in which we think today are so great that they cannot be overcome—*Scripture and Truth,* ed. Carson and Woodbridge, pp. 228–32.

20. Rogers and McKim give many fine quotations in which the language of accommoda-

tion is used by classical theologians in reference to the Scriptures. These have value whether or not they use them correctly in respect to the issue of inerrancy—*The Authority and Interpretation of the Bible*, chap. 1–2.

21. Charles Kraft goes into the dynamics of God revealing himself through culture—*Christianity in Culture*.

22. Bernard Ramm, "The Modality of the Divine Condescension," *Special Revelation and the Word of God*, chap. 2.

23. Wayne Grudem is very worried about any use of the term *accommodation* that might imply that inspiration might permit the smallest error—in Carson and Woodbridge, *Scripture and Truth*, pp. 53–57.

24. Paul R. Wells has a lengthy discussion about the use of the Christological analogy in *James Barr and the Bible: Critique of a New Liberalism*, pp. 9–33, 340–49.

25. See Bernard Ramm, *After Fundamentalism: The Future of Evangelical Theology*, pp. 89–95.

26. Hans Küng, *Infallible? An Inquiry*, pp. 215–16.

27. For the patristic and medieval images of inspiration, see Bruce Vawter, *Biblical Inspiration*, chaps. 2–3.

28. Wayne Grudem, in Carson and Woodbridge, *Scripture and Truth*, p. 54.

29. Gleason Archer thinks along these lines and has the ingenuity and the scholarship to make it seem to work. If he is to succeed, he will need to expand his *Encyclopedia of Bible Difficulties* to several additional volumes. On the other hand, the first one may be sufficient to convince many not to approach things this way.

30. William J. Abraham is getting at this point in *The Divine Inspiration of Holy Scripture*, chap. 1.

31. "If God wished to give his people a series of letters like Paul's, he prepared a Paul to write them, and the Paul he brought to the task was a Paul who spontaneously would write just such letters" (Warfield, *The Inspiration and Authority of the Bible*, p. 155). In my book I called this "biblical theism." I would now be inclined to call it "Calvinistic theism," *Biblical Revelation*, p. 92.

32. Coleman brings this out in *Issues of Theological Conflict: Evangelicals and Liberals*, pp. 163–65.

Chapter 5: The Human Dimension

1. Gleason L. Archer's book, *Encyclopedia of Bible Difficulties*, apart from its alarmist stance and over cautious approach to possible solutions, is a recent and in many ways helpful contribution to this literary genre.

2. George B. Caird, *The Language and Imagery of the Bible*.

3. Bernard Ramm, *The Christian View of Science and Scripture*, p. 54.

4. John W. Wenham, *The Goodness of God*, chap. 7.

5. James Orr, *Revelation and Inspiration*, pp. 175–77, and Richard J. Coleman, *Issue of Theological Conflict*, pp. 166–69.

6. Edward J. Carnell, *The Case for Orthodox Theology*, chap. 4.

7. Wenham treats this problem as well as anyone I have read in *The Goodness of God*, chap. 8.

8. Typical of the Chicago Statement, the next sentence reads: "We deny the legitimacy of any treatment of the text or quest for sources lying behind it that leads to relativizing, dehistorising, or discounting its teaching, or rejecting its claims to authorship." (Article XVIII). One feels a certain reluctance to accept certain literary forms even if the text suggests them.

9. This is a point made repeatedly by Northrop Frye in his book *The Great Code: The Bible and Literature*.

10. Article xiii. This comment is so generous, in fact, that some strict inerrantists will live to regret it simply because it allows a large degree of critical freedom. It is difficult to think of a liberal critical opinion that could not be worded to fit into this specification.

11. Hans Frei has called our attention to this fact in his important work *The Eclipse of Biblical Narrative: A Study in Eighteenth and Nineteenth Century Hermeneutics*.
12. Royce G. Gruenler has a fine discussion on Tolkien's liberating perspective on the good magic of the godspell in *New Approaches to Jesus and the Gospels: A Phenomenological and Exegetical Study of Synoptic Christology*, chap. 10.
13. Brevard S. Childs, *Myth and Reality in the Old Testament*.
14. George B. Caird, "The Language of Myth," in *The Language and Imagery of the Bible*, chap. 13.
15. Bernard Ramm supplies some ingenious explanations for phenomena that at that time he was unwilling to identify as legends—*The Christian View of Science and Scripture*.
16. Bruce Kaye, *The Supernatural in the New Testament*.
17. A good deal of James Barr's book *Fundamentalism* is devoted to making this point painfully clear.

Chapter 6: Biblical Criticism

1. Robert M. Price gives testimonies by Harry Fosdick, Robert Alley, and A. J. Mattill to this effect in *The Crisis of Biblical Authority*, pp. 41–42.
2. George E. Ladd, *The New Testament and Criticism*, p. 53.
3. Carl Henry speaks of "the uses and abuses of historical criticism" in *God, Revelation and Authority*, IV, chap. 17.
4. Hodgson and King, *Christian Theology: An Introduction to Its Traditions and Tasks*, p. ix.
5. Edgar Krentz, *The Historical Critical Method*, p. 55.
6. Edward Farley, *Ecclesial Reflection*, pp. 135–40.
7. Gerhard Hasel, *New Testament Theology: Basic Issues in the Current Debate*, pp. 18–28, 209–11.
8. Wellhausen knew that the manner in which he was studying the Bible would never lead anyone to hear God's Word from it. See Leon Morris, *I Believe in Revelation*, p. 101. For Barr the Bible is a human product only. The problem is that this was not Jesus' view of it or in a real sense the Bible's view of itself—James Barr, *The Bible in the Modern World*, p. 120.
9. Gerhard Ebeling, *Word and Faith*, p. 51.
10. Walter Wink makes this point in what Barr calls his "wild, thoughtless, and journalistic work" entitled *The Bible in Human Transformation*. See Barr, *Holy Scripture*, p. 107.
11. Royce Gruenler makes effective of Polanyi's postcritical hermeneutic in *New Approaches to Jesus and the Gospels*, chap. 8.
12. The approach to the philosophy of religion that I espouse is sketched out in *Reason Enough*.
13. James Barr is very concerned to defend critical freedom against a resurgence of dogmatic Bible reading both in *Holy Scripture* and *Fundamentalism*.
14. William J. Abraham is critical of those conservatives who appear to do so—*The Divine Inspiration of Holy Scripture*, chap. 1. Insofar as he himself expects the Bible to tell the truth, though, he is not completely free from the same dilemma.
15. J. A. T. Robinson, *Can We Trust the New Testament?* chap. 8.
16. Martin Hengel, *Acts and the History of Earliest Christianity*, pp. 134–5.
17. Raymond E. Brown, *The Critical Meaning of the Bible*, p. 25.
18. James Barr points to the common inconsistency of conservatives in this regard—*Fundamentalism*, chap. 8.
19. It looks as though J. Ramsey Michaels, recently dismissed from Gordon Conwell Theological Seminary, was insufficiently sensitive to classical fears and concerns. Alternatively, he may have just been tired of being sensitive to them.
20. Richard J. Coleman, *Issues of Theological Conflict*, pp. 144–50.
21. Howard Marshall has a most sensible discussion about being open to the actual data of the text in *Biblical Inspiration*, chap. 3.

Chapter 7: Word and Spirit

1. J. I. Packer sees the need for evangelicals to say more about the work of the Spirit when they discuss the inspiration and authority of the Bible—*Scripture and Truth*, ed. Carson and Woodbridge, pp. 347–48.
2. Bernard Ramm, *The Witness of the Spirit*, pp. 123–127.
3. Helmut Thielicke, *The Evangelical Faith* III, pp. 103–198.
4. Carl Henry subjects Kelsey's doctrine of functional authority to critical analysis—*God, Revelation, and ·Authority*, IV, pp. 470–75.
5. Bernard M. G. Reardon, *Religious Thought in the Reformation*, pp. 223–30.
6. Friedrich Schleiermacher, *The Christian Faith*, p. 78.
7. Jan Walgrave, *Unfolding Revelation*, pp. 226–29.
8. Karl Barth, *Church Dogmatics*, pp. 528–30.
9. Klaas Runia, *Karl Barth's Doctrine of Holy Scripture*; and Paul Helm, *The Divine Revelation*, pp. 40–47.
10. Walter Schmithals, *An Introduction to the Theology of Rudolf Bultmann*.
11. Rosemary Ruether, *The Church Against Itself*, pp. 119–20.
12. Claude Geffré, *A New Age in Theology*, p. 64.
13. Paul D. Hanson, *The Diversity of Scripture: A Theological Interpretation*, pp. xvii, 1–2, 16, 83, etc.
14. Hodgson and King present this revolution in theology in their volume *Christian Theology: An Introduction to its Traditions and Tasks*, chap. 2.
15. Bernard Ramm, *The Witness of the Spirit*.
16. James D. G. Dunn, *Jesus and the Spirit*, pp. 350–57.
17. Paul Tillich, *Systematic Theology* I, p. 42.
18. Bruce Yocum, Prophecy: Exercising the Prophetic Gifts of the Spirit in the Church Today.
19. Donald G. Bloesch, *Essentials of Evangelical Theology* II, pp. 269–75.
20. Jaroslav Pelikan, *The Christian Tradition: A History of the Development of Doctrine* I, p. 162; Geoffrey Wainwright, *Doxology: The Praise of God in Worship, Doctrine, and Life*, pp. 149–50.
21. Richard F. Lovelace, *Dynamics of Spiritual Life: An Evangelical Theology of Renewal*, p. 279.
22. David Tracy, *The Analogical Imagination: Christian Theology and the Culture of Pluralism*, p. 62.
23. Paul Helm, *The Divine Revelation*, pp. 71–88.
24. Paul Holmer seems to worry about this happening in conservative theology—*The Evangelicals: What They Believe, Who They Are, Where They Are Changing*, ed. David F. Wells and John D. Woodbridge, pp. 68–95.
25. James D. G. Dunn, *Jesus and the Spirit*, pp. 226–27.
26. E. D. Hirsch, *Validity in Interpretation*.
27. Walter Kaiser presses this necessity home at every opportunity—*Toward an Exegetical Theology: Biblical Exegesis for Preaching and Teaching*.
28. William L. Lane, *Commentary on the Gospel of Mark*, p. xii.
29. Anthony Thiselton, *The Two Horizons*, pp. 85–92.
30. Gruenler examines C. S. Lewis's hermeneutic in his *New Approaches to Jesus and the Gospels*, chap. 6.
31. Hans Küng, *The Church*, p. 202.
32. On pneumatic exegesis in the New Testament, see Earle E. Ellis, *Prophecy and Hermeneutic in Early Christianity*.
33. Paul Tillich, *Systematic Theology, vol. I*, p. 3.
34. Rodman Williams, *The Era of the Spirit*; and *The Pentecostal Reality*.
35. From "Come, Holy Ghost Our Hearts Inspire," published in *The Book of Praise* (Canada, Presbyterian Church of Canada, 1972).

Chapter 8: Unfolding Revelation

1. Gerhard Von Rad is particularly concerned to interpret the Old Testament as a process of refocusing the earlier traditions to show their fresh relevance to changing circumstances—*Old Testament Theology* I, p. 119.
2. This is one of the main points Paul Achtemeier brings out in *The Inspiration of Scripture*, pp. 76–93.
3. See J. A. Sanders, "Hermeneutics," *The Interpreter's Dictionary of the Bible*, suppl. vol., pp. 403–07; George W. Coats, *Canon and Authority*.
4. Gerhard Von Rad, *Old Testament Theology*, I, pp. 115–121.
5. Walter Kaiser, *Toward an Old Testament Theology*.
6. Ralph W. Klein, *Israel in Exile, a Theological Interpretation*.
7. See James D. Smart, *The Past, Present, and Future of Biblical Theology*, pp. 125–29.
8. O. Palmer Robertson, *The Christ of the Covenants*.
9. Richard N. Longenecker, *Biblical Exegesis in the Apostolic Period*, pp. 38–45.
10. R. T. France, *Jesus and the Old Testament*, chap. 3.
11. D. L. Baker, *Two Testaments, One Bible*, pp. 284–85.
12. J. I. Packer, "An Evangelical View of Progressive Revelation," in *Evangelical Roots*, ed. Kenneth S. Kantzer, pp. 143–58.
13. Edward J. Carnell, *The Case for Orthodox Theology*, p. 54.
14. Willard M. Swartley is well aware of this factor—*Slavery, Sabbath, War and Women*, pp. 139–42, 231–32.
15. An authoritative book on dating is John A. T. Robinson, *Redating the New Testament*.
16. Robert A. Guelich, "The Gospels: Portraits of Jesus and his Ministry," *Journal of the Evangelical Theological Society* 24 (1981), pp. 117–25.
17. In addition to the various New Testament introductions, see Jack Kingsbury, *Jesus Christ in Matthew, Mark, and Luke*.
18. Donald Guthrie presents the material thematically but observes the distinctives within each topic—*New Testament Theology*.
19. As George T. Montague does in *The Holy Spirit: Growth of a Biblical Tradition*.
20. James D. G. Dunn, *Unity and Diversity in the New Testament*, chap. 15.
21. Richard N. Longenecker, "The 'Faith of Abraham' Theme in Paul, James and Hebrews: A Study in the Circumstantial Nature of New Testament Teaching," *Journal of the Evangelical Theological Society* 20 (1977), pp. 203–12.
22. See Don Carson, in *Scripture and Truth*, pp. 84–85.
23. Loretta Dornisch, "Paul Ricoeur and Biblical Interpretation: A Selected Bibliography," in *Semeia* IV (1975), pp. 23–26.
24. Leonard F. Wheat was not too hard on Tillich when he saw his work as subtly disguised humanism—*Paul Tillich's Dialectical Humanism: Unmasking the God Above God*.
25. Avery Dulles, *Models of Revelation*, p. 143.
26. I. H. Marshall, *Luke: Historian and Theologian*.
27. E. D. Hirsch, *Validity in Interpretation*, chap. 1.
28. Raymond Brown, *The Sensus Plenior of Sacred Scripture*, p. 92.
29. William S. LaSor, "Prophecy, Inspiration, and Sensus Plenior," *Tyndale Bulletin* 29 (1978), pp. 49–60.
30. Bruce Vawter, *Biblical Inspiration*, pp. 113–19.
31. David Tracy, *The Analogical Imagination: Christian Theology and the Culture of Pluralism*, chaps. 3–5.
32. David C. Steinmetz, "The Superiority of Pre-Critical Exegesis," *Theology Today* 37 (1980), pp. 27–38.
33. Mortimer J. Adler picked this up and applied it to public education—*The Paideia Proposal: An Educational Manifesto*.
34. On the place of cognitive freedom, see James Richmond, *Theology and Metaphysics*; and John Hick, *Faith and Knowledge*.

Chapter 9: The Act of Interpretation

1. Anthony C. Thiselton, *The Two Horizons*, p. xix.
2. A. Berkeley Mickelsen, *Interpreting the Bible*, chap. 19.
3. Millard J. Erickson, *Christian Theology* I, p. 251.
4. Hendrikus Berkhof, *Christian Faith*, pp. 56–61.
5. For more data, see Earle E. Ellis, *Paul's Use of the Old Testament*.
6. George T. Montague, *The Holy Spirit*, p. 291.
7. Richard N. Longenecker, *Paul, Apostle of Liberty*, chap. 10.
8. Susan T. Foh, *Women and the Word of God*, pp. 238–40.
9. Krister Stendahl worries that this has been done, for example, to Paul and his doctrine of justification. See *Paul Among Jews and Gentiles*, pp. 78–96.
10. On evangelical hermeneutics, see J. I. Packer, "Infallible Scripture and the Role of Hermeneutics," in *Scripture and Truth*, ed. Carson and Woodbridge, pp. 325–56.
11. I. Howard Marshall, *Biblical Inspiration*, pp. 77–93.
12. Willard M. Swartley, *Slavery, Sabbath, War, and Women*, pp. 224–28.
13. See Walter C. Kaiser, *Toward an Exegetical Theology: Biblical Exegesis for Preaching and Teaching*.
14. Paul Tillich, *Systematic Theology* I, intro.
15. Edward Schillebeeckx, *Interim Report on the Books Jesus and Christ*, p. 3.
16. Helmut Thielicke seems to be getting at this crisis in contemporary theology when he speaks of Cartesian and non-Cartesian approaches—*The Evangelical Faith* I.
17. See Millard J. Erickson, *Christian Theology* I, pp. 112–25.
18. J. A. T. Robinson, *Truth is Two-Eyed*, chap. 5. The point will be made explicit in his forthcoming Gifford lectures, I am informed.
19. Donald Bloesch, *The Future of Evangelical Christianity*, p. 17.
20. John Macquarrie, *Principles of Christian Theology*, 2d ed., p. 12.
21. Gabriel Fackre, *The Christian Story: A Narrative Interpretation of Basic Christian Doctrine*, p. 17.
22. David H. Kelsey, *The Uses of Scripture in Recent Theology* pp. 185–92.
23. Charles Kraft, *Christianity in Culture*, chaps. 13–15.

Conclusion

1. *The Spiritual Exercises of Saint Ignatius*, trans. Anthony Mottola (Garden City, N.Y.: Doubleday, 1964), p. 47.
2. I think this is what Jack Rogers, Don McKim, Bernard Ramm, and now Howard Marshall have been trying to tell their fellow evangelicals. Had they made my next point too, they might have received a better hearing.
3. See, for example, Roger Nicole, "The Nature of Inerrancy," *Inerrancy and Common Sense*, ed. Nicole and Ramsey Michaels; and Paul D. Feinberg, "The Meaning of Inerrancy," in *Inerrancy*, ed. Norman L. Geisler (Grand Rapids: Zondervan, 1979).
4. James I, Packer has always upheld the importance of inerrancy while espousing a flexible understanding of how to apply it—*Beyond the Battle for the Bible*.
5. Millard Erickson shows himself very wise in his treatment of the inerrancy issue in *Christian Theology* I, chap. 10.
6. This ought to clarify the issue raised by Rex A. Koivisto, "Clark Pinnock and Inerrancy: A Change in Truth Theory?" *Journal of the Evangelical Theological Society* 24 (1981), pp. 139–51.

Bibliography
of the Works Cited

Abraham, William J. *The Divine Inspiration of Holy Scripture*. Oxford: Oxford University Press, 1981.
_____. *Divine Revelation and the Limits of Historical Criticism*. Oxford: Oxford University Press, 1982.
Achtemeier, Paul J. *The Inspiration of Scripture*. Philadelphia: Westminster Press, 1980.
Adler, Mortimer J. *The Angels and Us*. New York: Macmillan, 1982.
_____. *The Paideia Proposal: An Educational Manifesto*. New York: Macmillan, 1982.
Archer, Gleason L. *An Encyclopedia of Biblical Difficulties*. Grand Rapids: Zondervan, 1982.
Baillie, John. *The Idea of Revelation in Recent Thought*. New York: Columbia University Press, 1956.
Baker, David L. *Two Testaments, One Bible*. Downers Grove, Ill.: Inter Varsity Press, 1976.
Barr, James. *Fundamentalism*. London: SCM Press, 1977.
_____. *Holy Scripture: Canon, Authority, Criticism*. Philadelphia: Westminster Press, 1983.
_____. *The Bible in the Modern World*. London: SCM Press, 1973.
Barth, Karl. *Church Dogmatics*. Edinburgh: T. & T. Clark, 1936–1969.
Bauer, Walter. *Orthodoxy and Heresy in Earliest Christianity*. Philadelphia: Fortress Press, 1971.
Berkhof, Hendrikus. *The Christian Faith*. Grand Rapids: Eerdmans, 1979.
Berkouwer, G. C. *Holy Scripture*. Grand Rapids: Eerdmans, 1975.
Bloesch, Donald G. *Essentials of Evangelical Theology, I–II*. San Francisco: Harper & Row, 1978, 1979.
_____. *The Future of Evangelical Christianity*. Garden City, N.Y.: Doubleday, 1983.
Brown, Raymond E. *The Sensus Plenior of Sacred Scripture*. Baltimore: St. Mary's University, 1955.
_____. *The Critical Meaning of the Bible*. New York: Paulist Press, 1981.

Browning, Don S. *The Moral Context of Pastoral Care*. Philadelphia: Westminster Press, 1976.

Bruce, F. F. *Tradition: Old and New*. Exeter: Paternoster Press, 1970.

Bultmann, Rudolf. *Kerygma and Myth I*. Edited by H. W. Bartsch. New York: Harper & Row, 1961.

————. *Jesus Christ and Mythology*. London: SCM Press, 1958.

————. *Existence and Faith*. New York: World, 1960.

Caird, G. B. *The Language and Imagery of the Bible*. London: Gerald Duckworth, 1980.

Carnell, Edward J. *The Case for Orthodox Theology*. Philadelphia: Westminster Press, 1959.

Carson, D. A. *Divine Sovereignty and Human Responsibility*. Atlanta: John Knox, 1981.

Carson, D. A. and John D. Woodbridge, eds. *Scripture and Truth*. Grand Rapids: Zondervan, 1983.

Childs, Brevard S. *Biblical Theology in Crisis*. Philadelphia: Westminster Press, 1970.

————. *Introduction to the Old Testament as Scripture*. Philadelphia: Fortress Press, 1979.

Coats, George W. *Canon and Authority*. Philadelphia: Fortress Press, 1977.

Coleman, Richard J. *Issues of Theological Conflict: Evangelicals and Liberals*. Grand Rapids: Eerdmans, rev. 1980.

Cullmann, Oscar. *The Early Church*. London: SCM Press, 1956.

Davis, Stephen T. *The Debate about the Bible*. Philadelphia: Westminster Press, 1977.

———— *Logic and the Nature of God*. Grand Rapids: Eerdmans, 1983.

Demarest, Bruce A. *General Revelation: Historical Views and Contemporary Issues*. Grand Rapids: Zondervan, 1982.

DeMoor, J. C. *Towards a Biblically Theo-logical Method*. Kampen: J. H. Kok, 1980.

DeWolf, Harold L. *The Case for Theology in Liberal Perspective*. Philadelphia: Westminster Press, 1959.

Donner, Theo. "Some Thoughts on the History of the New Testament Canon." *Themelios* 7, no. 3 (1982), pp. 23–27.

Dornisch, Loretta. "Paul Ricoeur and Biblical Interpretation: A Selected Bibliography" *Semeia* 4 (1975), pp. 23–26.

Downing, F. Gerald. *Has Christianity a Revelation?* Philadelphia: Westminster Press, 1964.

Duilles, Avery. *Revelation and the Quest for Unity*. Washington: Corpus Books, 1968.

————. *Revelation Theology: A History*. New York: Herder and Herder, 1969.

————. *Models of Revelation*. Garden City, N.Y.: Doubleday, 1983.

Dunn, James D. G. *Jesus and the Spirit*. London: SCM Press, 1975.

————. *Unity and Diversity in the New Testament*. London: SCM Press, 1977.

————. *Christology in the Making*. Philadelphia: Westminster Press, 1980.

————. "The Authority of Scripture According to Scripture." *The Churchman* 96, no. 3–4 (1982).

Ebeling, Gerhard. *Word and Faith*. London: SCM Press, 1963.

Ellis, E. Earle. *Eschatology in Luke*. Philadelphia: Fortress Press, 1972.
––––––. *Paul's Uses of the Old Testament*. Grand Rapids: Eerdmans, 1957.
––––––. *Prophecy and Hermeneutic in Early Christianity*. Grand Rapids: Eerdmans, 1978.
Erickson, Millard. *Christian Theology I*. Grand Rapids: Baker Book House, 1983.
Evans, C. F. *Is "Holy Scripture" Christian?* London: SCM Press, 1971.
Fackre, Gabriel. *The Christian Story: A Narrative Interpretation of Basic Christian Doctrine*. Grand Rapids: Eerdmans, 1978.
Farley, Edward. *Ecclesial Reflection: An Anatomy of Theological Method*. Philadelphia: Fortress Press, 1982.
Flesseman-van Leer, Ellen. *The Bible: Its Authority and Interpretation in the Ecumenical Movement*. Geneva: World Council of Churches, 1980.
Foh, Susan T. *Women and the Word of God*. Phillipsburg, N.J.: Presbyterian and Reformed, 1979.
Fosdick, Harry E. *A Guide to Understanding the Bible*. New York: Harper & Brothers, 1938.
France, R. T. *Jesus and the Old Testament: His Application of Old Testament Passages to Himself and His Mission*. London: Tyndale Press, 1971.
Frei, Hans W. *The Eclipse of Biblical Narrative*. New Haven: Yale University Press, 1974.
Frye, Northrop. *The Great Code: The Bible and Literature*. New York: Harcourt Brace Jovanovich, 1982.
Geffré, Claude. *A New Age in Theology*. New York: Paulist Press, 1972.
Geisler, Norman L. *Decide for Yourself: How History Views the Bible*. Grand Rapids: Zondervan, 1982.
Gilkey, Langdon L. *Message and Existence*. New York: Seabury Press, 1979.
Glaser, Ida. "Towards a Mutual Understanding of Christian and Islamic Concepts of Revelation." *Themelios* 7, no. 3 (1982), pp. 16–22.
Goldingay, John. *Approaches to Old Testament Interpretation*. Downers Grove, Ill.: Inter Varsity Press, 1981.
Goodrick, Edward W. "Let's Put 2 Timothy 3:16 Back in the Bible." *Journal of the Evangelical Theological Society* 25 (1982), pp. 479–87.
Gottwald, Norman K. *The Tribes of Yahweh: A Sociology of the Religion of Liberated Israel*. Maryknoll, N.Y.: Orbis Books, 1979.
Gruenler, Royce G. *New Approaches to Jesus and the Gospels: A Phenomenological and Exegetical Study of Synoptic Christology*. Grand Rapids: Baker Book House, 1982.
––––––. *The Inexhaustible God: Biblical Faith and the Challenge of Process Theism*. Grand Rapids: Baker Book House, 1983.
Guelich, Robert A. "The Gospels: Portraits of Jesus and his Ministry" *Journal of the Evangelical Theological Society* 24 (1981), pp. 117–25.
Gundry, Robert H. *Matthew: A Commentary on his Literary and Theological Art*. Grand Rapid: Eerdmans, 1982.
Guthrie, Donald. *New Testament Introduction*. London: Tyndale Press, 1970.
––––––. *New Testament Theology*. Leicester: Inter Varsity Press, 1981.
Habermas, Gary R. *The Resurrection of Jesus: An Apologetic*. Grand Rapids: Baker Book House, 1980.

Hamilton, Kenneth. *Revolt Against Heaven*. Grand Rapids: Eerdmans, 1965.

Hanson, Paul D. *The Diversity of Scripture: A Theological Interpretation*. Philadelphia: Fortress Press, 1982.

————. *Dynamic Transcendence: The Correlation of Confessional Heritage and Contemporary Experience in a Biblical Model of Divine Activity*. Philadelphia: Fortress Press, 1978.

Harrison, R. K. *Introduction to the Old Testament*. Grand Rapids: Eerdmans, 1969.

Harvey, Van A. *The Historian and the Believer*. New York: Macmillan, 1966.

Hasel, Gerhard. *Old Testament: Theology: Basic Issues in the Current Debate*. Grand Rapids: Eerdmans, 1972.

————. *New Testament Theology: Basic Issues in the Current Debate*. Grand Rapids: Eerdmans, 1978.

Hatch, Nathan O. and Mark A. Noll, eds. *The Bible in America*. New York: Oxford University Press, 1982.

Helm, Paul. *The Divine Revelation*. Westchester, Ill.: Crossway Books, 1982.

Hengel, Martin. *Acts and the History of Earliest Christianity*. London: SCM Press, 1979.

Henry, Carl F. H. ed. *Revelation and the Bible*. Grand Rapids: Baker Book House, 1958.

————. *God, Revelation and Authority*. 6 vols. Waco, Tex.: Word Books, 1976–1983.

Hick, John. *Faith and Knowledge*. Ithaca, N.Y.: Cornell University Press, 1957.

Hirsch, E. D. *Validity in Interpretation*. New Haven: Yale University Press, 1967.

Hitchcock, James. *What is Secular Humanism?* Ann Arbor, Mich.: Servant Books, 1982.

Hodgson, Peter C., and Robert H. King, eds. *Christian Theology: An Introduction to Its Traditions and Tasks*. Philadelphia: Fortress Press, 1982.

Jeremias, Joachim. *New Testament Theology: The Proclamation of Jesus*. New York: Charles Scribner's Sons, 1971.

Jewett, Paul K. *Man as Male and Female*. Grand Rapids: Eerdmans, 1974.

Kaiser, Christopher B. *The Doctrine of God: An Historical Survey*. Westchester, Ill.: Crossway Books, 1982.

Kaiser, Walter C. *Toward an Old Testament Theology*. Grand Rapids: Zondervan, 1978.

————. *Toward an Exegetical Theology*. Grand Rapids: Baker Book House, 1981.

Kantzer, Kenneth S. ed. *Evangelical Roots*. New York: Thomas Nelson, 1978.

Kasemann, Ernst. *New Testament Questions of Today*. London: SCM Press, 1969.

Kaufman, Gordon D. *Theological Imagination: Constructing the Concept of God*. Philadelphia: Westminster Press, 1981.

Kaye, Bruce. *The Supernatural in the New Testament*. London: Lutterworth Press, 1977.

Kelsey, David H. *The Uses of Scripture in Recent Theology*. Philadelphia: Fortress Press, 1975.

Kingsbury, Jack. *Jesus Christ in Matthew, Mark and Luke*. Philadelphia: Fortress Press, 1981.

Klein, Ralph W. *Israel in Exile: A Theological Interpretation*. Philadelphia: Fortress Press, 1979.

Kline, Meredith G. *Treaty of the Great King*. Grand Rapids: Eerdmans, 1963.

_____. *The Structure of Biblical Authority*. Grand Rapids: Eerdmans, 1972.

Koivisto, Rex A. "Clark Pinnock and Inerrancy: A Change in Truth Theory?" *Journal of the Evangelical Theological Society* 24 (1981), pp. 139–51.

Kraft, Charles H. *Christianity in Culture: A Study in Dynamic Biblical Theologizing in Cross Cultural Perspective*. Maryknoll, N.Y.: Orbis Books, 1979.

Krentz, Edgar. *The Historical Critical Method*. Philadelphia: Fortress Press, 1975.

Kummel, W. G. *The New Testament: The History of the Investigation of Its Problems*. Nashville: Abingdon Press, 1972.

Kung, Hans. *The Church*. New York: Sheed and Ward, 1967.

_____. *Infallible?* An Inquiry. Garden City, N.Y.: Doubleday, 1971.

_____. *Signposts for the Future*. Garden City, N.Y.: Doubleday, 1979.

Ladd, George E. *The New Testament and Criticism*. Grand Rapids: Eerdmans, 1967.

Lane, William L. *Commentary on the Gospel of Mark*. Grand Rapids: Eerdmans, 1974.

LaSor, William S. "Prophecy, Inspiration, and Sensus Plenior." *Tyndale Bulletin* 29 (1978), pp. 49–60.

LaSor, William S., David A. Hubbard, and Frederic W. Bush. *Old Testament Survey: The Message, Form, and Background of the Old Testament*. Grand Rapids: Eerdmans, 1982.

Lewis, C. S. *Reflections on the Psalms*. London: Geoffrey Bles, 1958.

Lindsell, Harold. *Battle for the Bible*. Grand Rapids: Zondervan, 1976.

Loewen, Howard J. "Karl Barth and the Church Doctrine of Inspiration." Ph.D. diss., Fuller Theological Seminary, 1976.

Lonergan, Bernard. *Method in Theology*. New York: Herder and Herder, 1972.

Longenecker, Richard N. *Paul, Apostle of Liberty*. New York: Harper & Row, 1964.

_____. *Biblical Exegesis in the Apostolic Period*. Grand Rapids: Eerdmans, 1975.

_____. "The Faith of Abraham Theme in Paul, James and Hebrews," *Journal of the Evangelical Theological Society* 20 (1977), pp. 203–212.

_____. "Can We Reproduce the Exegesis of the New Testament?" *Tyndale Bulletin* 21 (1970), pp. 3–38.

Lovelace, Richard C. *Dynamics of Spiritual Life: An Evangelical Theology of Renewal*. Downers Grove, Ill.: Inter Varsity Press, 1979.

Macquarrie, John. *Principles of Christian Theology*. 2d ed. New York: Charles Scribner's Sons, 1977.

Marshall, I. Howard. *Biblical Inspiration*. Grand Rapids: Eerdmans, 1982.

_____. *Luke, Historian and Theologian*. Grand Rapids: Zondervan, 1970.

Martin, Brice L. "Some Reflections on the Unity of the New Testament." *Studies in Religion* 8 (1979), pp. 143–52.

Mickelsen, A. Berkeley. *Interpreting the Bible*. Grand Rapids: Eerdmans, 1963.

Miller, David E. *The Case for Liberal Christianity*. San Francisco: Harper & Row. 1979.

Montague, George T. *The Holy Spirit: Growth of a Biblical Tradition*. New York: Paulist Press, 1976.

Montgomery, John W. *The Suicide of Christian Theology*. Minneapolis, Minn.: Bethany Fellowship, 1970.

Morris, Leon. *I Believe in Revelation*. Grand Rapids: Eerdmans, 1976.

Nash, Ronald H. *The Word of God and the Mind of Man.* Grand Rapids: Zondervan, 1982.

Nicole, Roger R. and J. Ramsey Michaels, eds. *Inerrancy and Common Sense.* Grand Rapids: Baker Book House, 1980.

Novak, Michael. *Confessions of a Catholic.* San Francisco: Harper & Row, 1983.

Ogden, Schubert M. *Christ Without Myth.* New York: Harper & Row, 1961.

_____. *The Point of Christology.* San Francisco: Harper & Row, 1982.

Orr, James. *Revelation and Inspiration.* Grand Rapids: Eerdmans, 1952.

Owen, H. P. *The Christian Knowledge of God.* London: Athlone Press, 1969.

Packer, James I. *Beyond the Battle for the Bible.* Westchester, Ill.: Cornerstone Books, 1980.

_____. "Upholding the Unity of Scripture Today." *Journal of the Evangelical Theological Society* 25 (1982), pp. 409–414.

Pannenberg, Wolfhart. *Basic Questions in Theology I.* Philadelphia: Fortress Press, 1970.

Pelikan, Jaroslav. *The Christian Tradition: A History of the Development of Doctrine I.* Chicago: University of Chicago Press, 1971.

Pinnock, Clark H. *Biblical Revelation.* Chicago: Moody Press, 1971.

_____. *Reason Enough.* Downers Grove, Ill.: Inter Varsity Press, 1980.

Price, Robert M. "The Crisis of Biblical Authority: The Setting and Range of the Current Evangelical Crisis." Ph.D. diss. Drew University, 1981.

Rahner, Karl. *Foundations of Christian Faith; An Introduction to the Idea of Christianity.* New York: Seabury Press, 1978.

_____. *Inspiration in the Bible.* New York: Herder and Herder. 1966.

Ramm, Bernard. *The Christian View of Science and Scripture.* London: Paternoster press, 1955.

_____. *The Pattern of Authority.* Grand Rapids: Eerdmans, 1957.

_____. *The Witness of the Spirit.* Grand Rapids: Eerdmans, 1959.

_____. *Special Revelation and the Word of God.* Grand Rapids: Eerdmans, 1961.

_____. *After Fundamentalism: The Future of Evangelical Theology.* San Francisco: Harper & Row, 1983.

Reardon, Barnard M. G. *Religious Thought in the Reformation.* London: Longman Group, 1981.

Richardson, Peter. "I Say Not the Lord: Personal Opinion, Apostolic Authority and the Development of Early Christian Halakha." *Tyndale Bulletin* 31 (1980), pp. 65–86.

Richmond, James. *Theology and Metaphysics.* New York: Schocken Books, 1971.

Ridderbos, Herman. *Studies in Scripture and Its Authority.* Grand Rapids: Eerdmans, 1978.

Roberts, Robert C. *Rudolf Bultmann's Theology: A Critical Interpretation.* Grand Rapids: Eerdmans, 1976.

Robertson, O. Palmer. *The Christ of the Covenants.* Grand Rapids: Baker Book House, 1980.

Robinson, J. A. T. *Redating the New Testament.* Philadelphia: Westminster Press, 1976.

_____. *Can We Trust the New Testament?* Grand Rapids: Eerdmans, 1977.

_____. *Truth is Two-Eyed.* Philadelphia: Westminster Press, 1979.

_____. "Did Jesus have a distinctive use of Scripture?" *Christological Perspectives*, Robert F. Berkey and Sarah A. Edwards eds. New York: Pilgrim Press, 1982.

Rogers, Jack B., and Donald K. McKim. *The Authority and Interpretation of the Bible: An Historical Approach*. San Francisco: Harper & Row, 1979.

Ruether, Rosemary R. *The Church Against Itself*. New York: Herder and Herder, 1967.

_____. *To Change the World: Christology and Cultural Criticism*. New York: Crossroad, 1981.

Runia, Klaas. *Karl Barth's Doctrine of Holy Scripture*. Grand Rapids: Eerdmans, 1962.

Rushdoony, Rousas J. *The Institutes of Biblical Law*. Phillipsburg, N.J.: Craig Press, 1973.

Sabatier, Auguste. *Religions of Authority and Religions of the Spirit*. New York: McClure, Phillips, 1904.

Schaff, Philip. *Creeds of Christendom I–III*. Grand Rapids: Baker Book House, 1966.

Schillebeeckx, Edward. *Interim Report on the Books Jesus and Christ*. New York: Crossroad, 1982.

Schleiermacher, Friedrich. *The Christian Faith*. Edinburgh: T. & T. Clark, 1928.

Schmithals, Walter. *An Introduction to the Theology of Rudolf Bultmann*. Minneapolis, Minn.: Augsburg, 1968.

Smart, James D. *The Strange Silence of the Bible in the Church*. Philadelphia: Westminster Press, 1970.

_____. *The Past, Present, and Future of Biblical Theology*. Philadelphia: Westminster Press, 1979.

Smith, Barry. *Rudolf Bultmann's Hermeneutical Theory*. M. Div. diss. McMaster Divinity College, 1983.

Steinmetz, David C. "The Superiority of Pre-Critical Exegesis." *Theology Today* 37 (1980), pp. 27–38.

Stendahl, Krister. *Paul Among Jews and Gentiles*. London: SCM Press, 1977.

Stott, John R. W. *God's Book for God's People*. Downers Grove, Ill.: Inter Varsity Press, 1982.

Swartley, Willard M. *Slavery, Sabbath, War and Women*. Scottdale, Pa.: Herald Press, 1983.

Temple, William. *Nature, Man and God*. London: Macmillan, 1934.

Tenney, Merrill C. ed. *The Bible: The Living Word of Revelation*. Grand Rapids: Zondervan, 1968.

Thielicke, Helmut. *The Evangelical Faith I–III*. Grand Rapids: Eerdmans, 1974, 1977, 1982.

Thiselton, Anthony C. *The Two Horizons*. Exeter: Paternoster Press, 1980.

_____. "Truth." In *The New International Dictionary of New Testament Theology*, edited by Colin Brown. Grand Rapids: Zondervan, 1978.

_____. "Understanding God's Word Today." In *Obeying Christ in a Changing Word*, edited by John R. W. Stott. Glasgow: Collins, 1977.

Tillich, Paul. *Systematic Theology I–III*. Chicago: University of Chicago Press, 1951, 1957, 1963.

Tracy, David. *Blessed Rage for Order; The New Pluralism in Theology.* New York: Seabury Press, 1975.

_____. *The Analogical Imagination, Christian Theology and the Culture of Pluralism.* New York: Crossroad, 1981.

Turner, H. E. W. *Pattern of Christian Truth.* London: A. R. Mowbray, 1954.

Vawter, Bruce. *Biblical Inspiration.* Philadelphia: Westminster Press, 1972.

Von Rad, Gerhard. *Old Testament Theology I–II.* New York: Harper & Row, 1962, 1965.

Wainwright, Geoffrey. *Doxology: The Praise of God in Worship, Doctrine, and Life.* New York: Oxford University Press, 1980.

Walgrave, Jan. *Unfolding Revelation.* Philadelphia: Westminster Press, 1972.

Warfield, B. B. *The Inspiration and Authority of the Bible.* Philadelphia: Presbyterian and Reformed, 1948.

Wells, David F. and John D. Woodbridge. *The Evangelicals: What They Believe, Who They Are, Where They Are Changing.* Nashville: Abingdon Press, 1975.

Wells, Paul R. *James Barr and the Bible, Critique of a New Liberalism.* Phillipsburg, N.J.: Presbyterian and Reformed, 1980.

Wenham, David. "Jesus and the Law: An Exegesis on Matthew 5:17–20." *Themelios* 4, no. 3 (1979), pp. 92–96.

Wenham, John W. *Christ and the Bible.* London: Tyndale Press, 1972.

_____. *The Goodness of God.* Downers Grove, Ill.: Inter Varsity Press, 1974.

Westcott, B. F. *The Bible in the Church.* New York: Macmillan, 1964.

_____. *The Gospel According to St. John.* London: John Murray, 1881.

Wheat, Leonard F. *Paul Tillich's Dialectical Humanism: Unmasking the God Above God.* Baltimore: Johns Hopkins Press, 1970.

Wiles, Maurice. *The Remaking of Christian Doctrine.* Philadelphia: Westminster Press, 1978.

Williams, Rodman. *The Era of the Spirit.* Plainfield, N.J.: Logos International, 1971.

_____. *The Pentecostal Reality.* Plainfield, N.J.: Logos International, 1972.

Wink, Walter. *The Bible in Human Transformation.* Philadelphia: Fortress Press, 1973.

Woodbridge, John D. *Biblical Authority: A Critique of the Rogers/McKim Proposal.* Grand Rapids: Zondervan, 1982.

Yocum, Bruce. *Prophecy: Exercising the Prophetic Gifts of the Spirit in the Church Today.* Ann Arbor, Mich.: Word of Life, 1976.

Subject Index

Abraham, 8, 10, 11, 14, 32, 181, 201
Accommodation of revelation, 95–100, 106; risk of, 109–10
Adam, 67–68, 116–17, 119
Adultery, 114
Altizer, Thomas, 211
Amos, 32, 33
Apostles: church and, 47, 53; as New Testament writers, 46–47; Old Testament and, 36, 37, 39, 40, 42, 45, 56. *See also* Gospels
Apostolic authority, 47, 48–49, 50
Application of the Bible, 170–74, 185; in translation, 219
Aquinas, Thomas, 20
Athanasius, 19
Atheists, 151
Athenagoras, 63
Atonement, 110
Augustine, 20, 71, 79, 80, 88
Authority of Bible. *See* Biblical authority
Authority of church, 79–82

Baille, John, 21
Barr, James: on Biblical authority, xv; on Biblical text, 66; on inerrancy, 127; on salvation, xix; on scriptural religion, 15
Barth, James: On Bible as witness, 18; on errors in Scripture, 91–92; on mechanical view of Bible, xvi; on revelation, 6, 164; on saga, 123–24; on subjectivity, 158
Bauer, Walter, 70–71
Berkouwer, G. C., 159
Bias factor. See Cultural context
Bible: application of (*see* Application of the Bible); coherence of, 69–74, 186–87; collective aspect of, 187, 188, 189; complexity of, 185, 194–95; contradictions etc. in, 147, 186–87; cultural context of, 91, 92, 93, 95, 96, 108–15, 207; difficulties with (*see* Biblical

difficulties); dynamic quality of, 175–96, 202, 214, 215; errors in, 96–97, 98 (*see also* Inerrancy); factual reliability of, 74–79; functions of, 17–19, 55; historical context of (*see* Historical context of Bible); as human literature, 143–44; inconsistencies in, 120–21, 202; as individual texts, 187, 188, 189; King James Version, xxi, xxiii; as medium of Christian message, 17; proper use of, 64–68, 197, 205; study of (*see* Biblical criticism); symbolism in, 20, 116, 119, 189–91. *See also* New Testament; Old Testament
Biblical authority: over church, 81; defined, xiii; denial of, xvi–xx; inspiration and, 54–82; subjectivity and, 157–61; threat to, 90–95
Biblical criticism, xviii, 65, 66, 71, 130–52, 206, 207; belief in God and, 143; church and, 138, 139, 141, 150; dangers of, xviii, 131, 150–51; Enlightenment and, 130; Evangelicals and, 130, 214; faith and (*see* Faith); frameworks for, 139–43; Gospels and, 140, 141; guidance from God in, 173; negative, 131, 132, 143–50; positive, 89–90, 131, 136–43; the Spirit and, 168–69. *See also* Historical criticism; Liberal and conservative views; Liberal theology; Objectivity; Subjectivity
Biblical difficulties, 106–29; interpretation and, 187–89, 191, 195, 205–6; language and, 115–125
Biblical inspiration. *See* Inspiration
Biblical Revelation (Pinnock), 222
Biblical study. *See* Biblical criticism

Biblical teaching, 71–72
Biblical traditions, 175–79, 216–17; church and, 217; criticism and, 141; interpretation and, 141; in New Testament, 201, 202
Biblical witness, 29–60; New Testament to itself, 45–54; New Testament to Old Testament, 36–45; Old Testament to itself, 30–36
Blessings and curses, 112–115
Bloesch, Donald: on inerrancy, 78; on the Spirit, 164; on the Spirit of Christ, 213
Brandon, S. G. F., 132
Bromiley, Geoffrey, xiv, xvi
Brown, Raymond, 191–92
Bruce, F. F., 130–31
Bultmann, Rudolf: on Biblical gospel, 25; on miracles, 148–49; on modernity and Scripture, 211; on New Testament, 93–94, 124, 158–59, 160; on revelation, 4, 22–23; on transformers, 218; on virgin birth, 73
Buri, Fritz, 23

Calvin, John: on accommodation, 95; on Bible, xv; on Biblical authority, xiv; on faith, 165, 166; on revelation, 161, 163; on Spirit, 53; on transformer of culture, 209
Calvinism, 101–104
Canaanites, 110, 112
Canonical process, 45, 46, 54
Carnell, Edward J., 181
Case, Shirley Jackson, 149
Catholicism: church authority and, xvi, 79, 81; Evangelicalism and, 80
Celsus, 10
Chalcedon, xiv
Chicago Group for Biblical Inerrancy, 80
Chicago Statement, 119, 127, 225
Childs, Brevard S., 66
Church: authority of, 79–82; Biblical criticism and, 138, 139,

Scripture Index